MARKETING
INFORMATION
SYSTEMS

Pardot 1/8/94

MARKETING INFORMATION SYSTEMS

Kurt H. Schaffir
H. George Trentin

amacom
A DIVISION OF AMERICAN MANAGEMENT ASSOCIATION

International standard book number: 0-8144-5302-3
Library of Congress catalog card number: 72-78302

First printing

PREFACE

Perhaps no major management area has been neglected as much as marketing in the rush to develop and implement management information systems. The movement to such systems, which has been accelerating over the past five to ten years, has engulfed the financial areas of the business with refinements of accounting and reporting systems and new developments, such as corporate modeling. It has also begun to penetrate the manufacturing areas with data-based systems for products and operations to permit better planning and control. However, except for elaborations of the traditional analyses showing the who, what, where, and when of sales, and some refinements of forecasting techniques, marketing people have not been provided with the kinds of information which should flow logically from an integrated management information system and which would improve their effectiveness in planning and controlling marketing operations.

This condition may have its roots in the mistaken notion that marketing people operate by hunch or intuition, using a mystique which is incomprehensible to management in other areas of the business. It is true that marketing management has to deal in its judgments and predictions with more intangibles, such as the effectiveness of alternate methods of selling and distribution or customer preferences. But such judgments can be greatly improved if readily available opportunities for better marketing information are grasped when a company undertakes to update its overall management information systems.

The right view of such an undertaking is that it should serve all areas of the business in an integrated fashion. Most information flows start with the marketing function, in the form of forecasts and sales, and then flow through other functions to activate systems in the purchasing, manufacturing, financial, and other areas of the business. Accordingly, if marketing systems are neglected, all other systems operate at less than peak effectiveness.

This book first relates the marketing information system to an integrated total management system. It then explains in considerable detail how marketing information systems work. Since conditions in industrial and consumer markets differ, we present case studies covering both, as well as chapters dealing with specialized applications.

We have included a chapter on information needs in connection with government antitrust statutes, which generally prohibit business from selling to different customers at different prices unless they can be justified by cost differentials or as "good-faith defenses" against competitive price cuts. This is an area where knowing the nonmanufacturing costs by reasonable breaks in volume and by types of customers is a prerequisite to establishing selling prices.

Somewhat related are the emerging information needs of the new function typified by the "vice president for distribution." Many companies have discovered a no-man's-land of responsibility and knowledge from the point where the product leaves the manufacturing operation until it is delivered to the customer. The new function acquires its operations and responsibility from both the traditional manufacturing and marketing functions and usually finds a dearth of useful information to guide it. We have offered some illustrative approaches in this area.

The concepts and case studies presented in the book are derived from our experiences in the design and implementation of marketing information systems in business situations. In most cases, these systems have been in operation for over a year and serve effectively in meeting continuing management needs.

We acknowledge most gratefully the very substantial contributions of a number of our associates at Arthur Andersen & Co. in the preparation of this book. Their names together with the area with which each was most directly involved are Joseph Carr, Customer Service and Sales, Advertising and Promotion; Neil Doppelt, Advertising Agencies, Linkage with Other Areas of Operation; Granville Gargiulo, Operations Research; James Labick, Antitrust; Vincent Melore, Distribution; Peter Sillay, Finance and Banking; and Hans Willen, Linkage with EDP.

Our special thanks go to Charlotte Forsberg, without whose help the monumental task of assembling and organizing the manuscript could never have been completed, and to Evelyn Nethercott and her staff for their fine contribution in the preparation of graphics.

Finally, we acknowledge a great debt of gratitude to our clients. Their support—in every sense—made this book possible and gives it meaning. In a very real sense, it is their book.

The authors

CONTENTS

1

PLANNING AND REPORTING
MARKETING ACTIVITIES

WHAT IS A MARKETING INFORMATION SYSTEM?

In brief, marketing information systems are concerned with the collection of information which originates both from the customer and other outside sources, and from within the marketing organization itself, and with how this information is processed and used throughout the organization. This book deals with this internal management of information.

Marketing information takes many different forms, including orders (or the lack of them), reports from the field organization, periodically published trade or government statistics, and special studies or surveys which the company may undertake. The signals coming from these different sources are not always clear or consistent, and their interpretation and use require cross checking and correlation with each other, and also with the marketing programs and activities which have been planned or are under way. Sound information management depends on finding useful, meaningful ways of matching and comparing data.

To meet the needs of the marketing organization effectively, the information system cannot be merely a compilation of information, a collection of filing cabinets or punched cards or computer tapes, no matter how complete. It requires a set of procedures, manual, mechanized, or computerized as appropriate, for organizing and disseminating information, designed on the basis of careful analysis and anticipation of how information will be *used,* and directing it to the individual who needs it and will use it. In the final analysis, information is useful only to the extent that it leads to action, and it must be organized to direct attention toward opportunities for improved marketing activities.

HOW WILL IT HELP
THE MARKETING EXECUTIVE?

Management must judge its information systems, as it does other areas of operation, by whether and to what degree they contribute to achievement of the company's objectives of growth and profit. In marketing and sales, this specifically means the ability to contribute significantly to management's ability to:

1. Identify and improve sales performance of present accounts, products, or territories which do not meet reasonable or expected levels of sales, profit, share, or growth objectives.

2. Identify and activate profitable new accounts or dormant accounts.

3. Identify and implement needed changes in distribution structure and trade channels to achieve a proper balance of coverage and cost.

4. Monitor and maintain uniform application of a structure of pricing, discounts, and allowances which is competitive and consistent with marketing and financial objectives and antitrust regulations.

5. Establish and meet norms of customer service in terms of sales and service calls, planned availability of product, warranties, minimum order and shipping quantities, and performance against commitments, consistent with competitive requirements and economic considerations.

6. Promote performance and retention of good sales personnel through balanced, equitable, and effective assignment of territories and account objectives and responsibilities, and implementation of fair and attractive compensation arrangements.

7. Relate promotion and advertising activities to market norms and to the company's long- and short-term marketing and financial objectives.

8. Identify needs for new products and carry through their field testing and properly phased introduction.

9. Allocate available resources properly among brands, campaigns, geographical areas, distribution levels, media, and time periods.

Systems do not sell, of course—people do. But systems help management to direct activities toward areas of specific need and opportunity, and thereby generate additional sales or more profitable sales, guard against loss of business through failure to provide service, control costs, and strengthen the company's marketing position in both the short and long term.

PLANNING AND REPORTING

The application of systems concepts to the marketing and sales function requires the integration of three basic elements:

1. Information collection.
2. Planning and development of performance goals.
3. Performance and control reporting.

Effective quantitative planning is central to the development of the marketing information system because the planning process determines what internal and external data are required, how these are best collected and organized, and what standards will be used to measure performance. Before addressing ourselves to the technical aspects of systems development and concepts, which are explored in greater depth in the next chapter, some discussion of sales and marketing planning is in order. This is a vast subject, and a great deal has been written on it. We will cover it only to the degree necessary to show how planning needs and processes relate to the design of marketing information systems.

Management Objectives

Planning starts with top management because the marketing and selling function, like all areas of a business enterprise, must be responsive to management's overall goals and objectives. These relate principally to:

1. Earnings and growth of earnings.
2. Return on investment, in terms of both stockholders' equity and total assets.
3. Market position or share.
4. Company relations with the various elements of the business community, the government, and the general public.

In the present context, we shall be concerned primarily with the first three of these.

Management goals necessarily represent a balance of what is desired and what is possible. This balance is not achieved easily, but it evolves in the course of the planning process, which in different organizations may take many different forms. In a sense, planning is a continuous process since everyone is "always thinking ahead," but it is also true that when planning responsibilities are not clearly and specifically defined in terms of what everyone is supposed to do, nobody in fact does it. In order for plans to be adequately formulated, examined, tested, and coordinated for cohesive action, an organized step-by-step procedure is required.

Planning Horizons

There are normally at least two distinct levels of planning, long-term and short-term. Typically, short-term plans cover one year, usually, although not always, coincidental with the company's fiscal year. They may be reviewed and updated quarterly.

Because the marketing and sales plan is a necessary input to the preparation of the operating budget, it has to be completed before the budget can be put in final form. When the budgetary or fiscal year coincides with the calendar year, the marketing plan has to be available early in the fourth quarter. As a consequence, the bulk of the preparation has to take place during the third quarter, and this, in turn, necessitates the preparation of sales forecasts, on at least a preliminary basis, about midyear for the complete following budget year. With half, or possibly less, of the current year's results in hand, marketing management is severely handicapped in providing meaningful forecasts for the next year. Consequently, the ability to introduce forecast changes and to update the marketing plan, as well as the budget, on short notice later in the year can be a great asset; it therefore becomes an important feature in the design of a marketing information system.

The long-term plan covers a multiyear period, depending on the commitments management must make and on the time span these commitments cover. For purposes of this discussion, a five-year period will be implied unless otherwise specified. The availability of the long-term plan, together with the goals and objectives it incorporates, is an important factor in facilitating and speeding the preparation of the short-term plan and, of course, also adds an important element of overall perspective. Consequently, the long-term plan would typically be prepared during the second quarter, after the previous year's results have become available.

ORGANIZATIONAL STRUCTURES

As a basis for discussing the planning and operation of selling and marketing activities, it is of value to review the organizational context in which planning is carried out.

Marketing and sales functions may assume many different organizational forms, which reflect differences in types and number of products sold, channels of distribution, types of customers, and geographic areas covered. The two basic alternative structures are those that are oriented geographically or by trade channel (illustrated in Exhibit 1) and those that are oriented by products (illustrated in Exhibit 2).

In the geographically oriented structure, typical of many sales operations, men are assigned to territories and sell all product lines. Advertising, new product development, and market research staffs service all product lines. In the product-oriented marketing organization, on the other hand, each of its main product lines has specialists concentrating on a limited group of products and reporting to a product manager. This arrangement is preferred when each product serves the needs of a different group of customers or when the products are inherently complex and each requires a different technical specialist. Within the same organization, it is common to find marketing activities organized along product lines and the selling function organized geographically. A third variation, sometimes superimposed on geographic or product-line organization, involves assignment of special responsibilities for different trade channels or customer categories.

It is not our purpose here to explore in depth the advantages and disadvantages of alternative organizational structures. Rather, we wish to emphasize the importance of resolving organizational questions and establishing sound definitions of individual responsibilities at the outset, because (1) the organizational structure is a reflection of the underlying marketing environment in which a company operates, including products, geography, customers, and competition; (2) the organizational structure is the basic framework for executing the planning and control of the marketing system; and (3) the structure of the information system must correspond to the responsibilities defined by the organizational structure and must facilitate each organization's information requirements for planning and control.

Distribution Management

Historically, distribution of the product has been viewed as an extension of the manufacturing function because it involves labor, equipment, and materials (finished goods) in much the same way. Often, the production planning manager, traffic manager, or shipping and warehousing manager responsible for physical aspects of distribution takes direction from production management. The distribution and inventory functions have often been run with little concern for marketing strategies or

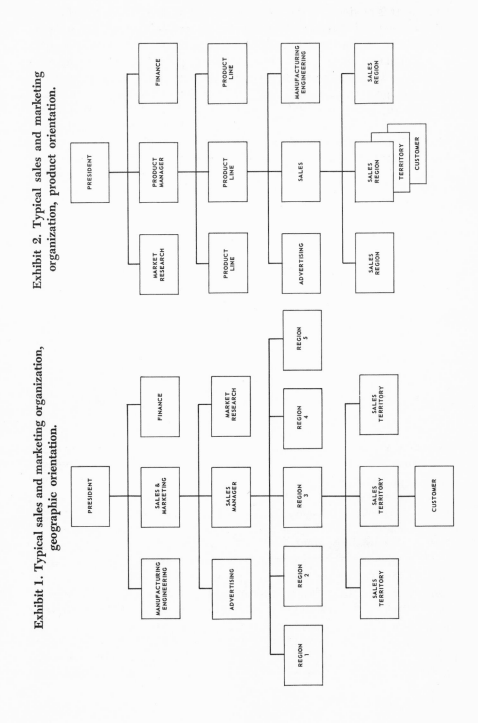

Exhibit 1. Typical sales and marketing organization, geographic orientation.

Exhibit 2. Typical sales and marketing organization, product orientation.

policies. It is obvious, on the other hand, that when and how a customer's orders are filled directly affect his future purchases and are, indeed, the concern of the marketing manager. The marketing manager should, at a minimum, have some voice in setting policy and regulating this function with regard to finished goods inventory levels, order processing, acknowledgments, scheduling, and warehousing. These areas of customer service are discussed in some detail in Chapter 3; Chapter 6 contains a full discussion of the distribution function. It is sufficient to point out here that information for planning and controlling the customer service function should be viewed as an element of the marketing information system, whether or not the company has formally placed management of the distribution function under marketing control.

DEVELOPING MARKETING PLANS

The flow chart illustrated in Exhibit 3 shows the basic components of each of the major marketing and sales planning activities. The detailed planning components shown on the left deal with the individual strategies to be included in the overall marketing plan and selling plan. Supporting systems, marked by an asterisk, include performance reporting, budgeting and profit analysis, and forecasting.

At the heart of the marketing information system is the need for integration of sectional plans with supporting systems and corporate objectives in the form of marketing and selling plans. These plans, in turn, trigger planning and contingent levels of activity in other areas, including inventory, distribution, manufacturing, finance, and raw materials purchasing. Together, these plans are aimed at providing marketing and selling programs which will meet levels of performance specified by management.

RECONCILING MANAGEMENT OBJECTIVES

Typically, corporate objectives are expressed in such terms as market share, gross sales, net profit, or number of sales units and reflect a desire for consistent growth in earnings per share for stockholders.

As illustrated in Exhibit 4, the objective of achieving consistent growth may at times be inconsistent with the life cycle of individual products or brands. Beginning with a small sales volume and negative profit contribution, new brands—if successful—may proceed through a period of rapid growth followed, after leveling off, by a slow decline

Exhibit 3. Overview, integration of marketing planning in the corporate planning process.

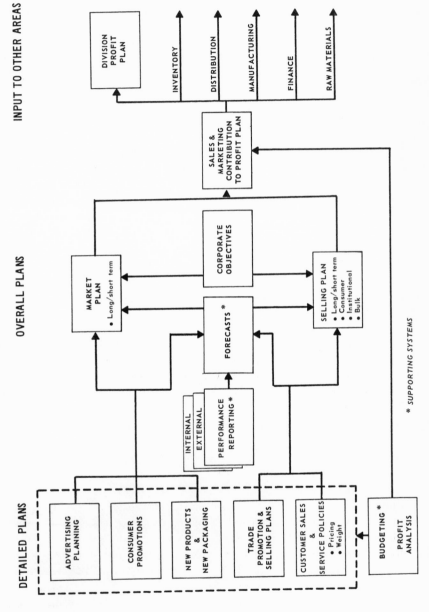

Exhibit 4. Relationship of product life cyle to management objectives.

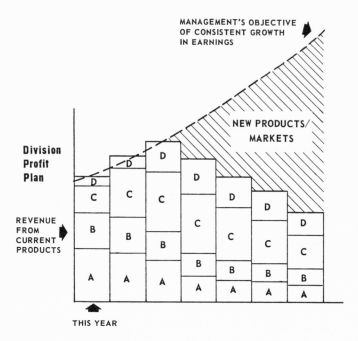

in both sales and net profit. Although time periods vary for different products, the general pattern is common. The decline can be caused by a variety of factors, primarily technological changes or the entry of competing brands or substitutes, which eventually lower sales volume. Thus, in order to achieve stable growth at any point in time, a number of brands at different stages of maturity are usually required. In Exhibit 4, this is illustrated by a divisional profit plan which assumes that new products will take up the slack when existing products cannot support the desired growth pattern.

Because growth during any particular period can be achieved in different ways, top management must provide more specific guidance in the development of marketing plans, and must coordinate marketing plans with other functions. Initially, specific guidelines should be established for not only sales and profit goals but also types of products, participation in specific markets, and productivity goals for both manufacturing and marketing operations.

The process by which marketing and sales management plans its operations to conform to these broad directives will next be illustrated in terms of the major elements of the marketing planning process.

LONG-RANGE MARKETING PLANS

The long-range marketing plan provides management with basic information to be used in establishing specific short-term objectives and formulating policies. It provides information about probable future market behavior and, in turn, forms the basis for developing plans for capitalizing on potential markets and for organizing company operations for anticipated sales efforts. Specific questions to be answered in the long-range plan are

- What are the sales growth potentials of the products or services?
- Are sales growth potentials soundly based?
- How much capital investment is required?
- What percentage return is expected on investment?
- What are resource requirements in terms of plant, personnel, and equipment?
- How risky is the situation (and are the risks reasonable)?
- What is the present and probable future competition?
- What are the profit implications?
- What external market or environmental factors must be taken into account?

The development of the long-range marketing plan usually includes

1. A long-term economic forecast of business environment.
2. A forecast of the market or market segments in which the company operates.
3. A forecast of the company's or brand's sales.
4. An evaluation of the rate of increase of company sales in terms of volume and market share relative to management's objectives.
5. A formulation of strategies for achieving these objectives.

Forecasts

It must be recognized that the basic market forecast is both a very crucial and a very sensitive element of the long-range plan, and also of the short-range plan. Forecasts must utilize all the pertinent information available to the planners and should be based on comprehensive study of the products, customers, and markets of the company and its competitors. Individual forecasts are usually made for each product line or group of products and are expressed in physical units and dollar volume. Historical price trends are applied with proper adjustment to reflect what is taking place in the market. Prices must also reflect management's judgments about competitors.

A projection of the overall economic environment in which the company operates is needed as part of the marketing plan to identify the principal factors influencing the size and composition of the company's total market. Government statistics and data from trade associations are valuable sources of information for such overall market forecasts. The economic forecast provides both a measure of the environment in which the company will operate and a statement of the assumptions upon which the plan is based. Together, the economic and internal forecasts

1. Define the external environment in which the company expects to operate.
2. Provide a common base for managerial decision making.
3. Enable management to formulate realistic planning objectives consistent with forecast conditions.

The forecast of company sales relative to the market provides a basis to start the *planning* process. It is important to differentiate between plan and forecast. The forecast is an estimate of the future based on current facts, while a plan is a program of intended action leading to desired results not necessarily directly derived from historical facts or current status.

Special techniques sometimes effectively used in forecasting long-term company growth include development of models for statistical projections. These may involve time series analysis to isolate cyclical, trend, and seasonal influences in industry and company sales, and multiple correlation to define the statistical relationship between product sales and the economic (external) variables and to construct mathematical equations for long-range sales forecasting.

Strategies

Once forecasts have been made, it is possible to evaluate the results in terms of management objectives and to consider alternative long-term strategies. In general, basic product and marketing strategies may include:

1. Increased market penetration with existing product lines, either by selling more to current customers or by finding new customers.
2. Market development, by adapting existing products to new markets or to additional commercial applications.
3. Product development, through programs of product innovation to serve traditional markets with new or different products.

4. Diversification to broaden the present product-market structure, by entering new markets with new products.

In general, the long-range marketing plan encompasses some elements of all these basic strategies stated in terms of:

1. Descriptive analysis of products and markets involved.
2. Enumeration and evaluation of principal determinants of demand.
3. Current market status and long-range outlook.
4. Company's place in industry, present and future.
5. Major opportunities and objectives versus competition, short- and long-term.
6. Current and anticipated problems in achieving objectives.
7. Proposed approach to accomplishing objectives.

Financial Projections

Exhibit 5 shows an example of the projected financial effects of a long-range plan for a leading consumer products company. The principal strategy illustrated here is new product development, shown by anticipated volume to be generated by present brands and new brands. These are related to anticipated increases in general and administrative expenses and management's earnings objective—shown here as 10% increase per year. This analysis develops the amount of funds which will be *available* for implementing marketing and sales strategies, both in introducing new products and in selling current brands.

Exhibit 5. Summary of long-range marketing plan (000 omitted).

(000) OMITTED

	19X0	19X1	19X2	19X3	19X4
SALES ($):					
Present Brands	53,000	52,500	52,000	51,500	51,000
New Brands	3,000	6,500	13,500	19,000	26,500
Total Brands	56,000	59,000	65,500	70,500	77,500
GROSS PROFIT (40%)	22,400	23,600	26,200	28,200	31,000
GEN. & ADMIN. (10%)	5,600	5,900	6,550	7,050	7,750
EARNINGS OBJECTIVE (Increases 10% per year)	5,600	6,160	6,776	7,453	8,198
AVAILABLE FOR SALES & MKTG. EXPENDITURES	11,200	10,940	12,874	13,697	15,052
SALES & MKTG. AS % OF SALES	20%	18.5%	19.6%	19.4%	19.4%

When the long-range plan is carefully reviewed and updated annually, it becomes a useful basis for new product plans and short-term marketing and selling plans.

NEW PRODUCT PLANNING

Systems for new product planning are closely related to the long-range plan. They will be covered here only briefly since they are discussed in depth in a later chapter.

The planning system, generally reviewed annually, provides a mechanism for the continuous identification and evaluation of new products, markets, or technologies which provide a basis for continuing growth. It provides also for evaluation of a company's strength in terms of technology, production capabilities, marketing, and distribution. As noted in connection with the long-range plan, these must be responsive to the changing economic environment.

The system should provide for collection and evaluation of marketing information with reference to specific new product concepts, the application of market and product testing techniques, and the establishment of administrative and financial control procedures to minimize risk and maximize return in the development and introduction of new products.

The introduction of a new product and, for that matter, efforts to get new customers or penetrate new markets often require heavy expenditure for some time before tangible results can be expected. Costs include research and development, capital investments for facilities and equipment, the costs of failures, and the costs of obsolescence of existing products resulting from the introduction of a new product.

From a systems standpoint, the process for new product introductions can be summarized as follows.

Search: Identification of new product concepts, including a continuous review of present products and markets to identify potentially profitable additions.

Screening: Preliminary analysis of new product ideas to eliminate weak proposals and to identify promising ones.

Evaluation: Careful, intensive analysis of new products in terms of market potential, compatibility with company policies, and harmony with present products and resources.

Development: Establishment of a program for the transformation of a new product idea into a prototype and the planning and organization of marketing and production resources.

Introduction: Review of test market results, modification of product and marketing strategies, planning and scheduling of action, and selling of the product on a national or regional basis.

At each step in the new product development process, information must be collected to support the evaluations necessary at that point. Exhibit 6 is an example of a new product proposal form used by a leading consumer products manufacturer. The form requires identification of types of changes in the product and an indication of the action taken. In addition to an initial review, this particular company maintains a file of those product ideas which were passed over so that they may be periodically reevaluated.

Another approach to the control of new product development is the progress checklist, which establishes target dates for each of the major steps in the new product planning process and for the specific activities which must take place; it also specifies the department responsible and the specific output expected at each step. A portion of such a checklist is illustrated in Exhibit 7 and shows the steps required for store or market tests.

In many companies, the new product development process is effectively controlled by concentrating responsibilities for overall progress and coordination under a new product manager.

Exhibit 6. Typical new product proposal form.

NEW PRODUCT SUGGESTION	DATE PREPARED _____
	PREPARED BY _____
	APPROVED BY _____

SUBMITTED BY _____   DEPARTMENT _____

SUGGESTION (DESCRIBE IN DETAIL)

TYPE OF SUGGESTION (CHECK ONE)

SPECIAL/NEW TYPE ☐	REFORMULATION ☐	OTHER ☐	_____
REPACKAGING ☐	EXTENSION OF PRESENT LINE ☐		_____
NEW USES ☐	REPLACE EXISTING PRODUCT ☐	WHICH	_____

MARKET / USERS OF NEW PRODUCT

REASONS FOR SUGGESTION

OTHER

ACTION:

REVIEWED BY _____   FURTHER EVALUATION ____   ASSIGNED TO_____

DATE _____   NO FURTHER EVALUATION ____   REASONS – ATTACH STATEMENT

Exhibit 7. New product development checklist, illustrative portion.

STORE AND MARKET TESTS	RESPONSIBILITY OF	OUTPUT
1. Determine need for store and/or market tests	MARKETING DEPARTMENT MARKETING SERVICES DEPT.	RECOMMENDATION
2. Establish checklist start/finish dates and responsibilities	MARKETING DEPARTMENT	CHECKLIST DETAIL TEST
3. Develop test market plans Advertising and promotion strategy Packaging Volume estimates Pricing Class of trade emphasis Selling aids	MARKETING DEPARTMENT	MARKET PLAN
4. Release production order	MANUFACTURING	PRODUCTION ORDER
5. Establish final advertising plans with agency, including deadlines	MARKETING	FINAL ADVERTISING PLAN
6. Solicit outside vendor bids for manufacturing, if necessary	MANUFACTURING	
7. Fix plant routing	ENGINEERING	PLANT ROUTING
8. Obtain necessary equipment (if over $10,000, seek Capital Projects Committee authorization)	MANUFACTURING	
9. Estimate production lead time for inventory purposes	MANUFACTURING, MARKETING	
10. Prepare bill of materials	MANUFACTURING	BILL OF MATERIALS
11. Estimate purchase lead times	PURCHASING, MANUFACTURING	
12. Establish marketing policies Discounts Freight policies	MARKETING DEPARTMENT	

CONTENT OF ANNUAL MARKETING PLAN

Moving on now to the process by which annual short-term marketing plans are developed, the following illustrates the procedures followed by the consumer products division of a major national manufacturing company.

The annual marketing planning system establishes the procedures by which marketing management, early in the second quarter of each year, analyzes division, industry, and environmental information and formulates a detailed marketing strategy for the coming year. It consists of six major phases.

1. Identification and collection of marketing information to be used in the planning process.
2. Comparative analysis of brand performance and evaluation in terms of long-range plans and division objectives.

3. Formulation of preliminary brand plans, budgets, volume, and distribution objectives.
4. Compilation of brand plans into a preliminary marketing plan and review with marketing and sales management.
5. Preparation of detailed plans for each brand, specifying the level of marketing activity, brand expenditures, and performance goals in terms of volume, distribution, shares of market, and brand contribution.
6. Review with top management and input of the approved annual marketing plan and budget into the profit planning system.

Preparation of the Marketing Plan

The annual marketing planning procedure begins with an analysis of current sales reports and the other planning systems:

Long-range planning system.
Top management plans and objectives.
New product planning system.
Research and strategic planning system.
Forecasting system.

These provide a variety of background information. They include historical brand activity on a district, regional, and national basis and summarize brand performance monthly by comparing actual sales volume and marketing expenditures with budgeted levels. They also include statements of market definition and division objectives, the marketing plans of former years against which actual results can be compared, and current long-range and new-product plans.

Other background data include penetration indices, environmental summaries, and competitive activity reports from the research and strategic planning department. The forecasting system provides an initial statistical forecast of performance by item and brand for the coming year, as well as other pertinent summaries.

This information is compiled and presented in a form which will facilitate its analysis by the brand managers and the director of marketing. The brand managers analyze this information and prepare a report evaluating historical performance, noting those brands which were either substantially above or below budget. In addition, they assess the future prospects for the current product line and measure this performance against long-range plans and division objectives to determine the need and marketing strategy for new products.

The director of marketing and the brand managers prepare preliminary plans and budgets for each brand and consolidate them into a preliminary marketing plan. The plans specify the projected level of sales and the marketing activities anticipated in order to achieve the planned sales level. The budget constitutes the translation of these marketing activities into dollars. These plans and budgets are evaluated by sales and marketing management to insure that marketing's contribution to the attainment of division objectives is sufficient to meet desired performance levels as developed in the long-range plan and transmitted in top management's annual guidance letter to sales and marketing.

Detailed Analysis

Prior to the production of the final marketing plan, the procedures provide for a detailed analysis of the major components of each brand's strategy, advertising and promotion plans, and market research and graphic arts projects.

The promotion planning process begins with an analysis of the apparent effect of promotions on past sales. On the basis of this analysis and his plans for future promotions, the brand manager outlines in detail what he anticipates the financial effects of these promotions will be.

In addition to specifying the expected costs of the promotion, the proposal requires a statement of objectives and a quantification of anticipated long- and short-run implications on the level of sales, distribution, and new purchasers for the brand.

The promotion planning functions must be coordinated with advertising planning so that the effect of one may reinforce the effect of the other. Advertising planning requires the same kind of analytical evaluation of sales and profit implications as other marketing activities. This highly complex process will be more fully described in a later chapter.

Another evaluative process, aimed at analyzing the merits of market research and graphic arts projects such as package design and displays, requires a detailed statement by the planner of their specific purpose and expected consequences. The anticipated results must be stipulated and related to the expenditures incurred to produce them.

These analyses, after appropriate reevaluations and reviews, lead to the formulation of the final annual marketing plan, which specifies by brand the:

1. Forecast sales volume.
2. Share of market and distribution objectives.
3. Price and discount structure.
4. Brand contribution to profit.

5. Scheduled marketing activities: advertising, promotion, and graphics/packaging charges.
6. Budgets.

As stated at the outset, the annual marketing planning system is an integral part of the total marketing information system. It establishes the goals and control procedures by which the marketing effort will be directed and monitored for the coming year. The final item forecasts and promotion and advertising plans which result from the marketing planning process provide a basis for planning the activity level of sales and other functional areas.

SALES PLANNING

Sales planning translates the overall sales and profit strategies outlined in the annual marketing plan into specific action plans and objectives to be undertaken at the territory and customer level.

The planning process includes statements of overall sales strategies for both present and potential customers. These, of course, may include a number of different types of objectives (none of which are mutually exclusive), such as increased territory sales volume, coverage of the full product line, elimination of small orders, establishment of new accounts, maximizing territory profitability, introduction of new products, maintenance of present customers, and increased retail availability of products.

In order for these goals to be consistent with overall company goals and marketing strategies, they must reflect analysis of the potential of territories and customer groups, the requirements of customers, in terms of service and coverage, and costs. Organizing the sales plan includes:

1. Identification and classification of present and prospective customers.
2. Determination of each customer's potential volume and grouping of customers as to potential.
3. Classification of customers by
   a. Type of selling effort (selling versus technical support).
   b. Level of support in terms of call frequency and duration.
4. Preparation of cost and profit analysis including
   a. Cost to serve present and potential customers.
   b. Expected volume and profit by types of market and class of customer.
   c. Estimate of the probability of success in selling.

5. Establishment of overall sales strategies, including the categories of accounts to be covered and the level of effort to be applied by category.
6. Development of district and region operating plans, including
   a. Customers to be serviced.
   b. Volume objective.
   c. Manpower requirements.
   d. Account selling plans.

The key element in the sales planning system is the required coordination and integration of detailed account and area plans with the overall strategies specified on the marketing plan.

Plans and strategies (activities and results) make up a portion of the information system, which then forms a standard against which what actually happens is compared. History (which is the starting point for preparing plans) is of secondary importance after the plan is prepared. The types of information required from the system, as well as the level of detail required, are defined when the plan has been prepared. The quality of the plan is dependent on the accuracy and the timeliness of data. Judgment in interpreting the data and detailing strategic actions is of key importance, but is apart from the structure of the plan itself.

The quality of the planning and reporting is also dependent on the resources (ability, time, and money) at the company's disposal and the degree of planning and reporting necessary.

Once a quantitative measure, such as sales dollars or number of calls, is expressed, there are various considerations of how performance against plan will be reported. The reporting system necessarily reflects the unique features of each company and of its informational resources in terms of availability, accuracy, timeliness, actionability, compatibility, and level of detail by responsibility.

By the proper analysis of variances between plan and performance, reporting systems can become effective control tools by identifying problem areas or potential problem areas. By the use of exception reports, based upon variances from plan, the planning and control action of management can be focused on those areas which require the greatest attention.

2

APPLYING SYSTEMS CONCEPTS TO MARKETING

The marketing information system is basically a framework for management. Every information system has this dual character: it is not only a mechanism for handling information but also a vehicle for the exercise of management control. Top management formulates the policies and objectives which give direction to an organization. Too often, soundly conceived policies fail in execution because of inadequate recognition of the gap between statement of policy and its interpretation through successive levels of the organization.

For example, a policy of maintaining close customer contact and a high level of customer service is subject to a wide range of interpretation. In order to be applied, it requires an information collection and reporting structure dealing with the specific objectives of selling operations, the approach to be taken with individual items of the product line, the required speed and completeness of delivery, and the incidence of returns and complaints. In addition, there must be means of periodically reviewing the costs associated with this policy and relating performance to that of competitors.

Similarly, when sales control or budgetary control efforts fail, the reason often proves to be lack of adequate consideration of the practical administrative and operating problems of preparing estimates, carrying out plans, gathering performance data, and relating information to action.

In short, effective management control requires an organized process for interpretation of top-level directives into programs of activity on one hand and expectations of results on the other, and for feedback of definitive information on both execution of programs and realization of results. The marketing information system provides the framework for this process of interpretation and feedback—for management by system.

HOW AND WHERE DO INFORMATION SYSTEMS FIT IN?

To understand the role information systems play, it is helpful to think of a five-link chain of logic (Exhibit 8) which leads from information (including data flowing in from external sources and internally generated plans, schedules, budgets, and forecasts), to systems which prepare it for use, to the people who use it, to the functions or purposes to which they apply the information, and finally to results. Results, in turn, give rise to information, completing the cycle.

We have outlined earlier the kinds of tangible results which management looks for and in terms of which it measures the adequacy of its information systems. Let us now turn to the users, and to the functions they must carry out to achieve these results.

Information Needs Relate to Organization

The organization chart in Exhibit 9 does not represent a specific company, but it offers a representative picture of the functional break-down of a medium-to-large marketing organization. A more complex

Exhibit 8. The role of information systems.

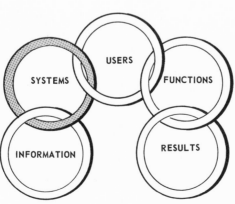

Exhibit 9. Organization of the sales and marketing function.

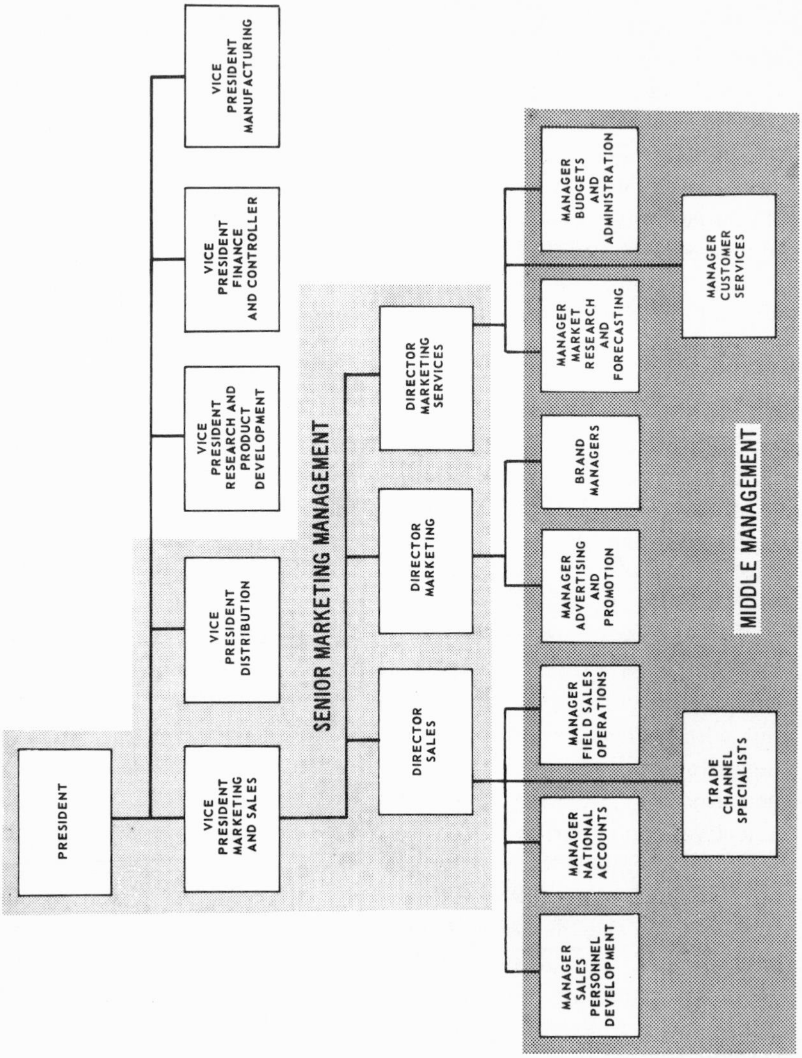

organization might have several distinct product divisions or selling divisions; a smaller or simpler organization might not require certain positions or functions, such as trade channel specialists or a customer service manager or a manager of advertising and promotion, or might combine several of these or other functions in a single position.

The chart defines three groups of users, representing three broad areas, or levels, in the organization. The middle-management level (the lowest level shown) represents the primary users of marketing information. It is here that plans are developed and executed, criteria are specified and applied, performance is reported and managed. In designing systems, we will be primarily concerned with the individual needs of this user group, particularly because much of the information used by others originates with them.

The information needs of senior marketing management, which as a practical matter often includes the presidential or senior vice presidential level, are related to the following.

1. Establishment of objectives.
2. Formulation of long-term plans and budgets.
3. Review of performance and compensation.
4. Organizational and personnel changes.
5. Flash reporting of key or critical events.

Normally, the information provided at this level represents a summarized version of middle-management reports. The design of top-management reports therefore generally follows the development of the more comprehensive, working-level requirements on which they are based, but with special emphasis on the tie-in of financial and marketing data regarding both objectives (growth in sales, earnings, market share) and performance. To be meaningful, the comparisons of statistical data about objectives and performance are generally accompanied by succinct written statements of reasons for major differences or changes.

The third broad area indicated in Exhibit 9 encompasses the operations outside the marketing function—primarily manufacturing, product development, and finance—which depend heavily on information supplied by marketing and in turn provide critical information relating primarily to production planning, scheduling, and inventory control (including purchased materials); planning, scheduling, and control of warehousing and transportation; product development; and budgeting of expense and cash flow, and profit planning.

The needs of all three major groups of marketing information users— senior marketing, middle marketing, and other-than-marketing management—must of course be fully considered. For the moment, however, let us focus on the middle marketing management group, which carries the primary burden of information management.

COMPONENTS OF THE MARKETING INFORMATION SYSTEM

Each line manager participates in a series of basic activities, or functions, through which marketing activities are managed. Principally, these are:

1. Long-range planning and product planning.
2. Development of current objectives and forecasts.
3. Operations planning to meet current objectives.
4. Budgeting and control of expenditures.
5. Implementation through issuance of information and directives internally and to others.
6. Activity reporting.
7. Performance reporting.

These activities are not necessarily of equal importance in each area, and each will receive substantially different treatment depending upon the nature of the business—that is, whether we are dealing with a consumer products operation, industrial selling to the private sector of the economy, marketing to military and government agencies, personal services, and so forth. But each occurs to some degree in every area of a marketing operation, and each requires systems support to some degree.

By way of example, consider sales planning, which is one of the principal activities under the more general heading of operations planning. Information normally required includes substantial detail on the following.

1. *Sales history* of individual customers, territories, districts, and regions.
2. *Background information* on major markets, customer categories, and individual major customers and on competitors' activities.
3. *Sales activity* on reports, customer assignments and number and types of calls made by class of customer.
4. *Cost* of sales operations in total and by class of customer in relation to revenue and profit, with analysis as to salary, commission, bonus, and expense overall and by salesman.

5. *Plans* for introduction of new products or promotions or extension of sales coverage.
6. *Personnel statistics* on recruiting and retention of salesmen and on availability of personnel by level of experience and capability, by location.

The collection and analysis of this information, its channeling through the various levels in the sales organization, and the preparation of a sales plan specifying call assignments and sales performance objectives, targets, or quotas in detail, together with appropriate budgetary information, must be coordinated and integrated through appropriate procedures. These procedures represent the sales planning subsystem—one of the key elements in most marketing information systems.

In every major area of marketing operations, we can think of each function as being supported by an information subsystem. This subsystem provides for the preparation of information for use by management and for the dissemination of plans, directives, and reports which represent the product of management effort in each area. The extent to which these procedures are thought through, organized, and formalized in actual practice varies a great deal, of course, from one organization to another.

INTEGRATION OF FUNCTIONS THROUGH SYSTEMS

What has just been described may be called the functional concept of marketing information systems. It represents a compartmentalized approach insofar as each function or job is viewed as supported by its own separate system. In actual practice, systems must be designed and implemented in an integrated way. They do not as a rule serve individual specialized functions, but cut across functions so as to provide for their coordination and internal consistency. They are most effective when they are designed to provide a common basis for interrelated planning and reporting functions.

Viewed in this context, individual subsystems, which form the building blocks of an overall systems structure, must be redefined in terms of the specific jobs they perform—such as historical reporting or forecasting or cost analysis—and as performing these jobs not just for a single function, such as sales planning, but in support of every function that requires that particular element of information.

Systems and procedures can be classified, then, according to the job they perform as distinct from the broader marketing function they serve.

Data collection and assimilation systems

1. From external sources (industry statistics, census, market research, advertising media, syndicated research).
2. Internally collected by marketing and sales organization (customer profile, competitive activity, call reporting).
3. Internal sales and inventory statistics.
4. Accounting and cost data.

Search and screening systems

1. Opportunities for increased sales based on buying patterns of current customers.
2. Potential customers in present and new markets.
3. Product opportunities for items used by customers but not marketed by company, or new products.
4. Competitive activity, including new products, price changes, promotions, and delivery performance.

Forecasting and projection systems

1. Statistical projections.
2. Models and simulations.
3. Economic analyses (long- and short-term).
4. Development and dissemination of management objectives.

Cost analysis and budgetary planning systems

Operations and activity planning systems

1. New product introductions.
2. Promotional activities.
3. Sales operations.
4. Advertising and media activities.
5. Warehousing and customer service activities.

Reporting systems

1. Sales and promotional activities.
2. Distribution activities.
3. Sales and profit performance.
4. Customer service performance.
5. Cost and financial performance.

Forecasting, as an example, draws on statistical data or generalized information from virtually every area of operation and, in turn, provides projections as a basis for planning and control to every area. So do

Exhibit 10. Systems serving multiple functions.

MARKETING MANAGEMENT FUNCTION	INFORMATION SYSTEMS					
	DATA COLLECTION	SEARCH & SCREENING	FORECASTING & PROJECTION	COST ANALYSIS & BUDGETARY PLANNING	OPERATIONS & ACTIVITY PLANNING	ACTIVITY & PERFORMANCE REPORTING
LONG RANGE AND NEW PRODUCT PLANNING	X	X	X	X	X	
OBJECTIVE SETTING AND FORECASTING	X	X	X	X	X	
OPERATIONS PLANNING	X	X		X	X	
- Sales	X	X		X	X	
- Adv. & Prom.	X	X		X	X	
- Distribution	X	X		X	X	
BUDGET PLANNING	X		X		X	
IMPLEMENTATION	X		X		X	
REPORTING						
- Sales Adv. & Prom. Activity	X	X		X		X
- Sales Performance	X	X		X		X
- Customer Service Performance	X	X	X	X		X
- Budget Performance	X	X	X			X

cost analysis and budgetary procedures, and so, to varying degrees, does each of the other systems. Coordination requires that information originating in each area be reviewed, reconciled, and redistributed in an organized way. Exhibit 10 shows, in broad outline, the interrelationship between major marketing functions and systems function.

WHY ARE MARKETING INFORMATION SYSTEMS NECESSARY?

In most companies the dimensions of the communications process are measured in terms of a staggering multiplicity of products, customers, sales personnel, and modes of marketing activities; hence the need for marketing information systems to provide for the organized flow of this massive and complex flood of communications.

The size and complexity of marketing operations in every type of business enterprise—be it a manufacturing, merchandising, or service organization—is growing also because of the mushrooming diversity of customer needs and of product lines, the multiplicity of distribution channels, and the geographic dispersion of operations domestically as well as overseas. Questions on where to apply company resources and efforts to best advantage in sales, promotion, advertising, or delivery or how to deal with product line and pricing decisions get more difficult because they require more detailed information and involve more people.

Another source of complexity is the increasing trend to specialization and definition of responsibility within the marketing function—between product management and sales operations, between brands and trade channels, between advertising, promotion, and research.

An integrated marketing information system provides the vehicle for coordinating operations and for assuring that problems and planning efforts throughout the organization are approached consistently and correctly, with full knowledge of relevant facts, and that the decisions, plans, and results which evolve are properly communicated and implemented.

BIGGER AND BETTER SYSTEMS—NEED OR LUXURY?

Like automobiles, marketing information systems come in different basic models, each available with or without various optional features. The popular "compact" model is represented by what we shall refer to as the byproduct system.

Many, if not most, of the existing information systems serving the marketing function depend primarily, or even exclusively, on information available as a byproduct of order handling, billing, and accounting operations. This normally includes such statistics as orders received, shipments and billings, receivables, sales revenue, various elements of selling and marketing expense, gross and net profit, and budgets and cost variances.

The appeal of byproduct systems for marketing is based on the notion that they cost little or nothing because they use information normally collected for accounting purposes, which is therefore "free" to the marketing organization. There are several pitfalls in this notion.

1. Information useful or necessary for marketing purposes is not necessarily captured in the order entry, billing, and accounting process unless special provisions are made for it. For example, elements of customer identity and product identity are often omitted because they are not needed in accounting summarizations of returns, credits, allowances, freight, and discounts. This may result in averaging of sales volume and profit contributions reported for individual customer categories or product categories.

2. Special marketing analyses and tabulations of sales or profits for particular groups of customers or products are generally not possible unless specific provisions for necessary coding have been built into the system. Even then, they may not be available in reasonable time unless output formats and computer programs have been prepared.

3. On-request reporting is slow, cumbersome, and expensive where possible requests have not been anticipated and, therefore, must be programmed on a one-at-a-time basis.

In short, effective systems are not really free even where the opportunity exists for using common input information available from accounting operations on a byproduct basis. Marketing information systems must be specifically planned, designed, and implemented to meet marketing needs, at some cost. But even the best byproduct systems cannot deal with the broad range of information needs characteristic of a modern marketing organization. Sales and marketing operations are, after all, inherently different from accounting and order handling, or for that matter from manufacturing operations, and have unique information needs of their own.

Considering the importance of marketing and sales functions in every business organization, what would constitute an information system specifically designed to meet their needs?

The question can, of course, only be answered with reference to a specific individual organization. It depends on the extent to which a recognized need exists for each of the many kinds of information systems we have identified (Exhibit 10). In general, byproduct systems are limited to internal phases of data collection, cost analysis, and performance reporting. They are severely lacking with respect to external market-oriented information and to search, screening, forecasting, and activity planning and reporting.

Cost-Benefit Considerations

Each system, to justify its development, should directly or indirectly provide economic benefits more than offsetting its costs. These benefits may be in terms of additional sales, more profitable sales, reduced cost, or improved customer service and customer relations, which strengthen the company's market position and competitive posture over the long term.

As was noted earlier, systems contribute to sales or profits by directing effort and attention—for example, toward the customer who is buying less than his potential, whose purchases are too heavily weighted with unprofitable items, or who receives inadequate service compared to competition. As will be illustrated, systems may in some situations also be expanded to provide specific direction as to selling or promotional action, and can, where appropriate, monitor activities to determine if action is taken.

In principle, benefits can be identified in terms of meaningful directions and signals and their potential results, recognizing that in marketing situations results do not follow with certainty but involve some element of probability. In practice, this is difficult to carry through. It will almost always be possible, however, to relate systems benefits in an order-of-magnitude way to one or more of the nine points we have listed near the beginning of Chapter 1 by which management judges the value of its information systems.

By way of example, one of the key subsystems in industrial products marketing information systems involves the development of customer profile data. These profiles are prepared and periodically updated by field sales personnel, generally with the assistance of their district supervisor and of marketing research personnel. Exhibit 11 partially illustrates typical profile data for a supplier of iron and steel furnace accessories. They provide a specific description of each operating location of all major customers and, to the degree obtainable, of present and potential customers. Each major furnace currently in place and planned for construction is listed, together with estimated throughput.

Exhibit 11. Input for customer profile subsystem.

CUSTOMER PROFILE _Blast Furnace Department_

CUSTOMER NAME _American Steel_   LOCATION _South Chicago_
PERSONS CONTACTED _Charles Jones (Supervisor) Frank Brown (Purchase Agent)_
NUMBER AND DIAMETER OF FURNACES _Two (#11, #12) #11-30', #12-29'1¾" at Bosh_
CAST CYCLE _#11-8.10, #12-7.92_ HRS.   CAST SIZE _#11-510, #12-495_ TONS
19X0 PRODUCTION _#11-349,700; #12-318,300_ TONS; 19X1 FORECAST _#11-316,000; #12-328,000_ TONS

REFRACTORY PRACTICE

ROW	PRODUCT	HEARTH	HEARTH WALLS	BOSH	STACK	STOVES	TRANSFER LADLES
1	FIRE CLAY	#11 – #12	#11, #12	#11, #12			
13	CLAY CASTABLE						#11, #12

TRANSFER LADLE TYPE _Plugh_   LADLE LIFE _150,000_ TONS HAULED
LADLE MAINTENANCE DESCRIPTION: _Scanned by crew after each heat; reviewed by foreman weekly; minor maintenance every 100 cast; major overhaul at 600 cast_
LADLE REFRACTORY, LINING _$.5512/_ TON HAULED, MAINTENANCE _$.0612/_ TON HAULED
COMMENTS (ANTICIPATED PRACTICE CHANGE THROUGH 19X5):
Will phase Blast Furnace #12 (built 1941) out in 19X2 Replacement not determined.

From these data, the replacement cycle and estimated annual usage of each item supplied by the manufacturer are determined. This in turn provides a basis for estimating market share information, long-term trends, and the probable effects of new technological developments, and for establishing individual salesmen's objectives and programs.

Of the nine payoff areas we have listed, the customer profile system has direct application in six, and it can be identified with potential sales on the order of several million dollars per year. The six areas of benefits are:

Sales coverage of present accounts.
Sales coverage of prospective accounts.
Customer service performance.
Sales personnel performance.
New product development.
Allocation of selling effort.

The customer profile information subsystem is characteristic of system elements not available in byproduct systems but commonly justifiable on a self-supporting basis.

MAKING USE OF COMPUTERS IN MARKETING INFORMATION SYSTEMS

Many, though by no means all, of the systems applications described here will make effective use of the massive data handling capabilities of computers; some, particularly in larger organizations, are predicated on the use of computers. Effective use of computers, conversely, requires special attention to marketing needs.

Even within the limited framework of byproduct systems, a great deal can usually be done to make the information more accessible and meaningful. This will be more fully explained and illustrated in subsequent chapters. Two key techniques, however, merit attention at this point; they are proper coding and the provision for on-request reporting in addition to regular periodic reporting.

Attention to special coding permits the grouping of customers according to trade channels, geography, sales department responsibility, or industry classification; or the grouping of products by source and use or Standard Industrial Classification (S.I.C.); or generally any grouping which facilitates recognition of relative strength and weakness in particular areas, or which provides a basis for comparison with external trade association, governmental, or other published statistics. Coding may be applied on orders or bills directly, or may be incorporated within a data processing system through a reference or look-up procedure.

ON-REQUEST REPORTING SYSTEMS

Marketing approaches and concepts have a way of changing, and as a result marketing management seems always to be looking for a new type of summary, cross-tabulation, or analysis. To those who observe the phenomenon over a few years, it becomes apparent that it has a cyclical character, with particular approaches going into and out of fashion periodically. The incidence of truly new and innovative concepts is relatively infrequent, at least in experienced organizations. Nevertheless, the cumulative requirement for different combinations and tabulations of information can be overwhelming.

On-request reporting can help to limit the proliferation of voluminous reports, each produced in great numbers on an indefinitely recurring schedule. Only a select number of reports and analyses are distributed on a regular periodic basis. The remainder are available as needed on short notice—normally a few days or, occasionally, overnight. The primary benefit sought through this type of system is often not the elimination of unnecessary paper—even though this is a welcome side effect— but rather the careful anticipation of and readiness for a wide range of information needs. In other words, the on-request reporting concept reduces the volume of reports on hand at a given time, but does not eliminate the need or the ability to have all reasonably expected report formats, clerical instructions, or computer programs fully developed in advance. Indeed, it is the maintenance of a system fully capable of producing any of the on-request reports quickly which makes it possible to limit publication of regular periodic reports to those which are routinely used.

Two novel features of on-request reporting from a computer system are beginning to find greater application. The first is on-line accessibility which provides for input/output keyboards located within the marketing area. The keyboards are connected by telephone lines directly to a computer which keeps selected data files continuously and instantly available. A simple typed instruction produces the desired report in minutes. Use of cathode ray tubes for display of information in place of keyboard devices is also possible.

The second novel feature is personalized reporting. Here the executive can in effect design his own report on the spur of the moment and, with the more sophisticated systems, have considerable flexibility in calling not only for listings and cross-tabulations but also for selective printing, calculation of simple ratios, cumulative totals, and so on. Obviously, these special features add to the cost of mechanized systems and their economic practicality has not as yet been fully tested.

Regardless of whether the marketing-oriented features to be provided are of a basic character, such as provision for appropriate coding, or of an advanced nature involving on-line capabilities, the costs of providing them are at a minimum when the job is done in conjunction with the conversion or redesign of the order handling and accounting systems—that is, as part of a more comprehensive implementation of management information systems or a conversion to a new computer configuration. Modification of an on-going system just to provide some additional elements needed from a marketing viewpoint is also feasible, of course, but may involve some redesign and reprogramming of major segments of the existing system.

CONTROL CONCEPTS IN MARKETING

Marketing information systems can, in some cases, provide direct guides to marketing action. This is possible where criteria can be defined in advance for deciding which of a number of possible actions is most appropriate under given circumstances. An example of broad potential application in the sales area is that of a national food products manufacturer and distributor who has established criteria regarding the length of time normally allowed between placement of orders by his major customers. These criteria are applied on a brand-by-brand basis. Failure of orders from specific customers to appear within the specified period results in an automatic signal for special sales action—a telephone call or an advancement in date of the next personal sales call, with special attention to the lagging brand. Wholesale slippage in the appearance of brand orders among a group of customers produces a "red alert" signal requiring closer examination and consideration of special promotional action.

Another feature of this system involves special week-to-week monitoring of sales during promotional periods to confirm looked-for effects, which may be increases in the number of accounts placing orders, or advancement in the timing of orders, or changes in the magnitude of orders. Relative success of different promotions with regard to these specific objectives can be directly observed. For seasonal or highly promoted items, daily review during the critical seasonal or promotional period may be necessary, together with daily adjustment of action criteria in conformance with a present cycle of objectives or action plans.

The idea of incorporating action limits in management reporting systems is by no means new. It is in fact nothing more than a form of exception reporting, or comparison of performance statistics with pre-established norms or standards of performance. These norms, to be useful, must, of course, be realistic and based on meaningful concepts. An example will be more fully described in Chapter 13.

Exception reporting is widely practiced in financial and budgetary reporting, and in sales reporting for comparison with quotas or targets. It will be a recurring element in this book. In most cases, however, exception reporting is presently used primarily to evoke explanations or reasons for variances or divergence between "actual" and "standard," and is not directly related to action. The idea of screening and search systems, based on identification of more direct links between exception reporting and action by seeking to define the specific alternatives possible in a particular marketing situation, has appeal and merit. It is finding growing application in the design and implementation of marketing information systems.

USING COMPUTERS IN FORECASTING AND PLANNING: MARKETING MODELS AND SIMULATION

The interest of marketing, perhaps more than of any other area of a company's operation, focuses on the future. From conception to realization, most major marketing moves extend over months and years. Careful planning is crucial and requires detailed consideration of all reasonable alternative approaches and of the responses each will evoke in the market.

In terms of marketing information, management normally has three or four basic reference points to help orient itself toward the future.

1. *Present company position* in terms of sales level, market share, and distribution coverage; and indications of latent strengths or weaknesses based on recent trends, research reports, and field sales reports.

2. *Market trend* in terms of overall growth, economic factors, and shifts toward or away from specific product categories.

3. *Statistical forecasts* reflecting continuation of historical trends of company sales.

4. *Financial objectives* or expectations defining what earnings are required and what funds are likely to be available to support marketing activities.

These are augmented by information on competitors' activities, governmental and regulatory actions or proposals, and technological developments.

It is supposedly the job of marketing management to combine and weigh this great mass of information, to relate it to specific pricing, promotion, advertising, product introduction, or selling actions, and to predict the results as a basis for establishing marketing plans and programs. As a practical matter, it is not physically possible for any individual or group to even begin to carry this out in a literal sense—that is, to trace through all these interrelated factors in numerical terms within the time span normally available. Consequently, marketing judgment—the application of individualized accumulation of experience of what seems to work and what does not—must bridge the gaps.

There is growing evidence, however, that the advent of organized logical techniques (under the headings of operations and marketing research) in combination with the prodigious powers of computers now makes it possible to carry out at least some of these analyses explicitly and quickly, supplementing the marketing manager's judgment.

The term "models" is commonly used to refer to these logical, analytical procedures (which may be carried out manually but are more often programmed for execution by computer) for translating proposed plans and assumptions into projections of their probable consequences. "Simulation" is the process of carrying through a particular analysis several times over, each time using a different set of plans or assumptions for the purpose of identifying either what assumptions are most consistent with known facts or experience, or given a set of assumptions, which plan or line of action appears to lead to the best results.

In undertaking an initial effort, it is seldom practical to develop a comprehensive model which deals with interrelations between individual marketing actions such as price changes, product introductions and advertising campaigns, and with interrelations of brands or sizes within a market. In general, a modular, building-block approach, tackling one area at time, has been found effective. Ultimately, individual models may be linked. This may require some reprogramming, but in light of the experimental or preliminary nature of most models now in use, this is very difficult to anticipate or avoid. In terms of economics, individual modular analytical programs or models can be made self-supporting more quickly, in much the same way as are other elements of the information system. Some illustrations are offered in Chapter 10.

Individual markets and marketing organizations offer different opportunities for application of these concepts, and few companies have begun to explore their full potential. Realization of the benefits of marketing information systems can be enhanced by, but does not depend upon,

application of sophisticated control concepts or models, and implementation of more basic data collection, analysis, and reporting systems is
often a necessary prerequisite to the application of more advanced
systems.

MASS DATA RETRIEVAL SYSTEMS

The sheer volume of statistics which sometimes needs to be digested
in planning is perhaps best illustrated by the marketing and media
planning activities of national advertisers and of the advertising agencies
serving them, as described in Chapter 14.

Mass distribution of consumer products in competitive markets requires that the manufacturer find means of getting his sales message
to the ultimate consumer in a way that is both effective and economical.
The variety of advertising vehicles at his disposal is staggering, particularly if we include direct mail, newspapers, catalogs, magazines and
periodicals, broadcast media, and public or point-of-sale displays. Brand
expenditures in this area outweigh profit margins and may exceed manufacturing costs. Management, therefore, is continually seeking better
ways of allocating advertising efforts and budgets among alternative
vehicles or methods.

The problem is to choose among hundreds, or perhaps thousands,
of different audience segments which overlap to varying degrees and
can be reached with different messages by different vehicles at different
times and at different costs. If the job is to be tackled systematically,
it requires the analysis of substantial amounts of complexly related
numerical data.

Large agencies and individual large advertisers have allocated substantial funds to the development of sophisticated data handling and
retrieval systems in support of manual or computer-based planning
procedures, sometimes involving use of mathematical models. For example, the geographic strategy for a brand may be developed by first
constructing a file of data on the demographic characteristics of the
population. Derived from census data and trade publications, this file
is usually on a county-by-county basis and contains estimates of current
population, the income, ages, household sizes, and estimated spending
patterns of the population, and some indicators of the relative importance of one county as opposed to another. This file may be in the
form of a book or set of tables, or may be on a computer tape.

A number of syndicated services collect information on the retail
and wholesale movement of brands. These services have generally

adopted the county as their basic geographic unit, although their reports contain information on groups of counties, such as metropolitan markets or television viewing areas. When consumer goods companies purchase this information, they or their agency may relate the retail movement reports to internal reports of sales volume. The resulting file of information, also on a geographic basis, contains actual sales for a brand and estimates of that brand's share of total market sales.

Similar massive files are maintained on audience characteristics and costs of individual media vehicles. Through a series of analytical steps of matching, in detail, audience to customer characteristics, and media costs to funds allotted, a media plan is evolved. The need for application of large-scale computers in this area is evident and quite advanced.

THE PEOPLE PROBLEM
IN MARKETING INFORMATION SYSTEMS

Systems development normally involves a variety of different specialized talents. In the case of marketing information systems, as the name suggests, success depends particularly on merging the activities of people with marketing and systems know-how, and this can be difficult in the light of the two groups' divergent backgrounds, approaches, and attitudes.

Individuals in marketing and sales management, as a group, tend to be as well organized, thorough, and quantitatively oriented as any other group in the company—probably more so. They have to be to work out complex business arrangements with their customers, to insure that their company's commitments and obligations for service are fully met, and to make effective use of their own time and that of their subordinates.

On the other hand, there tends to be a great deal of "reinventing the wheel" each time new plans or programs are developed because of insufficient documentation of how it was done the last time, aggravated by personnel turnover. Often several repeat passes are necessary because of uncertainty of what information management wanted, or simply in what format—an uncertainty which may originate with management. Much unnecessary and often unsuccessful searching is done for information which should be routinely available. Under pressure of time, there is a tendency to bypass the search for data in favor of reliance on memory and inductive reasoning bordering on guessing. Different forecasts or projections for the same items are made and used by different people in product management, sales, production planning,

and budgeting without coordination and sometimes without mutual awareness of the differences. To the systems man, there appears much need
for his services. However, he must be alert to some special aspects
concerning his role.

In marketing there is considerable emphasis on individuality. Sales
managers have their own approaches to the way they schedule sales
activity among large and small accounts, or between established customers and new prospects. Product managers approach the planning
and execution of promotions and advertising campaigns differently.
These differences are generally not merely a reflection of individual
idiosyncrasies, but exist at least in part by virtue of differences in product
line, facilities, marketing organization, or customer configuration. Every
company has, to some degree, its own unique approach to marketing
because it is a unique organization. This individual approach must be
served by the marketing information system—not changed by it, except
insofar as a better system can provide opportunities for refinement and
strengthening.

The marketing man's view of systems people may also involve some
distortions. These may derive from lack of familiarity with different
areas of specialization, such as systems design, operations research, or
programming. They may sometimes result from marketing people's real
concern for what they perceive as systems people's undue confidence
in the power of computers or their tendency towards oversimplification
of information management problems substantially more complex than
those normally encountered in accounting or order processing.

MARKETING MANAGEMENT'S ROLE

The answer to development of good systems lies in the organization
of project teams involving joint participation of marketing and systems
people which will promote understanding of their respective problems
and merge the special abilities each individual can bring to bear. The
responsibility of marketing personnel assigned to such an effort goes
substantially beyond that of simply passing on information to the systems
people. Marketing information systems do not sell products, nor do they
make marketing decisions. They do have a vital influence, however,
on how decisions will be made within the marketing organization because a comprehensive system, once installed, organizes and channels
the flow of information. That being the case, marketing management
plays an important role in setting the detailed specifications for the
system in just the same way as an industrial user of a highly complex

mechanism or machinery must set forth his specifications to a supplying organization. The systems organization can help by suggesting the probable costs and performance characteristics of the available alternatives and options so that the marketing user can arrive at his specifications in a fully informed way. Systems people must also define the format in which the systems specification needs to be presented in order for detail design and implementation to proceed effectively.

Because sales and the performance of marketing activities set the framework within which every other function in the company operates, the marketing information system transcends the organizational limits of the sales and marketing areas. For this reason it is also important that proper liaison is provided with other major functional areas, both at the technical and at the senior-management levels.

The systems approach is not new to management. Its application to marketing, however, has fallen far short of the real need which exists and of the opportunities which present themselves and which this book seeks to illustrate. In most marketing organizations, information collection and management has been a slow evolutionary process. The marketing information systems approaches described here represent a way of working more directly, subject to economic considerations, toward full satisfaction of management needs.

CUSTOMER SERVICE
AND SALES OPERATIONS

A reasonable working description of the customer service function is "all activities associated with order taking and order filling." This includes not only soliciting orders from customers and delivery of the product but also subsequent continuing customer service. To be effective, a sales operation requires information feedback to provide management with control tools and followup capability, and both internal and external data is needed in this process.

This chapter will review the marketing information system concept as it applies to customer service, sales performance, operational and financial control reports, and sales force compensation.

CUSTOMER SERVICE

For the purpose of this discussion customer service may be categorized by two types of activities: product service and order handling and filling. The first, product service, includes all activities needed to support the customer's initial and repeat purchases.

Product Service

The basic elements of product service include user training, product installation, and product maintenance or replacement. Of course, the relative importance of each element in the sales operation depends on the type of product. Little direct training is possible or required for users of most consumer products. On the other hand, many industrial products require heavy training; for example, successful marketing of data processing equipment requires that extensive user training programs be provided by manufacturers. Planning and controlling training expense is an extremely important element in the marketing mix of such industries. Effective planning and control of installation, maintenance, and repair—product service—have become increasingly important elements in the marketing mix.

The information collection and reporting system should provide management with sufficient information to allow for such product servicing decisions as:

1. Locating service parts.
2. Distributing training services and instructional material.
3. Establishing repair parts and service centers.
4. Training distributors and dealers or servicemen.
5. Determining the amounts of service parts to be stocked.
6. Scheduling service calls.

Each of these decisions requires feedback to the manufacturer on how his product performs after purchase by the customer.

Of particular importance in the area of product service are reports on product returns, warranty servicing, customer complaint letters, and special price or trade-in adjustments made by salesmen. Regularly solicited customer comments and special market research projects to obtain customers' views are also appropriate sources of information for planning and evaluating service policies. Such information, when effectively collected and reported, can help to identify potential product service problems as soon as possible and can provide data on the type and level of service provided by competitors. In addition, such data can be used to analyze the relationship between the appropriate level of product service and the other elements of the marketing mix.

The complaint/adjustment analysis report shown in Exhibit 12 is an example of the type of information which could be collected to monitor product service performance. The report, for a maker of consumer bakery products, shows, by manufacturing facility, the number of complaints received by week for each quarter by type of complaint (major categories only). In addition, it shows the total number of units of the order on which the complaints were based and the total number of units, if any, involved in an adjustment. A measure of plant product service performance is obtained by reporting the number of orders in-

Exhibit 12. Quarterly complaint/adjustment analysis report.

PRODUCT CHOC. COOKIES

CHICAGO PLANT

	WEEK 1	2	3	4	5	6	7	8	9	10	11	12	TOT.	ORDER SIZE (UNITS)	ADJ. (UNITS)	COST OF ADJ.$	COM-PLAINT %	ADJ. %	ADJ. COST %	PLANT SHIPMENTS
WRONG PRODUCT	1				2	1	1		2	2		1	8	240	40	175	1.0	–	.3	UNITS 24,000
WRONG SIZE	1	2		1		1	1		1	2			5	125	125	525	.5	.5	1.7	DOLLARS 49,000
STALE	3	2	4		3	3	1	1	7	2		4	26	650	650	2,400	2.7	2.7	4.8	
BROKEN		1					1		1				3	20	20	100	–	–	.2	
OTHER	1						1				–		2	15	–	60	–	–	–	
SUBTOTAL	6	5	4	2	1	4	4	–	8	5	–	5	44	1,050	835	3,260	3.9	3.4	6.6	

DALLAS PLANT

	WEEK 1	2	3	4	5	6	7	8	9	10	11	12	TOT.	ORDER SIZE (UNITS)	ADJ. (UNITS)	COST OF ADJ.$	COM-PLAINT %	ADJ. %	ADJ. COST %	PLANT SHIPMENTS
WRONG PRODUCT	2		4		2	2	2		4		2	2	16	480	80	350	2.0	–	.6	UNITS 24,000
WRONG SIZE	2	4		2				2					10	250	250	1,050	1.0	1.0	2.4	DOLLARS 49,000
STALE	6	4	8		6	2	2		14	4		8	52	1,300	1,300	4,800	5.4	5.4	9.0	
BROKEN	2				2		2						6	40	40	200	–	–	.4	
OTHER	2						2				–		4	30	–	120	–	–	–	
SUBTOTAL	12	10	8	4	8	8	8	–	16	10	–	10	88	2,100	1,670	6,520	7.8	6.9	13.2	

ALL PLANTS

	WEEK 1	2	3	4	5	6	7	8	9	10	11	12	TOT.	ORDER SIZE (UNITS)	ADJ. (UNITS)	COST OF ADJ.$	COM-PLAINT %	ADJ. %	ADJ. COST %	PLANT SHIPMENTS
WRONG PRODUCT	3		6		3	3	3		6			3	24	720	120	525	1.5	–	.5	UNITS 48,000
WRONG SIZE	3	6		3		3			3				15	375	375	1,575	.7	.7	1.5	DOLLARS 98,000
STALE	9	6	12		9	3	3		21	6		12	78	1,950	1,950	7,200	4.0	4.6	7.2	
BROKEN		3			3		3						9	60	60	300	–	–	.2	
OTHER	3						3				–		6	45	–	180	–	–	–	
TOTAL	18	15	12	6	3	12	12	–	24	15	–	15	132	3,150	2,505	9,780	6.5%	6.0%	9.8%	

volved in the complaint, the number of units of adjustment, and the value of those adjustments relative to the total shipments from the particular manufacturing location for the period. A similar analysis might be generated by sales office, service outlet, salesman, or serviceman, provided that procedures are established for the systematic collection of such information.

Order Handling and Filling

The second element of customer service which must be considered from the standpoint of information collection and reporting is the process of order handling and order filling. Again, effective policies can be implemented, and performance controlled, only when appropriate information is made available.

Exhibit 13 shows, from a conceptual standpoint, the key inputs and outputs of an integrated and fully automated order processing system. Information requirements include effective communication of orders, inventory, and shipping information among plants, warehouses, and other functional areas. The basic sequence of the events in the cycle is:

1. Entering a customer's order in the main office or branch and performing routine credit and inventory availability checks.

Exhibit 13. Integrated system for information processing (order handling and filling).

INPUT

MAIL ORDERS

PHONE ORDERS

ORDERS FROM COMMUNICATIONS SYSTEM

INQUIRIES

| Customer | ABC |
| Order No. | 4617 |

OUTPUT

WAREHOUSE REPLENISHMENT SCHEDULES

PRODUCTION SCHEDULING

BILL OF LADING

PLANT SHIPPING ORDER

INQUIRY RESPONSE
- Order Status
- Inventory Availability
- Order Backlog

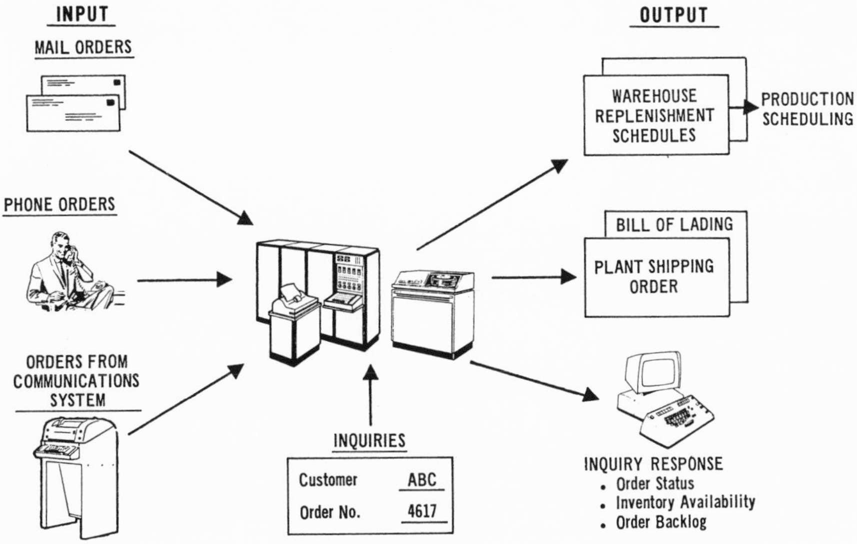

2. Producing a hard copy of the final order for the customer and salesman.
3. Preparing shipping documents (or warehouse releases) and bills of lading.
4. Shipping and reporting the shipments from stock point locations for inclusion into the billing and accounts receivable system.

This process may also be viewed in terms of the three basic operations of (1) prebilling, (2) order filling and delivery, and (3) post billing. Each of these has an impact on timeliness, cost and customer satisfaction. The order processing system must provide an inquiry capability to determine order status and inventory availability. Effective customer service also requires that marketing management have continuing, up-to-date information on product availability and anticipated delivery dates. This is especially true for special or seasonal products.

Effective control requires a system to provide performance data on the number of back orders and partial shipments by type of product and by customer as they relate to a company's customer service level objectives. Other elements of information which might be included in such reports are promised and actual delivery dates, analysis of the number of orders by size of order, and the number of days' supply of the product available for shipment.

Establishing the appropriate level of customer service requires information on customer expectations and on the levels of service provided by major competitors. Such information may be obtained in the course of salesmen's calls on customers, through special surveys, or through trade associations. It should be updated and evaluated periodically to insure that levels of service are comparable to those provided by others in the industry and, at the same time, that they are not excessively rigid and costly.

Some questions which should be considered in deciding on and maintaining an acceptable, competitive level of customer service include:

Reliability: Can customers depend on the completeness of shipments? Would they tolerate slower deliveries if they could depend on getting the product when promised? Are back orders a major source of complaint?

Communications: Are customers made aware of company policy on deliveries and of appropriate ways to complete order forms? Are written instructions to customers confusing?

Delivery time: Do customers view the company's order filling time as excessive?

Prior notification: Are customers notified when orders cannot be delivered as promised?

Claims and credits: Are credits and claims handled on an accurate and timely basis?

As with all other aspects of the marketing mix, better customer service usually means greater costs. Consider, for example, the costs associated with insuring that orders are filled and shipped exactly as specified by the customer. Since orders generally include a combination of slow-moving, low-volume items and fast-moving, high-volume items, an improved level of customer service, if applied to all items and types of orders, means an increase in the size of inventory and its carrying cost, as well as an increase in the number of products stocked.

The relationship between increases in customer service and increases in average inventory requirements is shown graphically in Exhibit 14. (In this particular example, 100% customer service could be defined as 100% of all orders delivered as ordered within an established competitive time period.) As indicated, the incremental costs associated with even small increases in a level of service above 90% are high. In this case, increasing the level of service from 95% to 97% required an increase in inventory levels of $10 million from $78 million to $88 million. Only the evaluation of a particular competitive situation can determine what level is appropriate. The information system should provide management with periodic reports on competitive practices and, in addition, should monitor internal customer service performance against the established level.

Specific examples of control reports for monitoring customer service performance are illustrated in Exhibit 15. Two reports are shown. The first indicates, by warehouse location, the amount of each product back-ordered (by customer), how long it has been back-ordered, and an assigned priority for filling the order. The second report indicates the overall level of customer service, showing the amount of product delivered, the time in excess of the established standard and the amount of product on back order, as well as the number of days in that status. A more complete analysis of the systems approach to management of the distribution function is provided in Chapter 5.

Some additional areas of the order filling process which require consideration as they relate to the selling operation are:

1. *Credit policies.* Information must be provided to allow the establishment of realistic credit policies. Reports on the number of negative credit checks handled should be provided in the information system as should reports, on an exception basis, for customers who exceed a credit limit.

Many companies do not make routine credit information available to salesmen, nor is it used in planning the selling operation, although such information could be of value in establishing customer potential

Exhibit 14. Level of service, breakeven analysis.

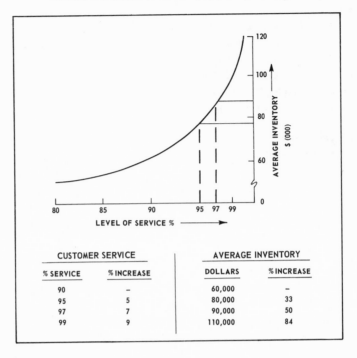

CUSTOMER SERVICE		AVERAGE INVENTORY	
% SERVICE	% INCREASE	DOLLARS	% INCREASE
90	–	60,000	–
95	5	80,000	33
97	7	90,000	50
99	9	110,000	84

Exhibit 15. Customer service reporting.

BACK ORDER STATUS REPORT
BY WAREHOUSE

WAREHOUSE———————LOCATION———————   DATE———————

PRODUCT	INVENTORY CLASS	CUSTOMER	CUSTOMER CODE	AMOUNT	DAYS	PRIORITY
07148	A	REAL CORP	1792–1A	1250	3	1
		SALE CORP	1824–1C	250	3	2
07149	A					
07150	B					
07155	B					

CUSTOMER SERVICE LEVEL REPORT
BY WAREHOUSE

WAREHOUSE———————LOCATION———————   DATE———————

TRADE CLASS	SIZE CLASS	CUSTOMER	CUSTOMER CODE	ORDER PLACED	DELIVERY TIME	UNITS ORDERED	% COMPLETE	BACK ORDER PRODUCT	DAYS
07	A	REAL CORP	1792–1A	8/6	8/9	5,000	65	1,250	3
	A	SALE CORP	1824–1C	8/4	8/8	1,000	75	250	3

and could be effective in eliminating calls on customers who are poor credit risks.

The credit department can contribute toward improvement of salesmen's effectiveness by tabulating account credit ratings and then providing the information to salesmen for use in scheduling prospect calls. For one particular company which sells women's apparel, a market where credit problems are common, this policy proved effective in eliminating many collection problems after the selling season as well.

2. *Credit problems.* The billing system should alert salesmen to potential credit problems. Also, feedback to the credit and marketing departments, through call reports, can pinpoint possible problems in maintaining credit policies. Salesmen can serve as a source of information on the length and type of credit extended to customers by competition.

3. *Collections.* Since a sale is not completed until the goods have been paid for, an effective information system should provide notification to customers of past-due bills.

4. *Order size.* Where there is a tendency on the part of many customers to place small orders, a requirement of the information system should be the identification of the cost of orders on an order-size basis so that action may be taken to increase the size of orders or reduce the number of small orders. Specific strategies such as the use of quantity discounts, establishment of minimum order size policies, add-on charges for small orders, or limiting the number of salesmen's calls on such customers, should be developed as part of the market planning process. Performance reports, including those which report sales performance on a per order basis, will be discussed later in this chapter.

In most cases, regular reports of the cost of orders by size are not required. But such data should be available on a special analysis basis for periodic reevaluation.

Information Required for Customer Service

To summarize the relationship between the marketing information system and customer servicing, the information system should

1. Identify those factors, such as training, maintenance, credit allowance, order size, and delivery time, which make up the important elements of the customer service mix.
2. Classify customers and products relative to their required customer service levels.
3. Monitor the continuing performance of the order filling function in terms of maintenance of specified service levels.
4. Evaluate, periodically, the adequacy of established levels of service on the basis of internal performance, competitive per-

formance, or periodic solicitation of customers and salesmen for comments.

SALES PERFORMANCE AND CONTROL REPORTING

As illustrated earlier, the collection and analysis of information on current and historical market performance is essential to the management of the sales operation. It contributes to development of overall management policies, determination of customer service levels, and formulation of specific plans and marketing strategies as well as, in planning, amount and allocation of a company's selling efforts. More specifically, the reporting of performance for each of the units in the sales operation provides a basis for establishing the relative importance of individual customers or types of customers and the strengths and weaknesses of individual markets or market segments. It can give a measure of company success in a market relative to the market's potential. For effective management of the marketing function, specific long-term and short-term marketing strategies must be based on such detailed performance data.

The performance reporting system provides a basis for evaluating and controlling sales and profit performance and the related success or failure of current marketing strategies. The most frequent uses of sales performance reporting are to monitor:

1. The performance of the field sales force in terms of individual or areas sales performance as related both to quota and to potential.
2. The volume and profit against plan for major products or product lines.
3. The volume and profit performance of markets, trade channels, or customers.
4. The effectiveness of particular marketing programs, such as advertising and promotional campaigns.
5. The effectiveness of the sales force in calling on and servicing current and potential accounts.

The traditional concept of the marketing information system, as discussed in Chapter 1, is limited to the reporting of company sales volume, by product or product grouping, for various geographic or organizational areas. The concept of performance reporting, in the context of a comprehensive marketing information system, however, includes the process of collecting, storing, analyzing, and reporting *all* relevant internal and external cost, revenue, and strategic information needed for planning and evaluating the selling and marketing operation.

Design of performance and control reports involves two basic questions: (1) What kinds of information, reported at what level of detail and with what frequency, are required? (2) How can such information be effectively identified, collected, and organized to provide an effective performance reporting system?

As a way of dealing with these questions, we will look at some of the types of performance reports developed by consumer, industrial, and service companies in the organization of their marketing information systems. It will not, of course, be possible to illustrate all of the various types of performance reports or reporting concepts used within the selling operation. However, some of the primary areas which will be included are

1. Customer analysis and customer and market sales performance.
2. Salesmen's activity.
3. Product and product group and market segment performance.
4. Promotion and advertising performance.

Customer Analysis and Customer and Market Sales Performance Reporting

At the start, an important part of any customer analysis system is the establishment of customer classification procedures. Meaningful codes must be based on an individual company's marketing environment. Although customer performance information is, for the most part, captured through transaction systems, such as billing, order processing, and accounts receivable, it is also important that customer coding be compatible with classifications used by industry, government, and trade associations.

Also, considerable refinement can be applied to developing an appropriate customer classification system. Some examples are:

Basic Customer Classifications

Size: Share of company volume or market volume.
Functional class, such as:

Basic	*Variations*
Manufacturer	Fabricator, OEM, processor
Wholesaler	Distributor, broker, jobber
Dealer	Chain, department store, discount
Consumer	Applicator, contractor

Location: Area served.
Affiliation.
Industry: By S.I.C. code.

Customer size classification. As illustrated in Exhibit 16, a typical distribution of customer size and sales volume indicates that a majority of sales volume, in this case 86%, comes from a minority (20%) of customers. The specific distribution will vary from one company to another, but the general relationship remains the same. This fact is important both in planning and directing the selling effort and in determining the structure of the performance reports for customers. This "key account," or "key customer," concept, placing maximum attention and effort on a relatively small number of accounts, as applied to planning is discussed in the last chapters.

From the standpoint of customer reporting and analysis, the key customer concept is used to provide more detailed and more frequent reports on major customers.

Individual product detail and information on past usage and potential can be maintained for this group with less detailed reports for individual smaller customers, or a single product detail report for all small customers as a group.

Generally, the sales coverage plan calls for more frequent coverage of major customers and salesmen require more frequent updating on

Exhibit 16. Application of the key customer concept.

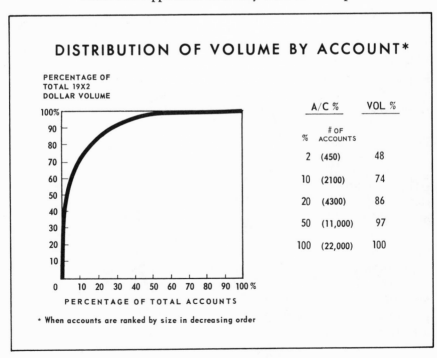

DISTRIBUTION OF VOLUME BY ACCOUNT*

PERCENTAGE OF
TOTAL 19X2
DOLLAR VOLUME

A/C %		VOL %
%	# OF ACCOUNTS	
2	(450)	48
10	(2100)	74
20	(4300)	86
50	(11,000)	97
100	(22,000)	100

PERCENTAGE OF TOTAL ACCOUNTS

* When accounts are ranked by size in decreasing order

such customer performance. One approach to customer report frequency is to provide weekly or monthly reporting on major customers and monthly or quarterly detail on minor customers. One major consumer products company, in an effort to discourage salesmen from calling on small, low profitability customers, provides its salesmen with only a single annual report on its smallest customer group.

It is important to keep in mind that the determination of a major customer should not be based on historical sales performance alone, but should consider the customer's position relative to the total market.

Customers fall into two obvious categories; those who are current customers and those who are inactive or dormant. The latter include those who (1) use the types of products sold by the company but purchase none of their requirements from it, (2) use all of the types of products sold by the company but purchase only some types from it, and (3) use types of products similar to those sold by the company but purchase none of the company's particular type.

The question of measuring their sales potential will be discussed in some detail later in this chapter.

Customer sales performance reports. The customer sales report in Exhibit 17 is an example of a detailed customer report by product. The monthly report, used by a consumer products manufacturer, includes sales of each product for the current period in comparison with both the established quota and the performance for the same period last year. Detailed information is provided on each of the major products, while all minor products are reported in aggregate. Groupings of lesser products are in dollars only, rather than in units and dollars, to provide a uniform reporting base. Another feature of this particular report is the highlighting of date of last purchase to call attention to those items which may require special selling effort. Figures are enclosed in parentheses to call attention to products whose performance is below plan. Other customer data includes the total discounts and allowances granted, by product (relating to pricing and special promotion). The relative importance of each product to total customer purchases is also shown and, in turn, the importance of the customer's sales relative to other customers in the territory serviced by the salesman.

Such detailed reports are prepared only for major customers, using the key customer concept. Reports for smaller customers are prepared both less frequently and with less detail.

Exhibit 18 is a summary customer report for each customer in a territory comparing performance against quota for sales and gross margin. In addition, this particular report indicates both the planned and actual share each customer represents of the territory's total volume

Exhibit 17. Monthly customer performance report.

CUSTOMER _____
LOCATION _____
CUSTOMER NUMBER _____

CUSTOMER CLASS CODE _____
INDUSTRY CODE _____
ANNUAL POTENTIAL _____

PRODUCT		MONTH			YEAR TO DATE						
		CURRENT MONTH	OVER (UNDER) PLAN	OVER (UNDER) LAST YR	CURRENT PERIOD	OVER (UNDER) PLAN	OVER (UNDER) LAST YR	DATE OF LAST PURCHASE	ALLOWANCE & DISCOUNTS TO DATE	% CUSTOMER PURCHASES	% DIST SALES
0120	UNITS	10,000	100	350	35,700	(6,500)	1,520	2/18	1,400	8.4	8.0
	$(000)	25,640	250	1,040	90,400	(18,400)	4,210				
0114	UNITS	5,250	(.50)	10	16,000	1,500	150	3/1	1,850	4.1	4.5
	$(000)	18,625	(150)	15	46,250	3,600	450				
0187	UNITS	2,400	150	250	7,000	(150)	—	2/18	750	2.3	6.2
	$(000)	6,240	450	700	20,150	(450)	520				
ALL OTHERS	$(000)	19,020	$(1,200)	(500)	44,000	(240)	1,000		215	4.0	1.5
TOTAL	$(000)	240,000	(21,600)	1,520	862,000	4,200	8,700		63,500	100.0	9.5

Exhibit 18. Monthly market share report, key customers.

TERRITORY _____

ASSIGNED TO _____

PERIOD _____

MARKET POTENTIAL $1,276,000

TARGET MARKET SHARE 300.0

ACTUAL SALES		DEDUCTIONS % OF NET	GROSS MARGIN		CUSTOMER		INVENTORY CODE	SHARE OF TERRITORY		UNIT SALES		MARKET SHARE %
GROSS	NET		% OF NET	BUDGET %				ACT	PLAN	ACTUAL	VARIANCE	
10,370	9,964	4.2	19.1	19.5	ABR CO.	12,849	01	21.0	20.1	18,460	1,460	39.0
79,608	77,352	2.9	21.6	21.7	AAB CO.	1,246	01	8.4	9.2	72,526	2,562	31.4
357,264	345,200	3.2	22.0	23.1	TOTAL			100	100	330,421	18,420	26.4

objective. Other variations of summary customer reporting would be to report only those accounts whose performance is under quota. A salesman's exception report is shown in Exhibit 19. Exhibit 20 is another variation of customer reporting. This annual report is used for territory planning. For each product, all customers are listed in three groups: (1) active customers, (2) lost customers, and (3) prospects. The report also shows sales potential, budget, and prior year's performance, as well as current share of business. Potential is reported in units and dollars.

Other types of customer-oriented sales performance reports include periodic reporting of lost customers or lost sales. These would be prepared quarterly or semiannually as a basis for sales planning.

Salesmen's Activity

In addition to the performance of customer and salesman in terms of volume and profit, the reporting of salesmen's activity as it relates to planned calls and sales is an important element in the performance reporting system. Such information about the selling activity can take a variety of forms but would generally include

- The number of customer or prospect calls (by type of call: visit, phone, letter).
- The number of active prospects.
- Merchandising activities (special in-store displays, promotions, and so on).
- The number of calls required to obtain an order.
- How time was spent (traveling, planning, writing orders, handling complaints).
- Call performance against plans or planned and unplanned calls.
- The number of orders per call.

The individual call report may contain all or some of the above information and represents a valuable source of performance measures. Exhibit 21 is an example of the three basic types of salesman's activity reports often included in the performance reporting system. The first is the itinerary of calls, or the call plan, which indicates the customers to be called on for a particular period. The document not only serves as a plan for covering customers, but also provides management with a convenient means of locating or contacting the salesman as required. The second document illustrated is the call report, which provides all the basic information reported by the salesman for accounts called on during the reporting period. Many firms require, as a matter of practice, the completion of an account call report immediately after the call is

(*Text continues on page 58*)

Exhibit 19. Monthly quota performance exception report.

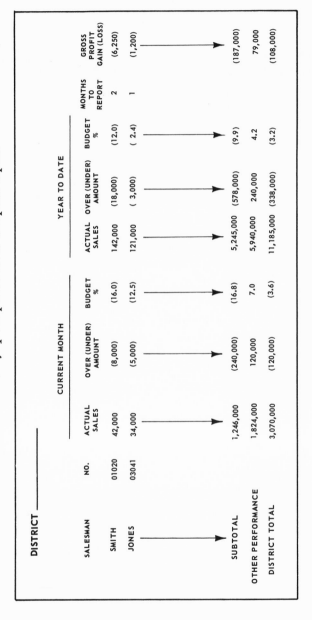

Exhibit 20. Annual customer/market planning report.

PRODUCT _____	SALES POTENTIAL		BUDGET		PERFORMANCE	MARKET SHARE			CURRENT POTENTIAL UNITS
	PRIOR YEAR	CURRENT YEAR	PRIOR YEAR	CURRENT YEAR	PRIOR YEAR	LAST PLAN	YEAR ACTUAL	CURRENT YEAR	
ACTIVE CUSTOMERS									
AA CO	$ 2,845	$ 2,990	$ 725	$ 800	$ 762	25.0 %	26.5 %	27.0 %	745
SUBTOTAL	48,400	54,640	12,100	14,200	12,700	25.0	24.8	25.0	21,400
LOST CUSTOMERS									
CCA CO	1,401	1,200	700		000	50.0	0.0		320
SUBTOTAL	3,600	3,700	1,800	900	000	50.0	0.0	23.0	1,000
PROSPECTS									
ABC CO	3,500	4,000							950
CBD CO	2,400	2,600							650
SUBTOTAL	32,000	36,000		4,000				8.5	10,000
TERRITORY TOTAL	$ 84,000	$ 94,340	$ 13,900	$ 19,100	$ 12,700	16.2 %	15.1 %	20.0 %	32,400

Exhibit 21. Activity reports.

WEEKLY ITINERARY

TO: _____ WEEK ENDING: _____
LOCATION: _____ ZONE: _____
FROM: _____ REGION: _____

ACCOUNT NAME	REASON FOR CALL
MON.	

CALL REPORT

REGIONAL SALES OFFICE COPY

DATE _____
TO: _____
LOCATION: _____
FROM: _____
ACCOUNT: _____
ADDRESS: _____

CONTACTS
NAME   TITLE

* - encircle applicable customer class number
** - encircle applicable symbol

REMARKS:

STATISTICAL INFORMATION - complete captions as applicable

SALES REPRESENTATIVES	CUSTOMER CLASS*	1 2 3 4 5 6
	TERRITORY NO.	
	P - PLANNED ** NP - NOT PLANNED	P NP
ALL FIELD SALES & TECHNICAL PERSONNEL	TOTAL CALL TIME	HRS.
	TRAVEL TIME	HRS.
OTHER	DEMONSTRATION & TRAINING	HRS.
	INSTALLATION	HRS.
	PROMOTION	HRS.
	SERVICE/REPAIR	HRS.
	OTHER	HRS.
DISTRIBUTOR REPRESENTATIVES	PRO-MOTION	HRS.
		HRS.
		HRS.
	OTHER	HRS.
REGIONAL SALES OFFICE	ACCOUNT CODE	

HOTEL/MOTEL
TUES.

HOTEL/MOTEL
WED.

HOTEL/MOTEL
THURS.

HOTEL/MOTEL
FRI.

HOTEL/MOTEL

PERFORMANCE SUMMARY

ZONE: _____
REGION: _____

MONTH & YEAR: _____

SALES REPRESENTATIVES	MISC. DAYS	DAYS RE-PORTS SUB-MITTED	TRAVEL TIME	TOTAL NO. OF CALLS	AVG. TRAVEL TIME	% PLAN'D CALLS MADE	AVG. CALLS PER DAY	MANAGER'S COMMENTS – NOTATIONS
TOTALS								

APPLICATION REPRESENTATIVES	MISC. DAYS	DAYS RE-PORTS SUB-MITTED	TRAVEL TIME	TOTAL NO. OF CALLS	AVG. TRAVEL TIME	AVG. CALL TIME	AVG. CALLS PER DAY	PROM.	DEMON. & TRNG.	INSTAL-LATION	SERV. & REPAIR OTHER
TOTALS											

made to insure that all the information relevant to the account is included. At a minimum, the report should include the types of activities performed (sales presentation, missionary calls, and so on), the name and location of the customer, time spent, significant orders obtained, and customer comments, if appropriate.

The operation of the call reporting system is closely related to an effective system for planning the call sequence. This requires the establishment of call frequencies appropriate for various sizes and classes of customers. In general, such frequencies can be established by sales management using a record of past call performance, the cost of various types of calls relative to the profit potential of each customer or customer group, and the salesman's or district manager's knowledge of specific customer requirements.

Since salesmen are generally burdened with a good deal of paperwork in the normal course of making sales, it is important that every effort be made to structure call performance reports to contain only that information which is of value in managing the sales operation. Call report forms should be simple and easy to complete.

The third document in the series is a performance summary, which summarizes for management all of the key performance activities for salesmen. Common types of performance summaries include comparisons of the relative effectiveness of salesmen, differences in the distribution of their time, and comparison of actual against planned or standard call frequency.

To keep travel and waiting time to a minimum, a few companies use fully automated routing and reporting systems which develop the planned call sequence considering types of account and geographic pattern. An individual preprinted form is automatically generated for each customer to be contacted, and the sequence of calling is suggested. The same form is then used for the call report which the salesman completes when calls have been made and for the report on which he indicates why a call was not made.

Product, Product Group, and Market Segment Performance Reports

Another major category of sales reports comprise product-oriented activity. These include the sale of specific products or product groupings by customer, territory, district, or other market segment with comparisons against plans or last year or total market potential. Exhibit 22 is an example of a product performance report for a consumer products company. Exhibit 23 (page 60) is a report geared to industrial products. Some variations of product reports would include product sales or profit

Exhibit 22. Product performance report, consumer products.

RESP. AREA: SWEET CHIPS			REPORT NAME: BRAND CONTRIBUTION			
RESP. OF: J.R. SMITH			REPORT NO: 12A–			
COST CENTER NO: 0 120			MONTH OF: MARCH 197X			

CURRENT MONTH				YEAR TO DATE		
BUDGET	ACTUAL	OVER (UNDER) PLAN	$ (000)	OVER (UNDER) PLAN	ACTUAL	BUDGET
2,415	2,604	189	GROSS SALES	733	6,014	5,281
1,634	1,690	56	STANDARD COST OF SALES	117	3,957	3,840
781	914	133	GROSS PROFIT	616	2,057	1,441
			DIRECT BRAND EXPENSES			
48	45	3	CONSUMER PROMOTION EXPENSE	(4)	104	100
80	85	(5)	TRADE PROMOTION EXPENSE	(15)	200	185
100	102	(2)	CONSUMER ADVERTISING EXPENSE	10	290	300
15	15	–	TRADE ADVERTISING EXPENSE	3	25	28
21	20	1	GRAPHICS EXPENSE	8	53	60
12	10	2	MARKET RESEARCH EXPENSE	(5)	20	15
276	277	1	TOTAL DIRECT BRAND EXPENSE	(4)	692	688
505	637	132	BRAND CONTRIBUTION	615	1,365	763
			EXPLANATION OF VARIANCE			
		28	PRICE	76		
		90	VOLUME	340		
		13	MIX	200		
		1	SPENDING	(4)		
		–	STANDARDS REVISION	–		
		132	TOTAL VARIANCE	612		
			KEY PERFORMANCE STATISTICS			
		.21	MARKET SHARE	.25		
		.82	RETAIL DISTRIBUTION	.86		
		.94	WHOLESALE DISTRIBUTION	.89		
			TOTAL ANNUAL BUDGET % TO DATE .21			

performance by class of customer, class of trade, distribution channel, branch office, or distributor.

As illustrated in both examples, key elements of product performance are (1) the overall profitability of the product or product group (once all appropriate expenses have been considered) and (2) the market position of the product relative to its competitors and the market as a whole. Both reports utilize the profit contribution concept in reporting product profitability. That is, marketing and selling expenses directly associated with the product are included in the calculation of profit contribution, while those operating expenses not directly identifiable by product are grouped into a general pool of overhead expense. The difficulties of identifying appropriate allocation bases for these expenses make the contribution concept more appealing as a tool for analyzing product profitability in the short term. More on the relationship between marketing and the accounting system appears in Chapter 9.

Promotion and Advertising Performance Reports

Still another area of sales and marketing performance relates to advertising and promotion. Advertising and promotion reports should pro-

Exhibit 23. Product performance report, industrial products.

BROWN COMPANY			REPORT NO. _____	
PRODUCT _____			PERIOD ENDED 6/30/XX	

	DESCRIPTION	CURRENT YEAR	VS. PLAN BETTER / WORSE	
			$/UNITS	%
SALES	UNIT SALES VOLUME–lbs.	200,000	5,000	2.6
	SALES DOLLARS	$405,500	$ 9,500	2.4
	DUE TO VOLUME		4,500	1.0
	DUE TO SALES MIX		2,500	.7
	DUE TO SELLING PRICE		2,500	.7
	NET SALES, ACTUAL	$395,000	4,250	
	LATEST ESTIMATE–			
	CURRENT YEAR NET SALES	$840,000	$45,000	5.6
MARKETING EXPENSE	GROSS PROFIT	$95,000	$2,600	2.7
	OPERATING EXPENSE			
	MARKETING EXPENSE			17.2
	MARKETING ADMINISTRATION	2,400	500	
	FIELD SELLING EXPENSE	5,700	(1,000)	(21.3)
	BROKERAGE	700	300	30.0
	ADVERTISING EXPENSE	1,500	(200)	(15.4)
	OTHER MARKETING EXPENSE	700	300	30.0
	TOTAL MARKETING EXPENSE	11,000	(100)	
	ADMINISTRATIVE & GENERAL	4,500	450	11.0
	RESEARCH EXPENSE	3,500	(300)	(9.6)
	TOTAL OPERATING EXPENSE	19,000	50	—
	OPERATING PROFIT CONTRIBUTION	$76,000	$2,650	3.6

vide more than expense statistics or comparisons with budget. They should include specific measures of what was advertised, how, and at what expense. Exhibit 24 shows an advertising performance report used by a consumer products manufacturer. The report shows, by type of medium, actual performance weighted by the number of commercial messages for each of the programs on which the product was advertised. The measures of performance include the average number of homes reached by the commercial message, the Nielsen ratings of the number of households watching at that time, and cost or budget performance, showing the cost of the commercial in total and per thousand message exposures.

As with all the other performance reports, effective reporting of advertising and promotional activity requires that specific performance goals and associated expense be planned in advance. More information on the planning and evaluation of advertising and promotion is provided in Chapter 4.

Exhibit 24. Advertising performance report.

MEDIA ANALYSIS REPORT PERIOD ENDING MEDIUM – TELEVISION					BRAND AGENCY	
NIGHTTIME NETWORK	NUMBER OF ANNOUNCEMENTS		AVER. HOMES REACHED	NIELSEN RATINGS	COST PER COMMERCIAL	COST PER THOUS. HOUSEHOLDS
PROGRAMS	30 SEC.	60 SEC.				
WEIGHTED AVERAGE						
DAYTIME NETWORK						

ORGANIZATION OF DATA FOR PERFORMANCE REPORTING

Development of the reporting systems for evaluating sales performance requires consideration of a number of basic questions:

1. What will the sales information be used for?
2. When and how often will the data be required?
3. How will sales be measured?
4. How will the data be grouped?
5. What form will the data take?
6. What will the basis for comparison be?

Defining the Sales Unit

In many companies, the word "sales" has connotations which vary from orders to bookings, shipments, cash receipts, dollar billings or even consumer purchases. When customer orders are shipped directly from stock, there is no substantial difference between orders and shipments, but those companies which take some time in filling orders generally use both terms. Retail cash-and-carry establishments concentrate on receipts, while most professional concerns, such as accountants, consultants, and advertising agencies, use billings or fees.

Most consumer products companies have need to keep careful stock of consumer purchases (as measured by store audits, warehouse withdrawals, or diary and panel data) since there is often considerable intermittent inventory building or liquidating. This data is most often provided by syndicated outside services or collected through salesmen's call reports.

In those instances where sales are reported in multiple units, or different units are used for different parts of the organization, it is essential that procedures be established to insure the convertibility of such information, both for ease of analysis and as a way of insuring the validity of the data.

Grouping of Information

A further question is the grouping of internal sales and other market data into appropriate categories, some of which include:

1. Product (major groups of products or product profit centers).
2. Geographical territory.
3. Market (class of customer, and use and trade channel).
4. Individual customers.
5. Sales unit (division, sales force, company-owned outlet, sales region, sales district, and salesman).

Such groupings should parallel customer groupings discussed earlier in this chapter. Which classes of information or combination of them a company uses in sales analyses depends not only on the company's circumstances with respect to diversity of product line, extent of geographic sales area, number of markets, and number of customers served, but also on factors such as the level of management to which the information is to be supplied and the difficulty of obtaining relevant external data for desired comparison.

Measuring and Using Potential

Effective reporting of sales performance requires that the information be reported in terms which relate to the total market. Knowing the size and characteristics of the market is vital to the marketing decision-making process. In performance reporting, the use of potential allows the focus of management attention to be directed outward to its position in the market rather than inward. Too often, sales goals are stated in such terms as "5 percent over last year" with little regard to true market growth or competitive conditions.

Potential may be defined as the total possible users in a given market at a given point in time. Market potential is not, in the short run, influenced by the amount of effort applied by a single seller in a given market. Consideration of potential must include the cross-elasticity or substitutability of one product for another. For example, the potential market for butter would include most present users of margarine. The amount of product already purchased must also be considered, particularly for durable goods. The potential market for home heating equipment, for example, would exclude those who had recently purchased such equipment.

The simplest measure of potential is, of course, total current usage of a product. However, this information is often not available and must be estimated from the relationship between the product and some other product or category for which such information is available. Many of the relationships between various industries are specified in the input/output tables prepared by the Department of Commerce. Generally speaking, population is the most commonly used index of potential for consumer products. Often, more than one variable is required in estimating potential. A general multiple variable index which is often used for consumer products marketers is the "Buying Power Index," which is produced annually in the *Sales Management's Survey of Buying Power Guide*. Three variables (population, effective buying income, and retail sales, weighted 2, 5, and 3 respectively) are combined to provide, on a city and county basis, estimates of potential for many consumer durables and nondurables. Primary uses of potentials are the identification of customers, industries, or areas which are undersold or oversold for a particular product. Using potential provides for the selective application of marketing effort and is an effective point of control. When total sales are not available, estimates of potential can be obtained by contacting the individual buyers. By asking buyers the amount of product they use, a projection of total usage can be made by a knowledgeable marketing manager.

Salesmen as Sources of Marketing Information

It is a common practice in many companies to use the salesman as the source for much marketing intelligence. Typically, the kinds of information generated by salesmen include:

1. Records of activity (sales calls, displays, presentations, shelf space, or facings).
2. Expense records.

3. Price comparisons to competition and other competitive activity.
4. Credit, adjustments, and special allowances.
5. Special assignments.

Although such information is often very valuable in the information system, there is a continuing complaint on the part of sales management that the salesman's job is "to generate orders and not to generate paper." Use of salesmen as sources of information does require careful evaluations, particularly to determine if, in fact, the information provides a basis for making decisions and taking action and is a necessary part of the order processing or bookkeeping process.

Another problem in the use of salesmen's activity reporting is the reliability of the information received. There is often some tendency to inflate accomplishments, particularly when performance is to be evaluated from the salesman's reports. By working with a salesman periodically, or by discussing the salesman's performance with customers, the field supervisor can audit his men's performance and evaluate the adequacy of data received on the sales activity reports.

Internal Cost and Sales Information

Yet another area of the marketing information system which requires attention from the standpoint of performance reporting is that of cost information. The specifics of budgets as a means of controlling and reporting performance will be discussed later. Concern here is with insuring that marketing and distribution costs are recorded within a system in such a way as to make it possible to view these costs as they relate to various segments of the business.

The traditional accounting approach has been to keep track of costs by type of expenditure, such as payroll, tax, selling expense, and so on. Information about marketing generally exists only as a byproduct. Marketers should know what is available from the accounting system and how it can be used. Information should usually be available on costs of:

Product and package variation.
Territories or information control units.
Channels of distribution.
Order size.
Size and type of customer.

As was discussed under product performance reporting, most analyses are on the basis of contribution to profit and unallocated (joint) costs.

Performance Reports, Budgets, and Forecasts

Budget reports should provide a basis for reviewing the performance of revenue and expenses for which the individual is responsible; they should also provide a basis for replanning, including taking advantage of economic opportunities as they develop.

Budgetary reports must facilitate control and replanning. The key is a good structure of reporting by responsibility and good variance analysis in explaining deviation from planned performance. Typical variance analysis would include sales price variances (deviations from budgeted selling prices), sales mix variances (deviations from budgeted product sales mix), and sales volume variances (deviations from budgeted sales volume). Exhibit 25 shows how such variances are calculated.

Plans and Forecasts

It is important to recognize the difference between plans and forecasts. The sales budget is not a sales forecast. A budget is a planning and control document which shows what management intends to accomplish. It is active rather than passive. A sales forecast is a projection, or estimate, of available customer demand. The forecast reflects the environmental and competitive situation facing the company, whereas the sales budget shows how management intends to react to this environmental and competitive situation. Good budgeting hinges on aggressive management control rather than passive acceptance of what the market has to offer. When the distinction is not made, the budget becomes more a figure exercise than a working tool.

Responsibility Reporting

Responsibility reporting is a system of planning and control which is tailored to an organization in order that activity data can be accumulated and reported by level of responsibility on a timely and factual basis. Responsibility reporting involves planning and reporting all costs and revenues to responsible individuals at all levels of the business who are in a position to exercise the most direct control over them. The fundamentals of responsibility reporting are:

1. Individuals in the organization are made responsible and held accountable for cost and revenue performance.
2. A business plan is developed that provides meaningful measures of performance.

Exhibit 25. Gross profit variance analysis.

PERIOD ENDING 10/03/XX   COMPANY CONFIDENTIAL

| | GROSS PROFIT | | VARIANCE SUMMARY | | | | 1 | 2 | VARIANCE ANALYSIS | | | | |
PRODUCT NO.	VARIANCE $	PERCENT O/U PLAN	PRICE VARIANCE	VOLUME VARIANCE	MIX VARIANCE	STDS REVISION VARIANCE	ACTUAL UNIT SALES	ACTUAL SALES O/U PLAN	3 AVERAGE ACT PRICE O/U PLAN	4 CURRENT STD COST O/U PLAN	5 PLANNED MARGIN O/U BR AV	% PLAN BRAND GR PFT	% ACT BRAND GR PFT
02150	4,672	27.6%	119–	4,601	421	231–	5,538	1,266	.02–	.04180	.3328	29.5%	36.0%
02184	17,441–	54.2%	109–	24,648–	7,408	92–	5,885	6,782	.02–	.01557	1.0923–	34.2%	4.6%
02246	3,199	14.7%	235–	2,355	1,273	195–	4,534	648	.05–	.04294	1.9650	37.3%	59.4%
BRAND TOTAL	9,570	24.7%	463–	17,692	9,102	518–	15,957	4,868					

VARIANCE ANALYSIS CALCULATIONS

MIX VARIANCE   COL. 5 (DIFFERENCE BETWEEN PRODUCT & BRAND AVERAGE MARGIN)
                X COL. 2 (DIFFERENCE BETWEEN PLANNED & ACTUAL UNIT VOLUME)

VOLUME VARIANCE   COL. 2 (DIFFERENCE BETWEEN PLANNED & ACTUAL UNIT VOLUME
                   X WEIGHTED AVERAGE BRAND GROSS PROFIT (NOT SHOWN ON REPORT)

PRICE VARIANCE   COL. 1 (ACTUAL UNIT SALES) X COL. 3 (DIFFERENCE BETWEEN
                  PLANNED & ACTUAL UNIT PRICE)

3. Performance is reported to specific individuals who exercise control over costs or revenues.
4. Individuals are held responsible only for those activities for which they exercise direct control.

The results of operations for all production and service areas are accumulated and reported in relation to the budget for all organization levels. Responsibility reports highlight the items of cost and revenue over which the individual has direct control. To support this, each individual receives a report which itemizes the detailed charges by type, amount and source of entry. Expense classifications that show significant variation from budgeted or expected performance can be analyzed immediately by reference to the supporting detailed responsibility reports. Where possible, expense responsibility and revenue or selling responsibility should of course be related and integrated in the reporting system.

SUMMARY—PERFORMANCE REPORTING

As a rule, it is difficult to generalize as to a particular company's requirements in the development of a performance system. However, these basic considerations should be made with respect to all performance and control reports. The information they contain must be sufficiently detailed, correct, and complete. In addition, the data must be manageable; that is, it must have consistency and comparability and must be capable of summarization and integration. And the system must provide for the matching of results with plans and objectives according to areas of responsibility.

SALES FORCE COMPENSATION

One key element in the selling operation is motivation of the sales force. This has a number of broad connotations, but the most important element is the compensation system. The marketing information system's performance and control reports must provide marketing management with information which will allow it to make decisions about both the type and the level of compensation to be used in directing the selling effort, and to insure that the system of compensation supports and enhances the achievement of the company's marketing objectives.

A definition of the objectives of sales force compensation provides a basis for discussion of the various types of compensation systems and the applicability of each in achieving a company's marketing goals. The general objectives of sales compensation systems can be summarized as follows.

1. To attract and hold good salesmen by providing the salesman with a standard of living in line with his training and abilities.
2. To stimulate the sales force to achieve the maximum attainable volume of profitable sales.
3. To control selling expenses.
4. To promote the full range of sales functions, including
   a. Effective coverage of sales territories.
   b. Promotion and sale of the full product line.
   c. Provision of adequate customer service.
   d. Solicitation of new accounts.
5. To achieve a desired level of customer service by supporting the customer's needs for service or maintenance calls or merchandising support.

This is by no means a comprehensive listing, nor does its sequence indicate any order of priority. It does, nevertheless, provide a point of departure for a discussion of the specifics of sales compensation systems. Since none of these broad goals is mutually exclusive, and all are, to some extent, contained in all sales organizations, the exact structure of the compensation system is often dependent upon its effectiveness in dealing with the company's immediate marketing strategies. For example, in order to stimulate sales of the full product line, higher commissions might be paid on the items in the line which are considered harder to sell. Compensation based on profit contribution might be most important where salesmen can influence profit: in negotiating prices, giving discounts, or accepting trade-ins. In instances where cooperation is important, a joint or group compensation scheme might be most effective.

Types of Compensation Systems

While there are thousands of different compensation systems in use in U.S. firms, they may be grouped into four general categories:

Salary plans
Straight commission plans
Bonus plans
Combination plans

Salary plans. Straight salary represents the simplest form of salesmen's compensation. It has a number of advantages in that it is easy to administer and easy to understand. The major advantage to management is that a salesman having a regular, predictable income can focus his attention on management's specific objectives and on customers' needs. A primary disadvantage, on the other hand, is that the salesman may lack sufficient direct incentive for increasing sales volume through individual effort. Straight salary plans provide maximum management control over salesmen's activities and are particularly appropriate where

1. Sales efforts are aimed at developing new markets or introducing new product lines.
2. New salesmen are being trained.
3. Customer service or technical service is a major part of the selling effort.
4. Maintaining customer relations is important, particularly where sales depend on relatively few large accounts.
5. Several individuals are involved in making and supporting a sale.
6. No clear relationship exists between the amount of sales effort applied and the final sale.

Straight commission plans. Straight commission plans provide income to the salesman solely on the basis of sales volume generated. Commissions may be on (1) a fixed rate, with the same commission percentage applied to all sales, (2) a progressive rate, with increasing rates applied to specific higher sales levels, or (3) a regressive rate, with the rate of commission decreasing beyond a specified volume level (generally to prevent high commission payments on windfall sales).

Frequently, drawing accounts are part of a commission plan, providing a minimum income to be credited against future earned commissions. In one variation of this, the draw is not paid back if a salesman does not earn sufficient commissions in a period; the drawing account is then a guaranteed minimum salary. Straight commission plans give maximum incentive for sales results and are important where

1. Companies have wide fluctuations in sales volume because of style or cyclical factors.
2. Little training, supervision, or control of the sales force is required in selling the product.
3. Customer service or technical support are not an important part of the selling process.
4. The relationship between the amount of effort and sales results is directly measurable.
5. Salesmen generally operate independently.

A major disadvantage of these plans is the inherent uncertainty of the amount of earnings for the salesman.

Bonus plans. Bonus plans provide for lump-sum compensation paid in addition to either salary or commission income. Generally, the bonus is tied to the achievement of specific marketing objectives, including sales volume levels, special product sales, special promotions, other accomplishments, or overall appraisal of individual sales efforts. Bonuses may be provided individually or on a shared, or group, basis. Frequently, bonuses are based on profit sharing.

The major advantage of bonus plans is the ability to direct effort to the accomplishment of specific selling goals. However, where a number of goals are combined for determining the bonus, the resultant complications in measurement and in administration may be a disadvantage.

Combination plans. As the term implies, combination plans, which are probably the most common type of compensation systems, combine salary with a commission or bonus program, or with both. The major advantage of combination plans is their flexibility in combining the security and control aspects of straight salary with the incentive and motivational aspects of bonus or commission plans. A major disadvantage is the resultant complexity and difficulty in understanding and administering combination plans.

Compensation and Performance Reporting Systems

Overall evaluation of the appropriateness of a specific compensation program should consider the features of the plans themselves. Major factors to consider are whether a plan is understandable, consistent and fair, and easy to administer. It is also important that a plan clearly emphasize the relationship between sales efforts, or sales results, and the amount of compensation.

A complex question is whether to reward a salesman for effort or for results. This goes back to the approaches to planning and establishing management's objectives, as discussed earlier. If marketing objectives are short term, the primary emphasis is on sales results. If they are long term in nature, with emphasis on building customer relationships through service and specialized marketing effort, the amount and type of effort applied may become an appropriate determinant of compensation.

If the compensation system is meant to reward effort, then some measures of performance relating to the quality and quantity of the salesman's effort should be developed for systematic reporting. In general, the criteria used to determine compensation must be consistent with the criteria used for performance appraisal, including the number of calls made on accounts, the number of new prospects contacted, and the total number of calls made in a period.

If results are to be measured, management must select among several criteria, including total sales, number of new accounts, gross margin contribution, and average order size.

Once the decision has been made to gear the compensation system to effort or results or both, it is the function of the information system to collect and report such information against performance goals. In all cases, information which provides the basis for administering the compensation system should measure those activities which relate to management's objectives, are capable of precise measurement, and are controllable by the salesman.

Summary—Sales Force Compensation

In summary, the type of compensation system appropriate to a given selling operation depends on consideration of

1. The functions management wishes the salesman to perform.
2. The amount of control over activities desired by the salesman.
3. The extent to which the salesman's effort is directly related to sales results and management's ability to measure the effort and results.
4. The balance desired between the security of a fixed income and the incentive of a variable income.
5. The existence of special selling objectives for the coming periods.

4

ADVERTISING
AND PROMOTION PLANNING

Two areas of marketing activity which have traditionally been viewed as the most subjective and least quantifiable are advertising and promotion. Visions of the "marketing mystique" or of "marketing's crystal ball" are often conjured up when the questions of planning and evaluating advertising and promotion are considered. As a result, these areas have frequently been bypassed in management information systems development. However, continuing efforts are made to provide better systems support in these areas, and there is increasing interest in the application of the systems approach to both advertising and promotion. Recent developments include expanded use of operations research techniques in marketing operations, development of more quantitative market research techniques, availability of larger quantities of detailed market, customer, and distributor information, and increased use of automated data processing to handle and analyze marketing information.

This chapter will highlight some of the key areas of advertising and promotion planning and control. In addition, it will deal with the types of information which sales and marketing managers require to support the planning and control process in this area. Consideration will also be given to the difficulties often encountered in making precise calculations and in obtaining accurate feedback when attempting to relate advertising and promotion effort to sales results. It should be kept in mind that, while this chapter deals specifically with advertising and promotion, these are only two of the elements of the marketing mix whose interaction must be considered in the marketing information system.

Since advertising and promotion play a more prominent role in consumer goods marketing, most of the following illustrations are developed in the context of consumer products companies.

DEFINING PROMOTIONS

Consumer product deals or promotions are special inducements in the form of reduced prices or extra merchandise offered for a limited period of time. Their purpose is to provide special stimulus in the market demand for a product. Characteristically, the inducement suggests to the consumer that he can get the product for less than the prevailing market price or get a bonus or premium with it which provides extra value.

At first glance, this may seem to be but a narrow facet of consumer goods marketing. But consumer deals are broadly used, are closely related to other marketing activities, and serve a broad range of strategic and tactical objectives. They therefore strongly influence the information requirements of the brand or product manager.

Dealing is costly—to deal usually means to sell for less than the established market price or to provide a product at greater cost than normal. Careful control is necessary to ascertain that marketing gains bear a reasonable relationship to cost.

As illustrated in Exhibit 26, dealing may be initiated by manufacturers or retailers. Types of deals include:

Retailer-initiated deals, often advertised through local media, aimed at generating store traffic. The objective here typically is to promote sales for a range of products through special pricing of one, which may at times be characterized as a "loss leader."

Manufacturer-initiated trade deals, aimed at the wholesaler or retailer rather than the ultimate consumer, seeking to induce stores to stock up and thereby assure product availability to the consumer.

Manufacturer-initiated consumer deals, seeking to create consumer demand for a specific product or product group, serving similar objectives as brand advertising.

Manufacturer-initiated deals coordinated to impact both the trade and consumer, combining the features of trade deals and consumer deals.

The last three of these, manufacturer-initiated and controlled deals directed at the retailer and the consumer, are of several forms, including price off (or more quantity for the same price), in-pack premium, coupon, and send-away premium. Contests or sweepstakes may be viewed

Exhibit 26. Types of consumer goods promotions.

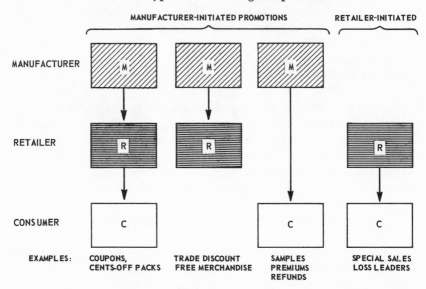

as variants of the coupon or send-away premium deal—they provide an extra value or potential value not directly reflected in the product.

COMPETITION IN THE MARKET

As stated earlier, both advertising and promotion must be viewed in the context of the total mix of marketing activities of which they are a part, and their individual effects cannot be fully isolated.

Two principal areas of interaction are immediately apparent. The first is the market in which the brand competes for its share of sales; the second is the manufacturer's product line with which the brand competes for its share of internal resources. Both these areas undergo constant and sometimes dramatic change. This change is primarily associated with the appearance of new brands or products. New brands, if successful, generally claim their share of sales in the market at the expense of existing brands, although a market expanding through normal population growth and growing consumer acceptance for the product may absorb new brands without loss of sales volume for those already established.

Deals are a means of providing or reinforcing stimulus for retailer and consumer interest and play a special role in the marketing mix.

A new product characteristic or a new advertising format more often than not depends on repetition for effectiveness. Through repeated exposure or usage, the consumer's identification of and with the brand is strengthened and reinforced. As a consequence, substantive modification of the product or of the advertising format can occur only infrequently. Deals, on the other hand, are by definition of limited duration and aim for immediate effect. They therefore provide a tool of great flexibility which can be used on short notice to deal with specific situations without establishing a requirement for continued application.

By the same token, the extensive use of deals by one competitor in a contested market is likely to provoke widespread imitation by other brands. Once consumer dealing becomes established as a regular activity by all major brands, it becomes difficult to stop or to differentiate between those brands which are leading the blows and those which are counter-punching. Through overuse, the special flexibility which dealing offers is therefore often lost, and—as with a price cut in which major competitors follow suit—all that remains is the reduction of profit resulting from assuming the burden of extra costs of dealing on a permanent basis. Appropriate feedback of deal performance becomes increasingly important as the frequency and extent of dealing increase.

APPLICATION OF FUNDS

The second major area of competition for deals is that for funds and resources within the company's product line. The mechanism by which the coordination of different brands' objectives within the company is accomplished is generally an annual plan—reviewed quarterly or monthly as conditions change—establishing the budget for advertising and promotional expenditures.

As discussed in Chapter 2, developing detailed plans and consolidating them into an overall marketing plan achieve the following results.

1. By consolidating individual brand budgets into an overall plan, the total marketing requirements are determined and may be reconciled with financial objectives.

2. By having two or more brands' promotions coordinated in terms of timing and advertising media, cost savings can be achieved. For example, coupons for several brands can be handled in a single mailing, or broadcast time can be purchased in larger increments and, therefore, at lower cost.

3. Similarly, combination of individual brand efforts into a joint cam-

paign provides greater total impact, particularly where not only the brand names but also the company name are important in building the desired image. Thereby both brand and institutional advertising objectives can be met in a single effort.

There is unanimous agreement on the need for the summarization and coordination which the annual plan provides, but not on the relative degree to which the perceived needs of an individual brand should be subordinated to an overall program. The point is made that deals are most effectively used for special purposes at special times and lose much of their value when they become a regular and recurring feature. Therefore, neither their form nor their precise timing should be dictated by overall program considerations. As a practical matter, the strong, growing brand is more likely to be permitted more independence in pursuing its own needs than smaller brands or those of limited potential.

DEAL STRATEGY

Consumer deals and promotions are undertaken for many purposes and reasons, and sometimes, it would seem, for no apparent special reason. We will try to cover those most commonly mentioned, without attempting an exhaustive catalog.

Introductory deals. Deals are often associated with major marketing moves such as the introduction of a new brand, a substantial product modification, or a fresh advertising campaign. Integrated and synchronized with other promotional vehicles, the deal provides a means of intensifying and concentrating the overall impact over a short period. Being clearly identified as a temporary feature, it permits the offer of special price or value inducements to be withdrawn after a short period without generating the negative reaction which might result from a price increase once the product is established in the market.

Product differentiation through dealing. Instead of modifying the product itself, the manufacturer may, for instance, devise a unique premium offer. Silverware or glassware premiums are examples and they offer the special advantage of inducing the consumer to make a whole series of purchases until she has completed the set.

Seasonal dealing. Deal action may be geared to seasonal needs as exemplified by heavy price-off dealing to meet early summer demand peaks in tea and suntan lotions, or winter demands in dry-packaged soups. The short or concentrated selling season intensifies competitive action much as if the product were being reintroduced each year.

Another special situation which may call for price-off dealing occurs where a basic ingredient is subject to substantial price fluctuations. Occasional periods of reduced commodity prices for coffee may, for example, induce producers to seek to expand brand or product acceptance through price-off consumer deals, again preserving the option to return to regular price levels later. Price competition in this area tends to be quickly matched by major brands.

The plain deal. In highly competitive market segments, such as soaps and detergents or cereals, deals have become rather a way of life. Brand market shares here are continuously monitored through syndicated surveys and are jealously watched. Marketing innovation in products, advertising, and promotion is virtually continuous and deals are commonly employed.

Characteristically, the brand marketing plan may provide from two to six deals or promotions a year, but the number and timing of deals and the effort or money expended on individual deals are subject to continual reevaluation.

In each case, effective control of the promotion requires that specific, detailed, measurable plans be established for each promotion. These may be expressed in such terms as increased market share, increased retail shelf space, number of repeat purchases, as well as costs and resultant profit contribution.

As an approach to determining the information requirements for promotion planning and evaluation, it is of some value to review the components of the promotion or dealing process.

Every deal involves two major phases, each of which can take substantially different forms; namely, (1) the manufacturer's offer of special inducement to the customer, and (2) the customer's action in taking advantage of this offer, or failing to.

The purchase of the product whose promotion is the underlying reason for the deal may be tied to either or both of these actions, or to neither. The offer, for example, may be made right on the package at point of sale as price-off, in-pack premium, imprinted coupon, or valuable box top; or it may be made by mail or other direct delivery to the home in the form of redeemable coupons or contest entry blanks; or it may be conveyed through advertising media in the form of coupons to be clipped from a newspaper or magazine. Each method differs both in cost and in effectiveness. Distributing material to the home involves an extra cost above imprinting the offer on the package. Furthermore, mailings of necessity cover both users and nonusers of the product and brand, and only 10% to 20% of those who receive the offer may capitalize on it. This is not to say that the major portion of the mailing cost is necessarily wasted; there will be a promotional impact even where the offer is not pursued. The offer, in effect, constitutes a form of advertising. Direct distribution to the home may be more specific in terms of desired demographic characteristic of recipients than magazine distributions, and it may be possible through combined mailing of coupons for a group of brands to make the cost per brand per thousand potential brand users reached comparable to media advertising rates.

In the absence of direct mailings to the home, a deal may be brought to the consumer's attention through advertising or special features and displays. Their form is often determined by the individual retailer, upon inducement by the manufacturer through promotional discounts or allowances for cooperative advertising. The cost of these discounts or allowances must be included in the evaluation of deal economics. The manufacturer's success in getting the retailer to "feature" his brand is a key element in dealing. The consumer's action in capitalizing on the deal offer may involve redemption of a coupon, submission of a contest entry blank, or simply purchase of the price-off package, and it constitutes an action quite distinct from purchase of the brand's regular package in the absence of the deal. This particular action of deal–offer–acceptance, at least in terms of total number of units, is often clearly observable. This step also adds a second element of cost. The cost of making good on the offer is the price the manufacturer pays for getting a number of users who would not otherwise have done so to try his product at least once.

Usually many or most of those taking advantage of the deal are the manufacturer's regular customers to begin with, and it is clear that the ratio of those deal buyers who would not otherwise have bought the brand to those who would have anyway is of critical importance in establishing the worthwhileness of a deal. If only one out of five deal purchases represents additional business, the price of each new trial is five times the unit cost of the deal. The second critical factor or ratio is the average number of "repeat" units or packages which those who were induced to try the brand once will buy after the deal expires. Many will immediately revert to their former brands or succumb to other brands' inducements. Others will remain as customers for varying numbers of successive cycles.

Brand loyalty is another important factor. A certain amount of brand switching, or trying of different brands, occurs at all times, and it can be defined in terms of the fraction of consumers who change—on any one purchase—to a brand different from the last one they bought. Marketing innovations increase this number, but some products or markets are normally characterized by greater switching propensity than others.

Deals usually, though not necessarily, increase total switching. They also change the direction, increasing the number who switch to the dealt brand and at the same time decreasing the number who would switch away from it. Knowing the general level of switching in the market to be, say, 20% provides a point of departure for estimating deal effects. The propensity for switching is known to be much greater for some users than others. A 20% average may result from very frequent switching on the part of half the users and very little by the other half. The new customers picked up by dealing may, therefore, be expected to switch away again on the next purchase with substantially more than the 20% average probability.

DEAL ECONOMICS

Since the basic facts needed to put a dollar value on a deal are not easily available, it is not surprising that in general practice deal actions are not justified in specific economic terms. The reasons most commonly advanced for engaging in deal activity are to maintain market share in the face of severe competitive pressures or to support the introduction or seasonal reintroduction of a new or modified product. However, consideration of how deal economics could be evaluated if the necessary facts were obtained will help establish what information is needed, as a step toward subsequent consideration of how this information can be obtained.

Consider, for example, the analysis of a 7-cents-off-regular-price deal on a can of shaving cream, with the deal offer imprinted on the individual cardboard box in which the can is sold (Exhibit 27). The item sells regularly for 69 cents, of which 25 cents represents contribution to the manufacturer's profit before advertising, promotion, and selling expense. The total number of units offered and sold under the deal is one million which represents—at 7 cents per unit—a deal payoff of $70,000. To this must be added special costs of printing and distribution of $5,000, for a total cost of $75,000. To break even, the number of units sold over what would have been sold without the deal would be $75,000 divided by 25 cents, or 300,000.

The mathematics works the same way for in-pack premiums, except that the cost of procurement and packaging of the premium item—offset by any price increase on the package—is substituted for the cost of giving 7 cents off the regular price. There may be an additional cost

Exhibit 27. Deal economics, promotion breakeven analysis.

PRODUCT   **SHAVING CREAM**   ALLOWANCE   **$.07/CASE**

REGULAR PRICE   **$.69**   FIXED COSTS   **$5,000.00**
                                                printing   distribution

VARIABLE MFG. EXPENSE   **$.44**

PROFIT CONTRIBUTION   **$.25**

TOTAL SALES (estimated) (units)	VARIABLE PROMO. EXP.	TOTAL PROMO. EXP.	REQUIRED BREAKEVEN VOLUME
800,000	56,000	61,000	244,000
900,000	63,000	68,000	272,000
1,000,000	70,000	75,000	300,000
1,100,000	77,000	82,000	328,000
1,200,000	84,000	89,000	336,000

if the premium merchandise offered elicits so little consumer interest that a portion of the deal packages is never sold. Send-away premiums, where the buyer must tear off or cut out a part of the package and return it (often with an additional payment) to receive his premium are similarly evaluated. However, customers who take up the offer will normally be only a fraction of those to whom the offer was made available. Announcement costs apply to all packages on which the deal was offered; redemption costs only to the fraction claimed. It must be assumed that the offer provided a real inducement only to those who took advantage of it, and any estimate of the number of new customers induced to try the brand should, therefore, be based on this smaller number.

In summary, the economics of deal management reduce to five basic values:

1. Announcement cost: the costs of printing, mailing, promotion, or media distribution of the deal offer in excess of regular packaging and distribution cost.
2. Premium or make-good cost: the costs in terms of cents off the regular price, coupon value, or premium cost, including all costs of handling redemptions.
3. Unit profit contribution at regular selling price, per package.
4. The total number of units sold under the conditions of the deal; that is, those on which the buyer actually obtained the benefits of the deal offer.

5. The fraction of buyers which represents added buyers who would otherwise have bought another brand.

TIME FACTORS IN DEALING

In planning a deal, two time periods are of critical importance: lead time and sell-off time. Lead time is the period necessary, as a practical minimum, to put a deal into effect. It covers initial planning, design, and approval of package modifications or material to be mailed or distributed to the home, preparation of conjunctive advertising and point-of-sale materials, notification of field sales personnel, establishment of allocations for individual distributors, purchasing and printing of special premiums or packaging materials, production of advance inventories and staging at distribution centers in preparation for release at a specific date, and, finally, the distribution to the retailer.

Special inducement offered to stock up on the product will often reduce subsequent purchases. The additional sales produced by the deal while it is in effect are to some degree borrowed from a later period, and a temporary reduction in sales may follow the deal peak. Any attempt to evaluate deals in terms of their effect on sales must, therefore, take into account this total deal period, including aftereffects.

In planning the timing of a deal, the frequency of purchase by the housewife is a key element. If the item is bought, on the average, every two weeks, sufficient deal merchandise should be provided for about a three-week period to assure exposure to the majority of users or potential users. If it is considered desirable to provide for not one but two successive purchases, the amount of deal merchandise must be correspondingly increased. In general, the less frequent the purchase, the longer the deal period must be and, as will become apparent, the more costly the deal may be.

Effective lead time can be reduced by preparing standby materials in advance, where the extra cost of storage and the risk of obsolescence is considered justified in the interest of being able to move quickly when the occasion requires.

Sell-off time starts at the date of release. Its termination is somewhat less definite. In the case of coupons, a final date for acceptance of redemptions is given, but later redemptions within reason are seldom challenged. Disappearance of price-off and in-pack premium packages may also tail off over a considerable period. As a practical matter, sell-off time is usually considered terminated when 90% to 95% of the deal merchandise has reached the hands of consumers. Characteristically, this involves a time span of one to two months.

MARKETING INFORMATION REQUIREMENTS

Marketing information needs for deal planning are summarized as follows.

Market

1. Definition of products and consumers which make up the market. Identification of submarkets and consumer groupings.
2. Geographic breakdown, with particular reference to possible deal boundaries.
3. Distribution channels; number and size classification of retail outlets.

Product and competition

1. Brands, price lines, sizes, packs.
2. Competitive coverage of different geographic areas, distribution channels.
3. Competitive deal history—number, frequency, duration, type of deal; wholesaler, retailer, and consumer orientation.

Sales and advertising coverage

1. Volume moving through covered outlets; adjusted market share.
2. Advertising coverage planned by region, metro-markets, and the like.

Deal requirements

1. Timing, coincidence with seasonal needs, coordination with other brands.
2. Financial restrictions.
3. Objectives, with geographic and consumer group breakdowns.

Deal options available

1. Types of deals—packs and sizes.
2. Lead time and response time.
3. History of effectiveness (percent change in weekly movement rate to retailer and to consumer).
4. Deal costs and breakeven points.

Deal performance

1. Weekly shipments of regular and deal merchandise versus objectives and forecast.
2. Retail shelf disappearance studies for consumer deals.
3. Retail shelf space allocation studies.
4. Consumer acceptance and repurchase studies.
5. Postevaluation reports.

With proper accounting techniques, the profitability and return on investment of individual brands can be determined within reasonable limits. To make this analysis, marketing management requires predeal, deal, and postdeal sales levels, marketing costs, and profit contribution by product within each major market. Each of these must be reported against some planned levels for each period.

Exhibit 28 shows a typical promotion specification form used by a confection manufacturer. This form, which must be completed by the product manager prior to the implementation of a promotion, requires both an identification of the type of promotion, with regional detail, and a statement of the specific objectives to be achieved.

One example of the type of information being developed to plan and evaluate promotions is shown in Exhibit 29. This is a sample output of a promotion forecasting model which reviews historical data on past promotion performance and prepares forecasts for prepromotion periods, promotion periods, and postpromotion periods. A base forecast for each period is estimated by actual case sales. Beneath it is an estimate of sales with the promotion. Incremental sales are further differentiated as to those subject to promotional allowance and those at regular price but included in promotional orders. The lower half of the output provides for calculation of the profit contribution impact of the promotion.

The principal requirements for establishing this type of reporting are (1) a definition of the promotional comparisons to be made, (2) determination of periods to be considered as predeal, deal, and postdeal, and (3) allocation of marketing costs, to the extent that they are not directly identifiable with the promotion. Establishing promotions on a project basis is an effective way of accounting for promotion expense.

Still another area of information which provides insight into promotion analysis is data on customer (wholesaler) buying patterns. Exhibit 30 is an example of a product-oriented report developed by a leading consumer products company. The report shows, on a trend basis, the percentage of major customers who regularly purchase the company's products. When shifts in trend occur, often as a result of competitor or company promotions, the report allows for an identification of the

Exhibit 28. Promotion specification form.

```
                   ┌──────────────────────────────────┐   DATE   3/15/XX
                   │  TRADE PROMOTION SPECIFICATION   │      # BC/7/XX
                   └──────────────────────────────────┘

    ITEM  0210  BRAND  BC  DIVISION  20

    PRICE  $ 10.00  /CASE

    GEOGRAPHIC COVERAGE   ALL REGIONS EXCEPT SF, SALT LAKE, SEATTLE

    PROMOTION TYPE  $1.00/CASE ALL REGIONS

    START/FINISH  6/1/XX /  8/1/XX

    GRACE PERIODS  + 2 WEEKS

    IS PROMOTION                        YES    NO     LIST OTHER ITEMS
         1. PART OF PACK TIME PROMOTION  [ ]   [X]
                                                       0200,0310,0350
         2. PART OF BRAND PROMOTION      [X]   [ ]
    GENERAL OBJECTIVES

         1. RAISE REGION 3,4 DISTRIBUTION ( "A" ACCOUNTS ) TO 65%
         2. MAINTAIN ALL OTHER REGIONS' DISTRIBUTION
         3. INCREASE "B" ACCOUNTS, REGION 1,2
```

Exhibit 29. Promotion contribution analysis.

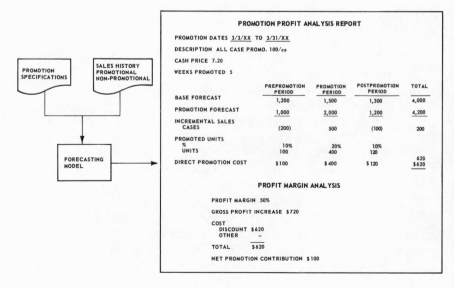

PROMOTION PROFIT ANALYSIS REPORT

PROMOTION DATES 3/3/XX TO 3/31/XX

DESCRIPTION ALL CASE PROMO. 100/cs

CASH PRICE 7.20

WEEKS PROMOTED 5

	PREPROMOTION PERIOD	PROMOTION PERIOD	POSTPROMOTION PERIOD	TOTAL
BASE FORECAST	1,200	1,500	1,300	4,000
PROMOTION FORECAST	1,000	2,000	1,200	4,200
INCREMENTAL SALES CASES	(200)	500	(100)	200
PROMOTED UNITS %	10%	20%	1.0%	
UNITS	100	400	120	620
DIRECT PROMOTION COST	$100	$400	$120	$620

PROFIT MARGIN ANALYSIS

PROFIT MARGIN 50%

GROSS PROFIT INCREASE $720

COST
    DISCOUNT $620
    OTHER –

TOTAL $620

NET PROMOTION CONTRIBUTION $100

PROMOTION SPECIFICATIONS

SALES HISTORY PROMOTIONAL NON-PROMOTIONAL

FORECASTING MODEL

Exhibit 30. National distribution trend summary.

REPORT DATE 1/10/XX							* PROMOTED THIS MONTH
ITEM	DESCRIPTION	DISTRIBUTION MEASURE END OF MONTH	NOV	DEC	JAN	FEB	MAR
2550	HS IN 1LB	% IN DIST	57	20	66*	74*	74
		VOL EXP	75	29	72	86	83
2590	HS IN 2LBS	% IN DIST	37	23	29*	34*	37
		VOL EXP	33	24	26	35	35
ABOVE ITEMS ONLY		% IN DIST	63	34	69	80	77
		VOL EXP	77	45	73	88	85
1460	ALM 144	% IN DIST	47	39	33	42	44*
		VOL EXP	35	35	27	34	38

THIS REPORT TRACKS NATIONAL DISTRIBUTION OF SELECTED ITEMS IN KEY ACCOUNTS. REPORTED CHANGES IN DISTRIBUTION ARE USED TO EVALUATE THE EFFECTS OF PROMOTIONS.

specific customers involved in the lost distribution. This provides a basis for specific action to be taken at the region and district levels.

SYSTEMS ELEMENTS OF ADVERTISING MANAGEMENT

Planning and controlling a company's advertising program requires three critical management decisions.

1. How much to spend on advertising: the establishment of the advertising budget and the overall objectives of the advertising program.

2. What to advertise: the allocation of the budget to specific products and the development of copy strategy.

3. When and where to place the message: the identification of the market segment (defined in terms of age, income, location, or other demographic characteristics) at which the message is aimed and the determination of the vehicle which provides the most effective and economical coverage of that market segment.

Many manufacturers, because they do not plan the goals of their advertising and promotion programs in sufficient detail, conclude that the effects of these programs cannot be usefully measured. Seldom are the objectives stated in quantitative terms. Too often, such objectives are not developed because operating managers demur, saying "advertising is an art and can't be evaluated," "advertising is just one element in a very complex marketing mix," or "advertising is a necessary business expense." Many marketing plans do not specify the objectives of the advertising program and, as a consequence, advertising plans are not evaluated.

PLANNING THE ADVERTISING EFFORT

Before attempting to define the information systems requirements for advertising, it is important to establish the alternative approaches which may be used to develop the advertising plan. In all cases, such planning should be based on factual information, analysis of past performance, analysis of markets and competitive behavior, knowledge of anticipated buyer behavior, and careful judgment about the type of product offered.

The specific advertising plan can only be developed after the basic marketing plan has been prepared because advertising must be coordinated with the other elements of the marketing mix, such as pricing, distribution, promotion, personal selling, and customer service.

It is important to differentiate carefully between the objectives of the marketing plan, such as increased sales, market share, or profit contribution, and the specific objectives of the advertising program. Will advertising programs be aimed at creating brand awareness, at increasing consumer purchases, at announcing a consumer promotion, or at introducing a new product? The plan should be specific in this regard.

DETERMINATION OF THE ADVERTISING BUDGET

In general, management's view of advertising planning is oriented to financial considerations, with fairly rigid standards for advertising-to-sales ratios. Some common financial approaches to advertising budgeting are the following.

Percentage of sales: Advertising expenses are established relative to the level of past company sales, forecast sales, or overall industry averages.

Competitive parity: Advertising levels are maintained at a constant ratio to the level achieved by leading competitors. This is sometimes characterized as maintaining a constant share of market and share of advertising.

Available funds: Advertising levels are determined by what is left after other expenses and management's profit objectives have been achieved.

Fixed sum per unit: Basically the same as a percentage of sales approach, but free of pricing considerations.

The consequence of these approaches is that the advertising plan, and in many cases the marketing plan, is established only after the level of advertising expense has been determined.

A more practical approach to the establishment of the advertising budget is to base the budget on profit opportunities in specific markets and anticipated results of the marketing plan. This "deterministic" approach to advertising planning requires that specific detailed plans be developed, including the following.

1. A summary of the marketing situation and the relationship of the advertising plan to the total marketing program.
2. A statement of specific objectives including the theme of the advertising message and the media best suited to reach the target market. To the extent possible, the objectives should be supported by past research and performance reports.
3. An estimate of the anticipated results considering market potential, past performance, and competitive action.
4. An estimate of the costs of the advertising program related to the level of planned sales and the resultant impact on profitability.
5. A statement of procedures to be followed to measure the performance of the plan.

This approach to determining advertising budgets places a considerable burden on information systems, particularly the accounting systems, to provide necessary detail. In addition to maintaining expenditure data by type of medium, such information may also be required on a region or district basis to make it possible for data to be related to external measures of activity such as audience reach and frequency reported as cost per thousand exposures.

Exhibits 31 and 32 illustrate two ways in which marketing reports may be developed to provide this information. The first report is a record comparing company advertising spending with that of competitors. The second report provides district detail for sales, market share, and advertising expense by medium. Much of the required input data can and should be provided by the advertising agency. However, it is necessary that agency reports be prepared in a form and level of detail compatible with other company information.

The marketing information system should provide marketing managers with detailed data for each advertising and promotion program. This includes information on sales, expenses, and contribution by area,

Exhibit 31. Competitive advertising spending, three-year summary ($000).

PRODUCT SWEET BISCUITS		TELEVISION				RADIO	PRINT	OTHER	ADVERTISING SPENDING CASE
		NETWORK		SPOT					
		DAYTIME	NIGHTTIME	DAYTIME	NIGHTTIME				
QI	1970	240	120	100	–	50	50	—	.26
	1971	280	80	120	50	–	100		.24
	1972	300	60	180	50	–	100	—	.32
QII	1970								
	1971								
	1972								
QIII	1970								
	1971								
	1972								
QIV	1970								
	1971								
	1972								
YEAR TOTAL	1970								
	1971								
	1972								
COMPETITORS DARK CHIPS									
QI	1970								
	1971								
	1972								
QII	1970								
	1971								
	1972								

Exhibit 32. Annual area advertising expense summary 19XX.

REGION	CASE SALES (000)		MARKET SHARE			ADVERTISING PER CASE 19XX CASE SALES				
	MARKET	PRODUCT	LAST YEAR	THIS YEAR	CHANGE	TELEVISION	RADIO	PRINT	OTHER	TOTAL
1	2,000	200	9.5%	10.0%	+ .5%	$.25	$.15	$.08	–	$.48
2	3,600	300	9.5	8.5	–1.0	.14	.10	–	$.10	.34
3										
4										
5										
6										
7										
20										
TOTAL	60,000	6,000	9.5	10.0	.5%	$.29	$.14	$.10	$.05	$.58

product, and type of advertising medium or promotion used. The systems approach also requires that specific, quantified plans be developed for each campaign or promotion. In effect, each should be handled as a separate project with all the relevant sales, expense, and external data coded with the appropriate project identification. This also requires a careful and consistent definition of the time periods included in the project. While the system will not necessarily establish a clear relationship between specific programs and sales increases, it will provide for improved control and evaluation of each project in relation to specific objectives.

5

DISTRIBUTION

Distribution concerns control of the flow of information and material to provide customer service. This flow starts the moment the customer makes his decision to buy the company's product and continues until it is delivered in satisfactory condition. Within this time frame, the distribution function must consider several basic elements, or steps.

Delivery time: The time elapsed from placement of the customer order to the delivery of that order.

Reliability: The probability that the customer will receive his order within the specified delivery time.

Communications: The ability to communicate order status and other information to the customer promptly and accurately.

Therefore, within this framework, distribution makes the product available to the user when he wants it. It provides service, which marketing men have come to realize is just as critical as price and quality in determining a company's market share.

Traditionally, in the areas of price and quality, the division of responsibilities between marketing and manufacturing has been reasonably clear. However, responsibilities for fulfilling the service needs of the market have not been as clearly defined. The customer service function is frequently divided between the marketing and manufacturing organizations. As a result, there is a loss of control both in performance and in associated costs.

Competitive pressures have forced increased attention to the service function. New customers are generated with superior service as well as with quality and price. Poor service is expensive because of both lost opportunities and unnecessary expense, and management's attention has more and more been focused on this area of a company's operation. To provide better control, some companies have organized service functions under a distribution manager. He provides the necessary full-time coordination between marketing and manufacturing. As part of his responsibilities, he determines how service can be provided most effectively at least cost. It will be helpful here to consider distribution as an integrated function reporting to one individual.

Within the distribution function there are two elements of service—internal and external. The internal element involves the relationship between the manufacturer and an intermediate distribution point before final distribution. The external element involves the relationship between the intermediate distribution point and the ultimate consumer or user. Since manufacturers need to exercise control or service influence over the complete flow to the end user, the scope of the distribution function should include both elements. The degree of control, however, depends on whether the intermediate distribution point is an independent wholesaler or retailer or a company-owned or company-operated distribution center. In the former case, a company can only expect to exert indirect control over the wholesaler's or retailer's operations. Where a company distributes products through its own operations, it can exercise direct control over the service elements. The scope of the distribution function increases as this influence becomes stronger. This chapter will focus on this aspect of distribution.

Pulling together these basic customer service elements in today's company organization is not an easy task. For example, within the element of delivery time, other time elements such as order processing and transportation must be considered. Since inventory availability and accessibility affect a company's delivery time and reliability response, the responsibility for inventory planning and location follows. If shipments are from finished goods, interaction with manufacturing may be limited to relating the inventory plan to the production plan. On the other hand, if any portion of the product must be manufactured after the customer's decision to buy, direct involvement of the distribution function in traditional manufacturing responsibilities becomes stronger.

As other elements in customer service, such as reliability, communications, credits and collections, and warranty response, are considered, the organizational implications become more pronounced. Consequently, as the distribution function emerges, it embraces a wide range of functions formerly associated not only with marketing and manufacturing but also with other organizational elements of the company. While it varies extensively from company to company, it is not uncommon to find distribution having responsibility for the functions listed.

Order processing	Production and inventory
Inventory control	planning
Plant and field	Customer and sales service
warehousing	Warehouse layout
Traffic	and location
Distribution center	Packaging
operations	Distribution cost analysis
Traffic research	and control
Materials handling	Distribution systems analysis

Each of these functions comprises many activities, and traditionally they have been dispersed throughout the organization. Examining some of these functions, we find the following.

Order processing involves not only the receiving and processing of customer orders but also such other activities as pricing, credit checking, inventory checking, customer acknowledgment, and communications. Typically, these activities are scattered throughout the organization; however, they are usually found in the marketing function.

The *inventory control* function generally provides stock status and determines when and by how much to replenish inventory. It may decide what items to inventory and where to keep them. These activities can be found under marketing, manufacturing, materials management, or any number of other functions depending on the company and the degree of decentralization of these activities.

Plant and field warehousing is generally concerned with those activities associated with the storage of goods. Within this function may be materials handling, storage, unloading and loading, and shipping activities. It is most concerned with the efficient operation of a warehouse and frequently becomes involved in the selection of additional warehouse space. The plant warehousing function generally falls under manufacturing; however, field warehousing functions have been found in the manufacturing, marketing, and distribution functions.

The traffic function has traditionally been involved in activities such as carrier and route selection, rate negotiations, private fleet operations, marine freight operations, and all activities in the movement of goods. These functions have been generally decentralized and are scattered throughout the organization. In the past, these functions have been cost-improvement oriented; however, as the distribution function emerges, we find increased emphasis on cost control and customer service improvement.

Distribution center operations, in the past, were called warehouse operations. As the need for customer service became more pronounced, many companies changed the name of warehouses to distribution centers and expanded this function's activities. These activities include not only the movement and storage of goods but also some sales, order processing, inventory control, and traffic functions. As the distribution center function evolved, it became primarily a marketing function.

The traffic research function is an expansion of the traffic function and generally becomes involved in the planning and design of new transportation methods and equipment. For example, containerization and the design of ships to accommodate such new containers would be among the responsibilities of the traffic research function.

The production and inventory planning function may become involved in all the production control or materials management activities usually found under manufacturing's responsibility. This could include such things as translating forecasts into plant capacity plans, allocating customer and inventory replenishment orders to manufacturing facilities, and setting inventory plans or levels for all the company's inventory locations.

The customer and sales service function has the role of promoting the growth of business through customer service programs. This could involve defining customer service objectives, reviewing the market and determining its needs, and monitoring customer service performance. In addition, other activities such as communications with the customer, credits and collections, and warranty response may be included.

The warehouse layout and location function could become involved in site selection and design or layout of a new warehouse in addition to development of location systems for efficient warehouse or distribution center operation. These functions have been scattered throughout the engineering and manufacturing organizations.

The distribution cost and analysis function pulls together under one organization all the distribution cost elements and provides for more meaningful analysis and effective control. For example, this function may develop standard freight costs to all customers and provide for actual freight cost comparisons.

There is strong argument for establishing the distribution function as a separate organizational element on a level with marketing and manufacturing. However, tradition is not easily overcome, and the movement in this direction has not been great. Many companies have been quick to recognize the merit of grouping these functions under one head; however, there is a natural tendency to let distribution develop within the organization that has most influenced it in the past and where its roots are deepest. As a result, in companies with heavy marketing orientation, such as consumer goods manufacturers, distribution is frequently found as part of marketing. Such an organizational alignment is frequently encountered in these companies since they were first to feel the need to respond to the service requirements of the market. On the other hand, with the more recent awareness of heavily manufacturing-oriented companies in this regard, the occurrence of a distribution function within the manufacturing organization is no longer a rarity.

Regardless of where the distribution function fits in the company structure, the logic for its continued existence and further development is overwhelming. The increased awareness of customer service, its cost, and its profit potential to the company all imply the need to manage it and to bring all the interrelated customer service activities under one function.

Marketing has a stake in customer service and, consequently, a significant role to play in the distribution function. Therefore, the rest of this chapter will attempt to define marketing's role in and relationship with the distribution function. To illustrate this, we will use an actual case study of how a distribution program was developed within a company.

DETERMINING THE SERVICE OBJECTIVES

Marketing's responsibility for recognizing and informing management of the needs in the marketplace is clear. Defining the product, price, and quality needs of the market is frequently accomplished in clear-cut and precise terms. Typically, marketing is relatively well informed of these factors and how they influence the company's share of the market. However, finding a company that is equally informed regarding the service needs of the market is the exception rather than the rule. More often than not, when service objectives have been set, they are a product of emotional response to customer pressure rather than of factual, objective evaluation of the market. Frequently these objectives are set without recognizing opportunities to seize a marketing advantage that improved service can provide. One of the best ways to set service objectives initially is through a survey of the market, commonly called a customer service survey. The survey should focus on all the elements of service— delivery time, reliability, and communications. This can best be accomplished by looking at the customer's needs and adopting his viewpoint. It is important here to look at distribution centers as if they were customers and determine if service is important to them. This will help in determining what the customer's problems are and if he is compensating for inferior or poor service. The objectives of such a survey are to (1) establish service requirements and necessary corrective action based on competitive levels, and (2) provide estimates of sales increases from improved levels of service.

The survey should ascertain specific and quantitative answers to such questions as the following.

What is the competition really doing? It is just as important to know your competition's level of service as its promotional activities. This information is an important consideration in developing and incurring the costs of your own service program.

What are the customer's problems? Knowing the space, handling, and quality restrictions of your customer if he is a manufacturer, as well as his inventory, distribution, and service requirements, is important in setting service objectives.

Why have past customers been lost? If price and quality are competitive, lost customers are inevitably a result of inadequate service.

Does the delivery requirement apply equally to all products? The importance of presenting a full line is basic to marketing. However, there are many instances where applying the same delivery time and reliability standards to all items in the line can be extremely costly. For example, should a company provide a two-day delivery service standard from its distribution center for all items? This would necessitate maintaining a full range of items in inventory. In many cases, the demands for some items are so infrequent that it is not justifiable to stock them at the distribution center. In this case, many companies elect to maintain these slow-moving items in a master inventory at the plant, where consolidated demands can justify stocking them. The delivery standard for these items would be greater since they would be shipped from the plant rather than the distribution center.

How important is communications to the customer? All too often, the importance of keeping a customer fully informed regarding the status of his order is overlooked, by everyone but the customer.

Is reliability more important in delivery than speed? Many companies, infatuated with the importance of speedy delivery, neglect the usually more important element of delivery schedule reliability. Many instances are found where customers are willing to sacrifice speed for assurance of delivery at the promised time. Opportunities for cost reduction in such situations are great.

Implicit in answering these questions is the extent to which improvements can produce realistic sales volume increases. Failure to do this adequately can result in incurring the costs of improved service without corresponding benefits.

It is possible to develop an information system to provide answers to these questions on a routine basis. This effort must be supplemented by periodic personal contact with the customer by persons outside the sales organization, preferably in the distribution function. There is a tendency to resist direct involvement with the customer by persons outside marketing; however, participation by distribution in customer surveys is frequently instrumental in gaining a better perspective of the relationship between delivery speed and reliability and of the importance of communications. Since the distribution representative is frequently well informed in inventory and its related problems, he is able to recognize customer problems in this area and how solutions can be developed to the mutual advantage of the customer and the company.

In summary, from a combination of customer survey and continuing information system, marketing must provide distribution with quantitative service objectives which clearly depict delivery objectives by product and geographic area, percent of conformance to these delivery objectives required, communications expectations of the customer, and other service yardsticks that might influence the market.

Given these objectives and a forecast of sales that may be expected, distribution must then evaluate the practicality and cost consequences of achieving these objectives.

GREAT LUMBER COMPANY

Great Lumber Company (not the real name) produces and markets a wide variety of lumber, wood paneling, hardboard, and other associated wood products. It has manufacturing facilities in the Southeast and Pacific Northwest. The company's sales offices are regionally located in seven major cities—Boston, New York, Atlanta, Cleveland, Chicago, Dallas, and Los Angeles. Sales are made either for direct shipments from Great Lumber's mills to its customers or through the company-owned distribution centers in the seven marketing regions. Direct sales and shipments are made to large building contractors and large independent lumber companies. Distribution center sales and shipments are made to local builders and smaller retail lumber companies.

For a number of years, management of Great Lumber was concerned over its increasing outbound freight and associated distribution costs and its deteriorating customer service image. Therefore, management decided to embark on a distribution program. It thought such a program could improve customer service without increasing costs, and possibly provide for major cost reductions.

A charter was developed and a task force was formed to work on the program. The program had two objectives: (1) Define and evaluate current customer service objectives in terms of competition, policies, facilities, equipment, cost, and procedures involved in the movement of materials and products to and from Great Lumber facilities. (2) Determine what steps must be taken to achieve optimum levels of customer service and insure the maximum return on investment; and recommend improvements in policy, organization, distribution methods, materials handling, facilities, and systems to achieve this goal. The task force was organized under a chairman who reported directly to the executive vice president. Reporting to the chairman were five major functions, each directed by company personnel knowledgeable in the areas of specialization. These functions were:

Customer service.
Storage efficiencies and standards.
Transportation efficiencies and standards.
Information systems.
Organization.

Outside consultants were engaged to assist the task force to accomplish many of the program objectives. In response to the first objective, the initial step of the task force was to conduct a customer service survey. The following case describes that survey.

Basic Objectives of the Survey

The customer service section of the distribution task force was charged with three basic assignments which constituted the primary objective. These were: (1) Establish customer service requirements, including delivery times, for certain major product lines by market region. (2) Recommend necessary corrective action to become competitive in the customer service area. (3) Provide estimated sales increases by product as a result of providing competitive customer service.

Scope of the Survey

The study covered three marketing groups—plywood, wood paneling, and hardboards. Exhibits 33 and 34 graphically illustrate the relative scope of the study within Great Lumber. The scope of the study was 36% of total Great Lumber sales dollars and 48% of the total tonnage.

Exhibit 33. Great Lumber Company,   Exhibit 34. Great Lumber Company,
   scope of distribution program   scope of distribution program
         (in sales tons).   by product line (in sales dollars).

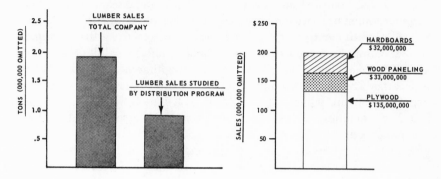

Survey Method

A customer questionnaire was designed to obtain specific answers about customer service and to gain an insight into the customers' needs. Each customer was asked to rate Great Lumber relative to the competition. The questionnaire was also designed to obtain quantitative estimates of expected sales increases if those needs were satisfied.

The complete survey was divided into three parts. First, representative customers and Great Lumber inside and outside salesmen handled by the Midwest regional office were surveyed. Then the findings were reviewed with the regional and product line managers, and each was asked to review the method and findings critically. Finally, the six remaining regional marketing areas were surveyed, and the findings, especially those of anticipated sales increase, were reviewed with the regional manager.

Customer interviews were arranged by the regional office or sales division involved. No calls were made without proper introduction, and very few calls were made without a representative of marketing present. Almost all inside and outside salesmen were also interviewed.

Findings of the Survey

Some of the general findings of the customer service survey were

1. Service problems increase in number and size in direct proportion to the number of products and number of customers of a given product line.
2. Customer service is adversely affected by the number of times a communication must be handled within the company.

3. Efficient inside sales personnel greatly minimize inefficiencies in the eyes of the customer.
4. Customer service is at its best when the output of the whole mill falls within one product line; it gradually deteriorates when additional product lines are sold from the same mill.
5. Customer service is at its best when customer-oriented decisions and answers are obtainable at the mill.
6. Great Lumber does not have any service policies, as such.
7. Great Lumber has a very poor customer service image.
8. Increase in customer service will have a favorable net effect on profit—somewhat intangible, but not as intangible as the effect of advertising dollars.

Conclusions from the Survey

In the interview, each customer and Great Lumber salesman was asked the following question: "Assuming price and quality are competitive, what increase in sales volume (by product) could we expect to achieve as a result of improved and competitive customer service? (Note: Customer service was defined as a total image of reliability and improved accuracy and speed of communications. The company quickly found that speed of delivery was not as important as these elements.)

The task force found that a potential sales increase of 8.3% over Great Lumber's present sales of $200 million per year could be achieved by providing better customer service. This amounted to additional sales of $16.5 million per year, which could result in pretax net profits of almost $3 million per year! Exhibit 35 shows these conclusions by product line.

In addition to these quantitative effects on sales and profits, the survey revealed that there were other intangible effects that could not be quantified.

The survey indicated that unaccountable dollars were being lost each day by the diversion of direct sales efforts in directions other than selling and the normal collateral duties expected of line sales. These included checking shipping dates and car numbers, following up on routings, and unnecessarily time-consuming litigation of claims and credits.

The survey also revealed that, in certain product lines, a substantial amount of potential business never reached the inquiry or the order state because of Great Lumber's past history of poor service.

Comments on service were too numerous to list. They ranged from outright disgust to shoulder-shrugging you-are-too-big-to-care responses. However, it must be stressed that the mere fact that Great Lumber asked about service evoked many favorable customer reactions.

Exhibit 35. Great Lumber Company, conclusions: total quantitative effect of service on profit.

PRODUCT LINE	GROSS SALES (000)	ESTIMATED SALES INCREASED FROM IMPROVED SERVICE	ADDITIONAL SALES POTENTIAL (000)	ADDITIONAL PROFIT CONTRIBUTION POTENTIAL (000)
PLYWOOD	$135,000	8.6%	$11,500	$2,200
WOOD PANELING	32,000	8.3	2,600	280
HARDBOARD	33,000	7.3	2,400	425
TOTALS	$200,000	8.25	$16,500	$2,905

With these conclusions and their substantial profit impact, Great Lumber management made two significant decisions: (1) continue the distribution program to determine the means and cost to achieve the service objectives, and (2) establish a customer sales service function. This function, as described earlier, would be to regularly talk to Great Lumber customers about service and inquire about its improvement.

Service Objectives Resulting from the Survey

An example of Great Lumber's service objectives for the plywood product line sold in the Midwest region is shown in Exhibit 36. In our discussion, we noted that speed of delivery was not as important to Great Lumber customers as reliability. Our example here shows that. The major sales potential would be achieved by improving reliability from a present level of 60% to 90%. Once this was accomplished, the delivery time standard would be reduced to six days. Although the Great Lumber customer service survey did not obtain estimates for a reduction of delivery time, we have shown what potential sales and profit improvements might be at five- and four-day delivery standards.

RESPONDING TO THE SERVICE OBJECTIVES

The first step of the distribution function is to examine the present flow and structure and determine how well it responds to the established time objectives. If improvements are required, as in the Great Lumber

Exhibit 36. Great Lumber Company, service objectives.

Product Line: __PLYWOOD__
Market Region: __MIDWEST__

CLASS OF SERVICE	DELIVERY RELIABILITY (% ON TIME)	DELIVERY TIME (DAYS)	ADDITIONAL IMPROVEMENT POTENTIAL	
			SALES (000)	PROFIT CONTRIBUTION (000)
CURRENT SERVICE LEVEL	60	7½		
IMPROVED RELIABILITY WITH				
1½ DAYS FASTER SERVICE	90	6	$1,650	$300
2½ DAYS FASTER SERVICE	90	5	2,700	500
3½ DAYS FASTER SERVICE	90	4	3,000	550

case, the next step is to determine the means and cost to modify the system.

To begin, let us examine the time elements of a typical distribution system, Exhibit 37. As we mentioned earlier, the cycle begins when the customer decides to place his order and it ends when he receives

Exhibit 37. A typical distribution system.

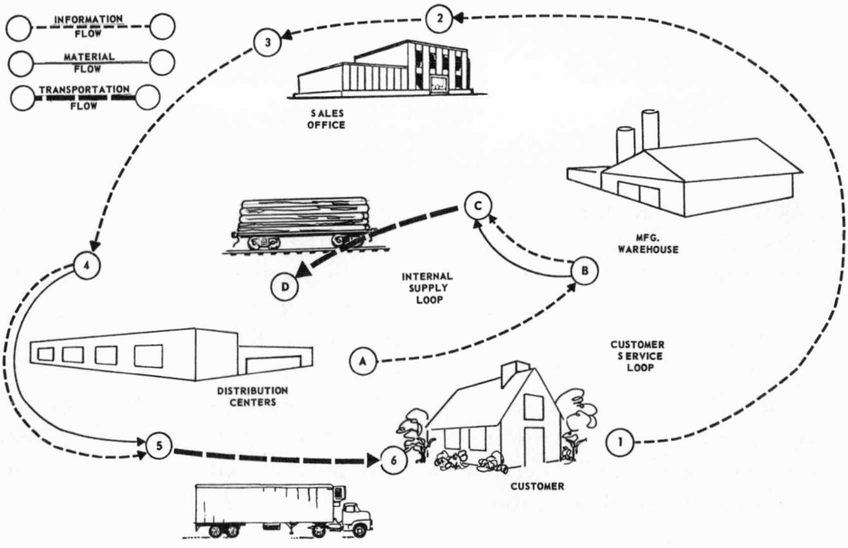

it (1 through 6). Assuming the need for an intermediate distribution point, our illustrated system depicts two distinct distribution circuits: the customer service loop (1 through 6) and the internal supply loop (A through D). Both are equally important in the total distribution system. The relationship between the distribution center and the customer is easy to establish. The manufacturing and the distribution center relationship is another dimension of customer service and must be treated accordingly. Time is important to both. How fast the customer is served from the distribution point has a direct impact on his inventory investment. How fast the company serves the distribution point has a direct relationship to inventory investment at the distribution center and to customer delivery reliability. Order entry is defined as the processing of orders from the customer through the sales organization until their receipt at the distribution center (1 through 4). Order entry could include, in addition to the mechanics of entering the orders, such functions as inventory control, production and inventory planning, customer and sales service, and traffic research. The planning activities take on more significance in the order entry portion of the internal supply loop (A to B).

When evaluating the order entry element, the distribution manager must be assured that there are no unnecessary time-consuming features in the present flow. For example:

1. Do salesmen communicate orders directly to the sales office or is input informal and uncontrolled?
2. Is mail service used to transmit orders or is some faster means available and at what cost?
3. Is there sufficient clerical depth at the sales office to assure uninterrupted flow of orders in the event of absences?
4. Is the format of the sales order designed to minimize order editing and transcription?

Beyond order entry, order processing and physical assembly time involves the time associated with processing the order through the distribution center to the shipping platform (4 to 5 and B to C). Here again, the inventory control function could be within the order processing element. However, functions, such as materials handling and warehousing, would be part of the distribution center operation. There is generally a greater delineation of these functional responsibilities in the manufacturing facility or, in our example, the internal supply loop. Exhibit 38 illustrates what usually happens within the distribution center or the finished goods operation of the manufacturing facility.

Exhibit 38. A typical distribution center system.

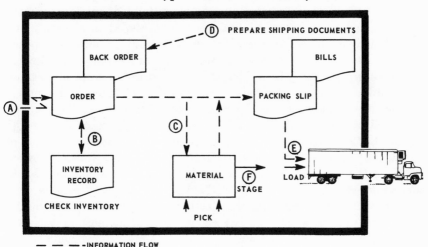

— — — -INFORMATION FLOW
————————MATERIAL FLOW

After an order is entered (A), some form of inventory checking is usually performed (B) before the order is sent out for picking. (In some cases, this is done in parallel with picking.) After the material is picked (C), or while it is being picked, the necessary shipping documents are created (D) and the material is loaded into the vehicle (E). A staging operation (F) may be performed to facilitate picking the complete order or waiting for a transport vehicle.

Note that we have distinguished between the actual order flow and the physical materials flow. There are two major reasons for this: (1) the costs within each element are independent and require different units of measure and techniques of control, and (2) the time elements are, in most cases, independent of each other.

In his evaluation of the order processing and physical assembly cycle of the order, the distribution manager must be assured, among other things, that the system provides for parallel processing of operations (inventory updating and order picking), that warehouse location systems provide for rapid and effective picking of orders, that all operations are effectively staffed and systems are designed for most effective utilization of time, and that there are no bottleneck operations that can be unduly affected by poor performance or absences.

The final time element is the period required to transport the orders from the distribution center to the customer by a specific mode of transportation (5 to 6 and C to D in Exhibit 37). For rail and truck shipments, this time generally includes point-to-point common carrier service. However, there are many cases where other elements of time are involved. For example, in cases of less-than-truckload (LTL) shipments, it may include the time required for the common carrier to consolidate and accumulate additional tonnage for shipment to the same city. At the other extreme, many customer orders may be pooled to achieve a full truckload for shipment into a geographic area. The orders would then be distributed to final destinations. Additional time is required to unload and then reload onto the vehicle that will distribute the material to the customer. The degree and extent of this additional time depends on the effectiveness of the common carrier's distribution system.

When evaluating this element of time, the distribution manager should be alert for opportunities to reduce time through the use of alternative modes of transportation. However, if major expenditures are made in this element to meet service objectives, consideration should be given to two areas.

Order size. The size of an order certainly affects a company's ability to produce and even transport it economically and must be included in a company's service consideration. Minimum and maximum order sizes, in units, line items, dollars, or weight, may fall under this constraint. For example, a company may set a transit time standard of two days, by truck, from its distribution center to all its customers in that general geographic location. Should this delivery standard apply to all orders regardless of size? Does it apply to less-than-truckload (LTL) orders? In other words, is the company willing to pay the additional costs of LTL shipments to provide the two-day service to all its customers? Or should it set a longer delivery standard that includes the normal time required to accumulate sufficient tonnage for a general geographic area to make shipments more economical?

Establishing price and service policies by order size is a way to control this. For example, a customer who ordered in full truckloads would be given the two-day service and pay the normal price. The company may allow him to consolidate a number of items to meet this policy. On the other hand, a customer who orders in less-than-truckload quantities may pay two penalties. One is the longer delivery time required to accumulate a full truckload, either by the carrier or the company. The other is a cost penalty to cover the additional cost of delivering the small order.

Order consolidation. A company's ability to consolidate items from one location to several customers, in a single shipment, also affects its ability to transport an order economically. Above, we talked about "normal time" to accumulate tonnage for a geographic region. This time standard is influenced by customer order frequency and geographic order volume patterns.

For example, three customers in a geographic region each order their requirements weekly from a company's distribution center. The consolidated requirements of the customers average 20,000 pounds, or the equivalent of one full truckload, per week. In this example, the company could expect normally to provide one-week delivery service to customers in that geographic region. If the total consolidated requirements of all three customers averaged only 15,000 pounds per week, the company could either provide weekly delivery service to its customers at a freight cost penalty by shipping 15,000 pounds when 20,000 pounds is optimum or provide delivery service less frequently at no freight cost penalty.

A more representative example has the three customers (A, B, and C) ordering their requirements differently: customer A orders 7,000 pounds weekly, B orders 13,000 pounds biweekly, and C orders 26,000 pounds monthly. The company ships to each customer as ordered, even though the total consolidated requirements into the geographic area average 80,000 pounds per month (the equivalent of four 20,000-pound truckloads per month). If the company had determined its customer needs, it probably would have developed order consolidation procedures to provide weekly truckload delivery service into that geographic area. Such delivery service would have been better for customers B and C, at less cost to them and to the company.

Order consolidation for entirely different purposes poses a far more complex problem. This involves a company's ability to consolidate from several locations to one customer in a single shipment. For example, a company allows its customer to consolidate his order, one product from plant X and the other from plant Z to achieve the full carload rate (90,000 pounds) in order to sell and service all his requirements. Assuming each plant can produce only one product, the company has three alternatives:

1. Ship from plant X to plant Z, and then to the customer.
2. Ship from plant Z to plant X, and then to the customer.
3. Ship separately, from plant X and plant Z, to the customer.

Not only are different distribution costs associated with each alternative, but the order processing, physical assembly, and transit time elements may be different. The point is that this company must balance the delivery times to its customers with the cost of providing that service before it establishes delivery objectives and order consolidation policies.

In summary, once service objectives have been identified, the distribution function must examine the present flow and evaluate the means and cost of achieving those objectives. For example, the results of this phase of work at Great Lumber Company is shown in Exhibit 39.

Exhibit 39. Great Lumber Company, time and cost elements.

Product Line:___PLYWOOD___
Market Region:__MIDWEST___

			TIME AND COST ELEMENTS							
			ORDER ENTRY (1)		ORDER PROCESSING (2)		PHYSICAL ASSEMBLY (3)		TRANSIT (4)	
CLASS OF SERVICE	DELIVERY RELIABILITY (% ON TIME)	DELIVERY TIME (DAYS)	TIME (DAYS)	COST (000)	TIME (DAYS)	COST (000)	TIME (DAYS)	COST (000)	TIME (DAYS)	COST (000)
CURRENT SERVICE LEVEL	60	7½	1½	$200	2½	$100	1½	$400	2	$450
IMPROVED RELIABILITY WITH:										
1½ DAYS' FASTER SERVICE	90	6	1	200	2	100	1	300	2	400
2½ DAYS' FASTER SERVICE	90	5	1	200	1	150	1	300	2	400
3½ DAYS' FASTER SERVICE	90	4	1	200	½	250	1	300	1½	500

(1) DEFINED AS STEPS 1 THROUGH 4 AND A AND B IN EXHIBIT 37
(2) DEFINED AS STEPS 4 THROUGH 5 AND B AND C IN EXHIBIT 37
(3) DEFINED AS STEPS 4 THROUGH 5 AND B AND C IN EXHIBIT 37
(4) DEFINED AS STEPS 5 THROUGH 6 AND C AND D IN EXHIBIT 37

Achieving the Objectives

Having evaluated all the time elements, the distribution manager should be constantly aware of where improvements can be made and the cost implications of these alternatives. As in Great Lumber's case, if the system is being examined for the first time, it is not unusual to discover opportunities to reduce time as well as costs.

For example, in Exhibit 39 we see that the physical assembly time is taking 1½ days at a cost of $400,000 per year. Earlier we defined this element as the physical movement of material from the warehouse to the shipping platform. Within this element is the time associated with inventory reliability, and the cost of keeping inventory. Great Lumber analyzed inventories, customer demands, safety stocks, and so on at its Midwest distribution center. It found the 1½ days was a result of improperly distributed inventory and higher than planned stockout rates. Also, inventory investment was much greater than necessary. Great Lumber revised its inventory control system and developed more responsive inventory levels. Through these steps alone, it was able to achieve a half-day time reduction, with less inventory investment and consequently less cost.

After a review of the Midwest regional sales office, Great Lumber found that the system for controlling paperwork was lacking some basic supervisory controls and standards of clerical performance. Orders could be found on the salesman's or clerk's desk for two to three days. Although some orders were entered and processed in less than one day, the average time was 1½ days. Here again, with no increase in cost, order entry time was reduced by half a day by installing supervisory control and performance measurements. A similar situation existed in the processing of orders at the Midwest distribution center. It was found that customer orders were first passed across the inventory records to determine availability prior to release for picking and shipping. A systems change to perform the availability and picking activities in parallel reduced total delivery time by another half day. As a result of this change, Great Lumber was able to check its inventory records when a discrepancy occurred. Consequently, customer communications were improved through more accurate response to product availability requests.

An examination of the transit time element revealed that of the $450,000 per year transportation costs, $50,000 was expended on premium freight costs. (Premium freight is the cost differential between shipping a 15,000-pound truckload when a 20,000-pound truckload is optimum.) Great Lumber determined that this additional cost was incurred because of customer delivery pressures to meet the six-day delivery and 90% on-time reliability commitments, and an ineffective order consolidation system. (The company waited until product was picked before it attempted to consolidate orders.) Here the company, through minor systems changes, was able to make a substantial cost improvement without impairing the two-day transit time standard.

Thus Great Lumber found it was possible to reduce delivery time by $1\frac{1}{2}$ days ($7\frac{1}{2}$ to 6), improve delivery schedule performance by 30% (60% to 90%), and reduce costs by $150,000 per year. But this is not the entire story. The projected potential in profit contribution from the improvement in service as shown in Exhibit 36 was $300,000. Therefore, the net contribution to profits amounted to $450,000 per year. This is shown in Exhibit 40.

Exhibit 40. Great Lumber Company, cost/profit opportunities.

Product line: __PLYWOOD__
Market region: __MIDWEST__

CLASS OF SERVICE	DELIVERY RELIABILITY (% ON TIME)	DELIVERY TIME (DAYS)	ANNUAL COST (000)	NET COST REDUCTION (000)	ADDITIONAL PROFIT CONTRIBUTION FROM INCREASED SALES (000)	NET PROFIT CONTRIBUTION (000)
CURRENT SERVICE LEVEL	60	7½	$1,150			
IMPROVED RELIABILITY WITH						
1½ DAYS FASTER SERVICE	90	6	1,000	$150	$300	$450
2½ DAYS FASTER SERVICE	90	5	1,100	50	500	550
3½ DAYS FASTER SERVICE	90	4	1,250	(100)	550	450

Although Great Lumber did not consider the possibility of reducing delivery time, we have carried our example through to show what the costs for each time element might have been. Note that with all the facts and estimated cost for reducing the six-day service level, profit contribution reaches a point of diminishing returns at four days. The additional profit potential in reducing the time from five to four days is completely offset by additional cost. Therefore, in this case, it is likely that a five-day objective will be agreed upon by management.

MEASURING PERFORMANCE

Once a company establishes the importance of customer service as a competitive strategy, a continuing system of performance measurement should be implemented. Without such a reporting system, the advantages of good distribution will rapidly be lost. A volume-oriented sales group may promise deliveries to costly geographic areas that are not consistent with the overall cost and profit objectives of the company. Therefore, once service objectives and policies have been agreed upon, the reporting system should highlight instances where orders have been promised in less than the standard delivery time. Similarly, the reporting system should identify instances where actual time and reliability performance is worse than standard. Distribution performance reporting may include such things as:

Measurement of the actual time experienced compared with the standard time by each identified time element.

Measurement of the percent of conformance or reliability to the standard time by element.

An identification of sales lost through customer service or inventory control inadequacies.

Periodic review and surveillance of the requirements of the marketplace (including competition).

Cost analysis of the normal distribution functions involved in the time/cost loop structured along the lines shown in Exhibit 39, to the extent practical. For example, off-site warehousing or distribution center cost would be within the physical assembly element.

An identification of premium freight cost or cost over the accepted transportation standard. For example, if rail is the normal mode of shipment, premium freight would be the additional cost to ship by truck.

Inventory performance reporting, which could include inventory investment compared with a developed standard, turnover comparisons, and identification of excess and slow-moving inventory.

For effective control, the distribution manager may not require routine performance reporting of all these items. It is desirable, however, to report at least those areas that are significant to insure that they are within plan. Exhibit 41 depicts such a monthly performance report which highlights actual performance compared with target. In this case, the distribution manager felt that service, inventory, and selected cost

Exhibit 41. Physical distribution, key indicator report.

Plant_____

For Month End_____

PERFORMANCE AREA	LAST MONTH	TARGET
CUSTOMER SERVICE		
% ON-TIME SHIPMENTS	80%	90%
% PARTIAL SHIPMENTS	8%	5%
CUSTOMER ORDERS BEYOND PROMISED DATE	100	75
POTENTIAL "LOST" SALES DUE TO STOCKOUTS (% OF NORMAL SALES)	6%	4%
INVENTORIES		
NO. OF STOCKKEEPING UNITS IN INVENTORY	385	350
INVENTORY TURNOVER	6.3	6.7
EXCESS INVENTORY (UNITS)	100	0
SLOW-MOVING INVENTORY (UNITS)	50	0
COST		
PREMIUM FREIGHT COST	$ 5,000	0
OFF-SITE WAREHOUSE COST	$40,000	$40,000
SHIPPING OVERTIME COST	$ 1,000	$ 2,000

Exhibit 42. Great Lumber Company, distribution program; key program indicators—service.

ON-TIME SHIPPING PERFORMANCE

TYPE OF SERVICE	PLANNED CAPABILITY	MILL A		MILL B		MILL C		MILL D	
		CURRENT LEVEL	BEFORE PROGRAM	CURRENT LEVEL	BEFORE PROGRAM	CURRENT LEVEL	BEFORE PROGRAM	CURRENT LEVEL	BEFORE PROGRAM
– – COMBINED	90–95%	89%	60%	90%	52%	76%	63%	83%	59%
– – MAKE TO ORDER	90–95%	88%	50%	90%	51%	82%	69%	80%	62%
– – STOCK ORDERS	95%	91%	67%	90%	54%	71%	56%	96%	52%

LEAD-TIME STATUS

TYPE OF DEMAND OR ACTIVITY	MILL A		MILL B		MILL C		MILL D	
	CURRENT LEVEL	BEFORE PROGRAM	CURRENT LEVEL	BEFORE PROGRAM	CURRENT LEVEL	BEFORE PROGRAM	CURRENT LEVEL	BEFORE PROGRAM
MAKE ORDERS (DAYS)	7	13.5	7	10.4	5	6.5	6	12.5
STOCK ORDERS (DAYS)	2	5.3	2	9	2.5	4.2	2.0	8.0
RAIL-SWITCHING TIME (DAYS)	1	2	1	2.3	1	1.5	N/A	N/A

measurements were sufficient to effectively monitor that particular plant or operation. Should a distribution cost or service category not identified by the report become a problem, an investigation of the causes would be in order. This may result in the addition of another performance measurement category or a change in the reporting format. Note the performance area "potential lost sales" because of stockouts. A system to report the actual lost sales generally requires considerable detail reporting in the sales offices and is often not very accurate. Consequently, this company reports potential lost sales, which is developed from one source—the inventory control system. Each time an inventory item is out of stock it is flagged. At the end of the month, the days-out-of-stock for each item is multiplied by its daily sales rate. This is considered a potential lost sale. The sum of all the potential lost sales is equated to the normal sales rate for all items to derive the percentage reported. This is then compared with the inventory control system target.

Exhibit 42 depicts a key indicator report in the customer service area. It evolved from Great Lumber's newly established customer sales service function. The report summarizes the reliability (percent on-time shipments) and time (lead-time status) performance of four mills. It not only compares current with planned levels, but also indicates the extent of improvement made through the distribution program efforts. Each mill within Great Lumber is measured identically, and the percents of improvement provide relative comparisons of performance, even though lead-time status is not comparable because each mill produces and distributes different products with different service requirements.

As marketing men have come to realize, customer service has a direct and measurable impact on a company's profits. Until recently, the elements and functions of customer service have been scattered throughout the organization. Now the trend is toward a separate and distinct distribution organization. The role of this function is to pull together and manage all the basic elements of customer service—time, reliability, and communications.

Marketing has a stake in customer service. Consequently, it must understand the role and objectives of the distribution function and its relationship to that function. As illustrated in this chapter, the most significant aspect of distribution is determining the service objectives. This is marketing's responsibility and links it with the distribution function. Without this step, distribution and customer service improvements become market response and competition response rather than company influence. The consequences are often cost increases rather than profit improvements.

6

PRODUCT LINE PLANNING
AND CONTROL

Product line modifications are becoming increasingly important as the mainstay of competitive position and acceptable profit levels. As the needs of the buying population change more rapidly, management must continually balance competitive position, growth, profitability, and risk in making product line decisions.

The purpose of this chapter is to illustrate how systems concepts can improve the management of this critical function. The chapter will cover the types of product line changes frequently recommended by marketing managers and the kinds of information systems required to support their suggestions.

Several case examples, drawn from the experiences of companies that have worked on such systems, will be used to demonstrate specific approaches.

TYPES OF PRODUCT LINE CHANGES

Most companies organize their planning of marketing activities around product lines, products, and items. Each of these represents a more detailed breakdown of the basic business of a company, as illustrated in Exhibit 43. Similar groupings of customer classifications, price ranges, and product "missions" have been used by some companies as means of identifying opportunities for new product line development or acquisition.

Exhibit 43. Product line structure.

PRIMARY MANUFACTURING CLASSIFICATION	REPRESENTATIVE PRODUCT LINE	REPRESENTATIVE PRODUCTS	REPRESENTATIVE ITEMS
Food products	Baked goods	White, rye, and whole wheat	3 loaf sizes
Textile products	Carpeting	Wool facing	6 patterns
Toys	Model car kits	Prepriced 89¢ kits	7 separate kits
Building supplies	Thermal and acoustical insulation	Acoustical insulation tiles	5 tile sizes
Automobiles	$3,200–$4,000 medium-priced	1973 "status" model	3 engine sizes

At any point in time, a company can be involved in product line modifications at all levels of its current product line structure.

1. Adding a completely *new product line* to serve new requirements of present customers or to enter completely new markets. In Exhibit 44, for example, the textile manufacturer considering a line of sheets and towels does not anticipate any major change in his basic customer group. On the other hand, the automobile company that enters the motorcycle market can expect a mixture of old and new customers for his new product line, although his product mission (private transportation) remains the same.

2. Adding a *new product* to an existing product line for sale to

Exhibit 44. Types of product line changes.

PRIMARY MANUFACTURING CLASSIFICATION	REPRESENTATIVE PRODUCT LINE		REPRESENTATIVE PRODUCTS		REPRESENTATIVE ITEMS	
	CURRENT	POSSIBLE ADDITION	CURRENT	POSSIBLE ADDITION OR REPLACEMENT	CURRENT	POSSIBLE ADDITION OR (DELETION)
Food products	Baked goods	Frozen pies	White, rye, whole wheat	Diet bread	3 loaf sizes	"Small family" loaf size
Textile products	Carpeting	Sheets and towels	Wool facing	Polyester facing	6 patterns	"Caribe" ("Mosaic")
Toys	Model car kits	Outdoor sports equipment	89¢ kits	$1.39 kits	7 separate kits	Packages of 3 kits
Building supplies	Thermal and acoustical insulation	Bathroom fixtures	Acoustical insulation tiles	Ceiling hardware	5 tile sizes	Colored tiles (3½ X 3½)
Automobiles	$3,200–$4,000 medium-priced	Motorcycles	1973 "status" model	1974 "status" model	3 engine sizes	375 H.P. (285 H.P.)

current customers. These changes are usually implemented to maintain or broaden the appeal of a company, as illustrated in Exhibit 44 by the food products manufacturer who adds a diet bread to three current bread products. Product addition or replacement is often regular and predictable in fashion goods industries as older products become less popular; the carpet manufacturer in Exhibit 44, for example, may add polyester facing to supplement or replace wool.

3. Adding a *new item variation* to those already offered. Item modifications are the most common type of product line change, and include new styles, colors, sizes, packaging, formulation, or performance characteristics. These changes are usually designed to meet new customer needs or to switch buyers away from a competitive supplier, as illustrated in Exhibit 44 by the toy manufacturer who combines three kits into a single package or the bread manufacturer who offers a new-size loaf. The basic characteristics of the products themselves are changed very little, if at all. At the consumer level, item changes often provide the basis for advertising and promotion campaigns.

4. *Deleting an item or a product* from the current line. Weeding out is essential to the control of slow-moving or low-margin products that have been kept in the line beyond their period of economic justification. Difficult marketing decisions are associated with deletion, however, since the requirements of key customers or market segments are often affected.

Each type of product line decision requires careful evaluation of marketing and financial risks. Thus, the designs of both financial and marketing information systems need to contain elements of performance measurement and analysis that will permit effective control of the product line itself.

NEW PRODUCT LINE PLANNING

The objectives of new product planning boil down to obtaining satisfactory and reliable answers to these key questions:

- What is the market potential for the product line?
- What is the economic feasibility of the product line?
- What is the timetable for the product line in terms of specific development checkpoints, financial requirements, and anticipated sales and profit results?

The management personnel responsible for product line planning must continually refine the answers to these questions, drawing upon

Exhibit 45. New product line entry strategies.

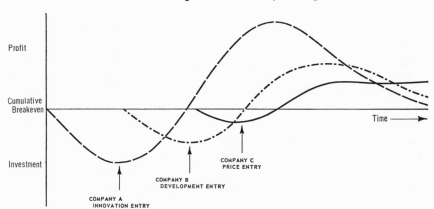

DIFFERENT ENTRY STRATEGIES FOR THE SAME PRODUCT INVOLVE
VARIATIONS IN TIMING, INVESTMENT LEVELS, AND PROFIT OPPORTUNITIES.

their experience and upon information gathered as the product line addition project proceeds through well-defined development stages.

The effort and money expended on the key questions depend to a large degree on the "newness" of the new product line under consideration, as illustrated in Exhibit 45. Assuming that company A has innovated a new product or process, that company can expect to reap the benefits of being first (if the product line is successful) in exchange for substantial initial losses while the product line is being tested and refined. Company A may also profit from royalty and license revenues if the product line has unique and protectable features. Company B is second into the market, having developed the product line idea a little beyond A's original concept. Capitalizing on A's investments in educating and attracting customers, B can get to market more cheaply (instant coffee is a good example of this). Depending on the relative reputations, resources, and marketing skills of A and B, B may or may not be able to overcome A's advantage. Company C may not innovate at all and could be content to copy A or B exactly and depend on price advantages for market penetration. Without heavy research, advertising, and promotion investments to recover, C's return on the new product line may actually exceed that of A or B despite lower sales volume and unit profit.

All three companies have carried out careful assessments of the potential volume, entry costs, production economics, and the timetable for profitable sales. While each may get significantly different answers to these questions, their actions depend on where they stand or expect to stand as innovators, developers, or price competitors for the new product line.

Most organizations that consider product line additions are in the categories of company B or company C—they are developers or efficient producers or marketers, but not necessarily originators. For such companies, continuous monitoring of customer activity, as well as competitive activity, is a basic requirement for successful product line growth. When marketing a new product line, it is normally more difficult to solicit a new customer group for that line than to appeal to current customers. Thus the usual logic for product line additions calls for sales to existing customers who are prospective users of the product line or to customers who, although they are users, may not be direct purchasers (such as a supplier of original equipment who enters the leasing market). The customer profile technique detailed in Chapter 12 is particularly appropriate for identifying new product line possibilities among existing customers. Procedures for maintaining up-to-date profiles provide valuable information on what customers are buying from other suppliers, on the characteristics of competitive products, and on the changes in the buying habits and policies of key customers.

The product life cycle sketched out in Exhibit 45 provides the basis for an approximation of anticipated product profitability over time, as illustrated in Exhibit 46. A projection of this kind, refined and updated as new information becomes available, is essential to the management

Exhibit 46. New product line planning.

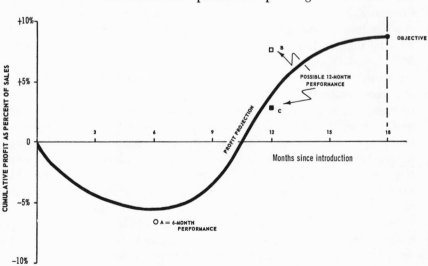

A PREESTABLISHED PROFIT PROJECTION ENABLES MANAGEMENT
TO COMPARE ACTUAL RESULTS AGAINST PERFORMANCE BENCHMARKS

of product line additions. It establishes a series of bench marks, in this example in terms of cumulative profitability, against which progress can be measured. The detailed plans behind such a projection should include cost, volume, and unit profitability estimates, as well as program budgets for each phase of new product line development, testing, and market introduction.

To illustrate the usefulness of the planning technique shown in Exhibit 46, assume that at the end of the first six months of full-scale sales effort the new line shows a cumulative loss of 5% (point A in Exhibit 46). While this is not a particularly positive result taken by itself, marketing management gains the proper perspective by comparing the 5% loss to the *planned* cumulative loss, which is close to the actual results in this example. Another reading, at the end of a year, might show a cumulative profit higher than planned (point B), or lower (point C). If performance is better than expected, management can consider revising strategies to take advantage of favorable response—perhaps more advertising and promotion to gain additional volume while maintaining profitability. If results are poor (point C), a reevaluation could lead to cuts in promotional expenses in an attempt to bring cumulative profits to an acceptable level. Continued poor performance versus plan might result in the prompt termination of the new product line effort, rather than continuing to reach for objectives that look more and more unattainable. Decisions on all these alternatives must rely on comparison with a preestablished plan in order to be effective.

Of course, one of the basic information requirements for new product line profit projections is objective appraisal of market conditions and consideration of possible competitive responses. Periodic studies of new product failures and successes, as conducted by The Conference Board, Inc., continually identify "inadequate market analysis" as the principal cause of failure. Even with the extensive and expensive market research efforts common in some consumer goods companies, good data can lead to the wrong answers concerning the number of prospective customers and their interests in a particular product idea. Small and medium-size industrial goods companies face an even tougher task in evaluating market potential, since they must attempt to gauge probable success without the financial resources or marketing research capabilities normally required; however, these handicaps of size are often offset by an advantage of compactness: the ability of a small management group to reach decisions quickly and initiate action when conditions seem favorable.

In the industrial environment, too, the new product sometimes emerges from research and development almost as a surprise. As a technological innovation, it has a great appeal to engineering and top management, and optimism carries the day. Under such circumstances, even a superior product faces long odds since careful planning and testing, and the setting of volume and profit bench marks, are ignored in the rush to market.

LEWIS STAMPING COMPANY

Such an atmosphere of enthusiasm prevailed at Lewis Stamping Company, a pseudonym for an actual organization whose experiences are described here for illustrative purposes.

The company's primary business is the fabrication of various metals and alloys using precision dies. Over the years, the owners had tried to take advantage of new and more efficient punches and presses and had built their operation to an annual volume of just over $20 million. One of their biggest operating problems involved damage and down time on high-speed equipment when parts jammed because of misaligned raw stock. Even skilled operators occasionally positioned a plate or bar incorrectly, and the fabricated piece did not release cleanly from the punch or press, causing frequent shutdown for inspection and repair.

To help protect the expensive production equipment, and the machine crews as well, the Lewis engineers devised an automatically controlled feed system. The system monitored raw stock alignment and included control features that activated alarms or shutoff mechanisms when it detected feed problems. This special device seemed to offer unique advantages for any user of high-speed punches and presses. Lewis management determined to produce the control unit as a new product line and market it to the metal stamping industry.

The president of Lewis contacted Bernick Brothers, a firm of manufacturing representatives that handled punch and press equipment for a number of manufacturers. He provided the Bernick sales manager with a technical specification sheet on the device (now dubbed the "Lewis Protektor"). The Bernick sales manager agreed that the Protektor had a bright future, and he agreed to add it to his product list and to solicit firms with high-speed equipment.

By providing Bernick Brothers with a margin of $250 on each $2000 sale, Lewis felt sure that the representatives would pursue prospective customers aggressively; besides, the $1,750 left after commission still provided Lewis with $250 profit contribution over manufacturing costs of $1,500 per unit. Lewis management eagerly awaited orders and profits.

At the end of the first year's activity on the Protektor, results were not particularly encouraging, as shown in Exhibit 47. A total of 310

Exhibit 47. Lewis Protektor, total revenues at end of first year, 19XX.

NEW UNIT SALES	**$ 620,000**
NEW ACCESSORY SALES	**23,700**
SUBTOTAL: $ 643,700	
UNIT REPAIR REVENUES	**52,500**
PARTS SALES AND PARTS REPAIR REVENUES	**39,500**
EXCHANGES	**6,500**
REWORK / CONVERSION	**5,800**
TOTAL	**$ 748,000**

Exhibit 48. Metal-forming machines, 1968, by machine type (000).

	POSSIBLE PROTEKTOR APPLICATIONS, 1968	PERCENT INCREASE /(DECREASE) SINCE 1963
HYDRAULIC PRESSES	51.5	16.0%
MECHANICAL PRESSES		
INCLINABLE, SINGLE ACTION	178.8	16.8
STRAIGHT SIDE (ALL TYPES)	47.3	(26.6)
GAP / C-FRAME	43.4	12.1
ROTARY DIE	2.7	32.7
MULTIPLE TRANSFER	2.8	4.5
MULTIPLE PLUNGER	3.6	15.5
PUNCHING AND SHEARING MACHINES	3.0	N/A
FORGING MACHINES	13.1	(3.6)
TOTAL POSSIBLE PROTEKTOR APPLICATIONS	346.2	
ALL OTHER MACHINES	328.3	
TOTAL	674.5	3.3%

SOURCE: *INVENTORY OF METAL WORKING EQUIPMENT*
(NEW YORK: *AMERICAN MACHINIST*, McGRAW-HILL, 1968).

units had been sold, but Lewis felt that this was only a tiny fraction of the potential business—having been in the business for many years, the president was certain that "thousands" of potential customers were available and that even a market penetration of only 10% or 15% would yield unit sales several times the first year's actual volume. He seriously considered dropping the Protektor entirely; his engineering staff was spending considerable time installing the few units that were sold and trying to modify the product to meet specific customer needs.

The president asked his own sales manager to gather as much factual information as he could find about the market for the Protektor. The sales manager, in turn, located a survey by an industry trade publication that estimated the total number of metal-forming machines as of 1968 by type, as well as by general industry classification (S.I.C. code) and geographic location. The survey is summarized in Exhibits 48 and 49, which highlight possible Protektor applications.

As the president and his associates had suspected, there were "thousands" of prospective customers, both in terms of machines to be fed automatically and in terms of individual firms operating several such machines. However, a close examination of the 310 orders received (Exhibit 50) showed that the Protektor's activity did not seem to parallel the potential estimated from the trade publication survey. For example, the Protektor had done well in applications for straight side mechanical presses, but these machines accounted for only about 14% of possible applications, and their usage was declining relative to other applications. On the other hand, very few sales had been made for use with single action mechanical presses, which represented the largest single application area. The same pattern applied to industry penetration; most of the current customers were classified as either metal stampings (S.I.C. 346) or automotive parts (S.I.C. 3717) companies, which together account for about 14% of potential customers. Very few sales had been made to companies in other high-potential industries, such as fabricated structural metals, cutlery, or metal furniture.

The president, thinking back to his ideas about the Protektor and his instructions to Bernick Brothers, could understand this situation. He had directed Bernick to solicit prospective customers that were similar to Lewis; and Bernick's salesmen had seen detailed demonstrations on Lewis Company equipment only. The same situation applied to geographic market coverage, where the president noted large potential markets outside Bernick's usual territories. Overall, however, he gave Bernick credit for good performance.

Having reviewed a more complete analysis of the market for the Protektor, Lewis management concluded that the new product line had not been given a fair chance. The sales manager drew up a series of

Exhibit 49. Metal-forming machines with possible Protektor applications only, 1968.

BY INDUSTRY

S.I.C. NO.	INDUSTRY	PERCENT OF TOTAL	NO. OF FIRMS	AVERAGE MACHINES PER FIRM
344	Fabricated structural metal	10.6%	9,791	3.8
346	Metal stampings	9.8	2,678	12.7
342	Cutlery, hand tools, etc.	5.6	1,805	10.8
3717	Automotive parts	4.3	1,849	8.1
2514	Metal furniture	3.9	1,112	12.3
345	Screw machine products	3.8	2,427	5.4
364	Electric wiring and equipment	3.6	1,853	6.8
349	Fabricated wire products	3.4	2,575	4.6
362	Electrical apparatus	3.2	1,302	8.4
363	Household appliances	1.6	625	9.1
341	Metal cans	1.5	329	15.3
334	Ferrous/nonferrous metals	1.3	388	11.7
3722	Aircraft parts	1.0	242	14.7
	All others	46.4	71,075	2.2
	Total	100.0%	98,051	
	Weighted average			3.5

BY GEOGRAPHIC AREA

AREA	PERCENT OF TOTAL MACHINES
Chicago	14.3%
New York/Newark	11.8
Detroit	7.9
Los Angeles	6.9
Philadelphia/Camden	5.8
Boston	5.7
Cleveland	5.2
Atlanta/New Orleans	4.8
Bridgeport/Hartford	4.2
Milwaukee	3.6
Indianapolis	3.4
Buffalo/Syracuse	3.4
Cincinnati/Louisville	3.3
All others	19.7
Total	100.0%

SOURCE: *INVENTORY OF METAL WORKING EQUIPMENT*
(NEW YORK: *AMERICAN MACHINIST*, McGRAW-HILL, 1968).

Analysis of potential based on external data enables marketing managers to plan selling efforts and to establish realistic estimates of potential.

Exhibit 50. Lewis Protektor, new unit sales summary, 19XX.

APPLICATION AREA	NUMBER SOLD	PERCENT OF TOTAL
HYDRAULIC PRESSES (total)	40	9.8%
MECHANICAL PRESSES		
STRAIGHT SIDE (all types)	132	42.6
INCLINABLE, SINGLE ACTION	51	16.4
GAP, C-FRAME	34	11.0
MULTIPLE TRANSFER	12	3.9
MULTIPLE PLUNGER	9	2.9
ALL OTHERS	72	23.2
UNIT TOTALS	310	100.0%
INDUSTRY		
METAL STAMPING	82	26.4%
AUTOMOTIVE PARTS	48	15.5
METAL CANS	21	6.8
ALL OTHERS	159	51.3
UNIT TOTALS	310	100.0%
GEOGRAPHIC AREA		
PHILADELPHIA/CAMDEN	143	46.1
NEW YORK/NEWARK	61	19.7
BUFFALO/SYRACUSE	55	17.7
ALL OTHERS	51	16.5
UNIT TOTALS	310	100.0%

These analyses, requiring a detailed review of sales records, permit direct comparison between external data (Exhibit 49) and internal data. Defining appropriate breakdowns of customers and market segments as part of overall information systems design allows for the regular and economical collection of sales analysis statistics.

action plans he felt would contribute substantially to future marketing success. These included:

1. Developing specification sheets and promotional material directed at specific applications where large numbers of potential installations were available, such as single action and C-frame presses, and individual industries as identified in the survey.

2. Carrying out more extensive training of manufacturers' representatives engaged to solicit prospective customers.

3. Engaging other representatives for wide industry and geographic coverage.

4. Monitoring progress by application type, customer type, and location against planned market penetration, with the plan, in turn, based on the most recent survey of industry activity and a realistic appraisal of Protektor potential.

5. Initiating more detailed reports of in-house time spent on installation, repair, and modification for use in future pricing decisions.

The Lewis Stamping Company example highlights some important features of a successful new product line development effort. First, even the most limited kind of market research and prospective customer identification are required for directing new product line marketing activities. Second, the results of initial marketing programs must be evaluated against a preestablished plan that specifies both volume and profitability as key bench marks; the plan should also spell out just where and under what conditions sales success is expected. Finally, existing marketing and financial information systems may need to be modified so that they provide rapid updates for new product lines. Information on sales force activity, costs, technical problems, and competitive activity is particularly critical during the market introduction period.

NEW PRODUCT PLANNING

The dividing line between new products and new product lines tends to be hazy. New products (as opposed to whole new lines) usually use existing facilities, sales manpower, and distribution channels. The same general group of customers is usually solicited both for new products and current products, and surveys of prospective customer interest are more easily carried out for this reason. The key information needs for new products are the same as for an entirely new product line. A grocery products manufacturer considering a new line of desserts and a bank considering adding a credit card should both undertake the detailed planning, budgeting, and bench-mark setting described previously for a completely new line of merchandise.

In many cases the primary rationale behind a new product addition has to do with accommodating customers. No marketing manager can ignore the sight of customers who patronize another supplier for some products when (he reasons) he could easily supply those items and increase both total volume and profits by doing so.

The supplementary (or accommodation) product can be marketed first as a resale item purchased from another supplier. Many grocery products, apparel items, and some durable household goods such as TV sets and phonographs are marketed under these circumstances either as private brands or under the brand name of the original supplier. Once the volume of a resale product begins to become sizable, it is logical to carry out a make or buy analysis and consider manufacturing rather than resale. If the manufacturing decision is made, the now-displaced supplier can be expected to launch promotional activities or lower his prices (or both) so as to make entry into the manufacturing end of the business as difficult as possible.

The development of new products through the resale tactic is a well-established and growing marketing technique. Financial risks are reduced considerably in comparison with the direct manufacturing route, and there is a strong parallel in the minds of marketing managers to the use of brokers to open up a new sales territory. In both cases the unit profitability expected has definite limitations, but out-of-pocket expenses should vary directly with volume.

GREAT LUMBER COMPANY

The decision to market a product on a resale basis can involve as little as a memo to the purchasing agent and revisions to a catalog or price list. It is possible to lose control over this type of new product addition activity when risks look low and profits look high, as illustrated in the case of Great Lumber Company.

As described in Chapter 5, Great Lumber manufactures and markets a wide variety of wood products, such as untreated wood, unfinished furniture, plywood, paneling, and unfinished ready-to-install cabinets. Sales are made through a contract sales force that calls on architects, specifiers, and contractors. Great Lumber also sells through a chain of branch stores in the Midwest, where local contractors and the general public buy wood products and supplies under the Great Lumber brand name.

The product line available at each branch grew substantially as Great Lumber added new types of plywood, paneling, moldings, and finished and semifinished wood products. While this type of product line expansion was taking place, the branches also began to handle many of the accessories required by the small contractor or do-it-yourself customer, such as woodworking tools, brackets, nails and bolts, and decorative trims. The usual procedure for adding such products was for divisional managers with responsibility for branch marketing policies to survey branch managers twice a year, asking them whether they had any requests for product additions. The Great Lumber purchasing agent would then be instructed to negotiate contracts with suppliers and arrange for shipment to Great Lumber distribution points in the regions requesting specific new products.

The "one stop" reputation of Great Lumber branches began to grow, particularly in larger branches in Chicago, Detroit, and Milwaukee where supplementary products were stocked in great variety. At the same time, divisional managers noted rapidly growing inventory levels in these branches, and increasing reorder problems for the large number of low-value, low-volume products stocked at distribution points and warehouses. Most importantly, several key branches were showing level or declining margins despite steadily rising volume. The average branch exhibited a performance profile as shown in Exhibit 51.

Although branch-controllable expenses varied widely from one location to another, further analysis showed that the number of line items processed in a year provided the most consistent indicator of such expenses, as shown in Exhibit 52. As expected, the high-volume branches with high expenses (and profit problems) had the greatest catalog of available items and the largest numbers of line items per invoice. Divisional managers concluded that this indicated a direct relationship between the size of the product line and branch-controllable expenses, and they authorized a more detailed study of product profitability to pin down specific corrective actions.

Working with broad breakdowns of branch expenses, divisional and product management personnel estimated branch margins for major product groups. This process required the allocation of branch expenses as logically as possible among product groups. The various approaches

Exhibit 51. Great Lumber Company, annual branch performance profile.

SALES VOLUME	$ 3,000,000
GROSS MARGIN	900,000
BRANCH-CONTROLLABLE EXPENSES	−450,000
BRANCH MARGIN	$ 450,000
GENERAL AND ALLOCATED OVERHEAD	−300,000
NET PROFIT BEFORE TAX	$ 150,000

Exhibit 52. Great Lumber Company, relationship between size of product line and branch-controllable expenses.

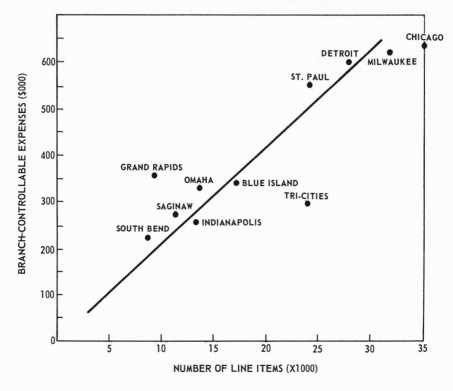

Exhibit 53. Great Lumber Company, branch expense allocation.

BRANCH-CONTROLLABLE EXPENSE CATEGORY	BASIS OF ALLOCATION TO PRODUCT GROUP					
	DIRECT	LINE ITEMS	UNIT SALES	AVERAGE INVENTORY	CUBIC FEET	DOLLAR SALES
SELLING	X	X				X
SHIPPING			X			
WAREHOUSING	X		X	X	X	
OFFICE ADMINIS- TRATION	X	X				
OTHER				X		X

used are summarized in Exhibit 53; in most cases more than one allocation basis was tried in order to provide a "reasonableness" cross check. For example, warehouse expenses were allocated directly for some product groups stored in special locations. For those products in mixed storage facilities, the number of line items, unit sales volume, average inventory levels, and estimated cubic foot requirements were all used as indicators of proportional warehousing costs.

Exhibit 54 shows the results of branch expense allocations to product groups. Decorative moldings and hardware showed a loss at the branch margin level, and coatings, glues, and painting supplies contributed very little to branch performance. These categories, of course, were heavily stocked with resale products added steadily in response to branch managers' requests. A closer inspection of the products in these problem groups identified 140 individual products that actually detracted from branch profit contribution although they contributed 12% of the average branch's sales volume. Estimated performance for the average branch without these 140 products is shown in Exhibit 55.

Several factors contribute to the margin improvement of about 8%. Elimination of the poorer 140 products was estimated to improve overall margins from 30% to 32% of sales volume. Branch controllable expenses, particularly for warehousing and order filling, were estimated to decline about 20% with the 12% sales volume decrease.

Great Lumber did not want to damage its full-service approach by

Exhibit 54. Great Lumber Company, product group profitability.

PRODUCT GROUP	PERCENT OF SALES	PERCENT OF BRANCH MARGIN
UNFINISHED WOOD	10%	14%
REGULAR PLYWOOD	30	28
TREATED/STAINED PLYWOOD	20	40
DOORS, WINDOWS	15	25
COATINGS, PAINTS, SUPPLIES	10	4
DECORATIVE MOLDINGS	5	(3)
HARDWARE	10	(8)
	100%	100%

Exhibit 55. Great Lumber Company, annual branch performance profile.

	PRO FORMA	CURRENT
SALES VOLUME	$ 2,640,000	$ 3,000,000
GROSS MARGIN	$ 845,000	$ 900,000
BRANCH-CONTROLLABLE EXPENSES	−360,000	−450,000
BRANCH MARGIN	$ 485,000	$ 450,000

dropping all these resale products automatically. Instead, branch managers were instructed as follows:

For low-margin products with price problems because of competition, attempts should again be made to raise prices.

For low-margin products with inventory cost and warehouse expense problems, inventories should be cut and orders taken for bulk shipment only.

Customers should be offered the option of ordering deleted products for future delivery if order quantities are above specified minimums.

As these policies were being implemented, regional and divisional managers arranged for problem products to be monitored throughout the company twice a month. They also established objectives for any resale product by defining volume and branch margin levels that additional products should meet after an initial test period.

The Great Lumber Company example illustrates several key points concerning new product additions.

1. Control over new product additions manufactured or purchased for resale requires a formal set of procedures. Planning and information systems that facilitate this control process need not be elaborate; basic steps would be to define management responsibility, follow short checklists of approval points, establish minimum volume and profit objectives, and check progress against objectives regularly.

2. The profitability of each product in the line should be examined periodically beyond the gross margin level. Logical allocations of some overhead expenses, such as selling, warehousing, and order processing, can help identify opportunities for improvement.

3. The rationale for maintaining current levels of product variety should also be examined objectively once or twice a year.

These control procedures can help to eliminate unnecessary and unprofitable product variety while still encouraging full consideration of market opportunities.

ADDING AND DELETING ITEMS

Changes at the item level—the point of smallest differentiation between product variations—are the most common kind of product line activity. The increasing numbers of colors, sizes, package types, and minor quality differences are usually rationalized in terms of customer accommodation. Life would be a lot simpler if customers were satisfied with black automobiles and economy-size jars of peanut butter. However, most manufacturers are not in a position to dictate what the customer will buy and are faced with more and more items that must be produced and inventoried to meet "nonfunctional" needs. The magnitude of the problem in any particular company can be most easily gauged by arranging items in order of decreasing sales volume and then plotting cumulative item sales against cumulative number of items. Examples of this analysis are shown in Exhibit 56, which is based on actual data of three companies. The sales volume contribution of the last 50% of the items ranges from 20% down to about 5%—proportions that are typical of both consumer goods and industrial goods companies.

Another eye-opener for management is a plot of item count over time, showing the growth in the number of different "things" offered for sale. The inventory of items tends to grow without anybody in particular noticing it. Special items for individual customers become standard; accessories, spare parts, and even premiums and give-aways are absorbed into the system as inventory investments go up and inventory turnover goes down.

Demonstrating that the small-volume items are numerous is only a start toward understanding the complications of item proliferation. Each variety requires a slightly different series of manufacturing, finishing, or packaging operations. Even a small batch of a low-volume item requires some setups in the manufacturing process and associated down time before and after the setups, as well as waste and scrap allowances. Inventory levels, too, tend to balloon as item count increases, since each item offered for sale is normally backed up by replacement inventory or spare parts, as well as raw materials, semifinished goods, and packaging supplies. Overhead areas are also influenced by the number of items in the line. Clerical and management time is required to prepare and maintain bills of materials, cost sheets, product codes, catalogs, and price lists.

Exhibit 56. Item/volume concentration.

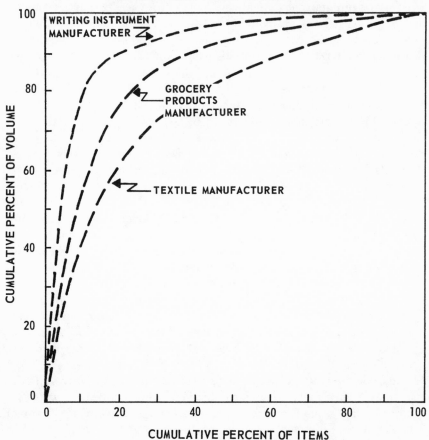

High volume concentration in a small proportion of items is common in many manufacturing companies. This graphic approach is a convenient way to gauge the magnitude of the "small item" problem; marketing and financial analysis is required to
identify just which items should be deleted.

Since it is quite difficult to determine the full costs of a particular
item, including its share of manufacturing and general overhead, most
companies rely on gross margin measures to judge item value. This
is only an approximate measure, however, and product managers must
remember that the other costs, although not precisely defined at the
item level, are nonetheless real expenses. For this reason, small-volume
items might well have higher gross margin objectives than larger-volume
items, as insurance against building an inefficient level of product line
variety.

Marketing information plays a major part in establishing item needs. Aggressive sales managers are always looking for ways to gain a competitive edge by offering a more attractive variety than other suppliers. This objective often translates into high item addition rates. A careful survey of competition in terms of width and depth of line provides the factual basis for both expanding and contracting item levels.

HIGHPOINT TEXTILE COMPANY

Highpoint Textile Company (a fictitious name) manufactures several types of fabric in a wide variety of patterns for sale to cutters, who in turn convert the fabric into apparel for women and children. The product line consists of several stable patterns, with estimated life cycles of two or three years, and a number of more fashion-oriented patterns that may be good for one or two seasons only before requiring replacement. Each pattern is manufactured in a number of colors, ranging from 10 to 18, and in one or two or three widths. Considering these possible product variations, total item count is calculated by multiplying patterns by average colors per pattern by average widths per pattern.

The continual rotation of new patterns to replace outdated ones and new colors for each pattern kept Highpoint production planners awake nights; their capacity was limited in the finishing department, and they were having trouble scheduling at least a short run of every item in time to replenish inventory. Each item required a different setup in both the weaving and finishing departments, and machine utilization measurements showed less and less actual production time and more and more down time for setups.

Highpoint's senior management concluded that new item additions were getting out of hand, and called upon the marketing managers to demonstrate just how additional items would make the company more "competitive." At the same time, the controller was asked to prepare estimates of the actual costs of adding a new pattern to the existing product line.

After a number of lengthy discussions, the marketing managers concluded that a competitive position could be defined as meeting the needs of the marketplace, and that those needs could be estimated by careful monitoring of competitive product lines. If new trends developed in consumer demand, product lines would change in a noticeable way. They agreed that the consumer ultimately determined the variety of products offered to him, and that the competitors could be expected to have just as good an idea of consumer interests as Highpoint. A program to monitor competitive conditions was established as follows.

1. Identify all existing and planned Highpoint products in terms of market segments (such as primary consumer group), price range within segment, and style category within price range.
2. Identify the major competitors in each market segment.
3. Collect and evaluate information on each competitor's product line.
4. Compare existing and planned Highpoint item and pattern additions, and their effect on the total Highpoint line, to the average of competitive offerings.
5. Revise new pattern and item plans for basic market segments where planned lines exceed the average of major competitors.

For example, a market segment might be defined as cotton/polyester fabric for women's wear, sold at $2.50 to $3.00 per yard. Average competitive offerings might include 10 patterns with 12 colors each, available in 48- and 60-inch widths. If Highpoint's plans called for 14 patterns with 18 colors each, in three widths, that plan might require revision.

Exhibits 57 and 58 show part of the resulting competitive analysis. In Exhibit 57, Highpoint's current product line in the C market segment is shown, including scheduled pattern, color, and width additions. The average of major competitors was determined by examining the catalogs of seven other suppliers that Highpoint sales personnel considered their stiffest competition; competitors offering substantially different lines or soliciting different customers were not considered major competitors.

On the basis of the competitive analysis, a new plan was devised to serve market segment C, as shown in Exhibit 58. The new product plan called for about the same number of patterns in total (20 versus 21) but a new grouping of fabrics and reduced numbers of colors and widths per pattern. The total item count reduction amounted to 150 stock-keeping units. A substantial side benefit of the competitive analysis was the identification of a trend away from nylon patterns in this segment, and some evidence that competitors were copying Highpoint's new fabric. These pieces of information were incorporated into the revised plan.

While marketing managers were finding ways to whittle down and reshuffle items and patterns, the controller was working to identify new pattern introduction costs. His analysis focused on several types of new pattern expenses.

1. Styling, sample development, and pilot plant operations necessary to test and develop a new pattern.
2. Inventory and receivables carrying costs for new patterns.

Exhibit 57. Highpoint Textile Company, current product line for market segment C (including scheduled pattern and item additions).

Fabric Type	NO. OF PATTERNS	NO. OF COLORS PER PATTERN	NO. OF WIDTHS PER PATTERN
Cotton/Polyester blend	4	15	1.5
Acetate	9	15	2.0
Nylon	5	15	1.5
New Fabric	3	14	2.0
Total No. of Patterns	21		
Average for all Fabrics		14.7	1.8
Major Competitors, Average for all Fabrics	17	13	1.6

A key step in determining where and why products or items should be deleted requires an analysis of the strongest competitive product lines. New market development or significant technical advantage can support a product line larger than those of strong competitors. If these factors are not present, some line trimming may be in order.

Exhibit 58. Highpoint Textile Company, planned product line for market segment C.

Fabric Type	NUMBER OF PATTERNS	NUMBER OF COLORS PER PATTERN	NUMBER OF WIDTHS PER PATTERN
Cotton/Polyester Blend	5	13	1.6
Acetate	8	13	1.9
Nylon	2	12	1.6
New Fabric	5	13	1.4
Total No. of Patterns	20		
Average for all Fabrics		12.9	1.6
Net Change from Original Plan	−1	−2 per pattern	−0.2 per pattern
Estimated Total Stock Unit Change: − 150			

Relatively small changes in the product variety can result in substantial swings in the number of different inventory items required.

3. Average write-downs on obsolete inventory at the end of a pattern's life cycle.
4. Scrap, waste, direct labor, and variable plant overhead costs incurred during setups for a new pattern during the time that pattern is in actual production.

The controller also distinguished between capacity and under-capacity conditions in the plant. At or near full capacity, any new item or pattern would mean a loss of production time because of the setup requirements of the new item. Thus, two other factors would need to be considered for those additions being made when the plant was near full capacity.

1. Underabsorption of overhead because of lost production time.
2. Lost profit from current items that could have been produced (and sold at a profit) during the time that a new item would require for setups.

Exhibit 59. Highpoint Textile Company, new pattern cost analysis.

	ADDITION COSTS PER PATTERN	CONTINUATION COSTS PER PATTERN
1. Styling, sample development, and pilot plant operations	$ 2,000	
2. Inventory and receivables carrying charges	1,000	$1,000
3. Disposal costs at deletion (inventory write-down)	1,500	
4. Setup costs: direct labor, materials, and variable overhead	4,000	4,000
5. Overhead not absorbed because of increased setups*	2,000	2,000
6. Profit lost by not producing other, profitable patterns during setup time*	8,500	
Totals	$19,000	$7,000
Breakeven volume @ $.50 per yard profit contribution:	38,000 yards	14,000 yards

*APPLIES ONLY AT OR NEAR FULL CAPACITY

All these costs were calculated for an average pattern, as shown in Exhibit 59. The controller found that this type of cost analysis provided a useful tool for evaluating current patterns, as well as proposed additions. The costs of carrying inventory and receivables, direct change-over labor and materials, and underabsorbed overhead applied for current products. He then calculated breakeven volumes for a typical pattern with a $.50 per yard profit contribution. The breakeven volumes recover the addition or continuation costs.

With this analysis in hand, he then posed the following questions to marketing management: Is the forecasted annual volume for a planned new pattern sufficient to cover all introduction costs? Is the forecasted annual volume for a current pattern sufficient to cover continuation costs?

These two tools—the detailed answer to what is competitive and the analysis of introduction and continuation costs—helped Highpoint achieve stronger control over product and item additions without sacrificing market mobility. Periodic updating of these tools will continue to provide objective criteria for product line decisions.

The examples used in this chapter all point to the need for quantitative, factually based information to guide the product line planning and control process. The costs of providing for the regular collection of such data through marketing and financial information systems are small in comparison to the benefits of better decisions.

Some flexibility is required, of course, in applying hard numbers to a bright product proposition. Realistic estimates of market potential, entry cost, and profitability serve as checks against the accumulated experience of marketing managers and salesmen.

A final point on this subject involves organizing the new product development effort. This function, like inventory control, does not have a secure home in many organizations. Marketing management usually has responsibility for identifying new product needs, and marketing also has a strong voice in decisions to delete products or items from the current line. Engineering, production management, and finance also have important contributions to make toward the effective control of the product line. In those cases where actual responsibility is undefined or assigned to less experienced managers, the function can become an optional or occasional business activity. With the company's future so heavily dependent on success in this area, explicit definition of overall responsibility should be the first order of business for senior management.

7

ANTITRUST AND
MARKETING INFORMATION NEEDS

A major company, in a private suit by one of its customers, was required to justify a volume-discount schedule under which it granted discounts of from 1% to 5% on annual purchases valued at from $500,000 to $7 million. The maximum discount was received by only three customers, thus instigating the legal action. The court awarded the complainant $220,000 for damages incurred through the discrimination.

In another action, affirming the decision of a lower court, the Fifth Circuit Court did not discuss the cost defense in detail, but stated that any system of discounts in which 98% of the customers qualify for no discount whatever imposes a heavy burden of justification on its proponent.

This particular case shows that antitrust laws can present some very difficult and confusing problems to the marketing executive. Today one cannot read the business pages without seeing mention of one type of court action or another. Federal and state antitrust laws affect the marketing operations of every company. At the same time, most problems which arise with respect to antitrust laws are avoidable if they are anticipated. What then are the information requirements necessary to minimize the possibility of liability under the law as a result of marketing decisions?

This chapter reviews the supporting requirements for pricing differentials and cost justification, not from a legal but from a cost analysis point of view, to help the marketing manager in avoiding the pitfalls inherent in today's antitrust laws. The chapter is organized into three main areas: The first area deals with the antitrust legislation itself. The major acts are summarized and the implications inherent in specific sections discussed. The next part of the chapter develops the kind of information systems marketing managers may wish to consider in order to comply with the requirements of the acts described. The chapter closes with a case history describing the details of a cost justification project.

ANTITRUST LEGISLATION

Antitrust is a complex and highly technical portion of the law. Its origins lie in English common law. However, only since 1890, with the passage of the Sherman Act, has it become a force in shaping U.S. business practices.

Through the years, the original legislation has been strengthened to a point where all firms involved in interstate commerce must be cognizant of its major provisions. Should a firm become involved in any type of antitrust action, the management must be guided by a skilled attorney. Often, however, the material requirement for a successful defense resides within the accounting area. Unless a company has the ability to accumulate and analyze costs in a credible manner, the attorney's task will be much more difficult, if not impossible.

A brief discussion of the major acts and their key provisions follows.

The Sherman Act

The Sherman Act, passed in 1890, is the original and one of the most important federal statutes covering restraint of trade and monopolization. It was enacted because of public clamor over the tactics of big business. The language of the act is broad and not well defined. It has been sharpened through the years, however, through litigation and by specific amendments.

The Act consists of two sections. The first declares illegal every contract, combination, or conspiracy in restraint of trade among the several states or with foreign nations. Agreement among competitors to fix prices or to boycott a price cutter is considered unlawful per se. Agreements which may restrain trade in other, less obvious ways are subject to the "rule of reason."

Section 2 of the Sherman Act forbids monopolization and attempts to monopolize. In applying Section 2, the courts have experienced difficulty in differentiating between aggressive competition and predatory practices. The former is healthy, the latter illegal. However, it is often difficult to ascertain which is which. A summary of the provisions of this Act is given.

THE SHERMAN ACT
HIGHLIGHTS AND MAJOR FEATURES

Importance

The Sherman Act is the keystone of all United States antitrust legislation.

Major Features

Section 1:   Declares restraint of trade illegal.
Section 2:   Forbids monopolization and attempts to monopolize.

Penalties

- Violation of the Act is a federal crime punishable by fine or imprisonment or both. Since 1955, the maximum fine is $50,000 for each violation.
- Empowers the federal government to obtain injunctions. Failure to obey subjects the defendant to contempt proceedings.
- Injured parties are given the right to collect three times the damages plus attorney fees and court costs.
- Property transported from one state to another in violation of Section 1 of the Act can be seized and forfeited to the United States.

The Clayton Act

After the Sherman Act was in effect for several years, it came under heavy criticism for not preventing practices which *tended* to reduce competition or were *conducive* to creating monopolies.

On October 15, 1914, Congress enacted supplementary legislation commonly known as the Clayton Act. This legislation contains more than 20 sections, but most of them simply qualify the more important sections. Four of the main sections are discussed below.

Section 2 deals with price discrimination. Since this section was substantially amended by the Robinson-Patman Act, it will be discussed as part of that legislation.

Section 3 deals with two closely allied practices. The first is that of tying the sale of one product to another. For example, it is unlawful to require the potential purchaser of a machine for dispensing salt tablets to also purchase salt from the seller. The second is that of requirements contracts. The law is intended to prevent a manufacturer from foreclosing his rivals from markets at the wholesale or retail level.

Section 7 of the Clayton Act, amended in 1950, is designed to prevent mergers (and other acquisitions) which may have an adverse effect upon competition. This section can apply to a vertical acquisition, as well as to a horizontal one. Thus, if a manufacturer buys up a distributor or supplier of raw materials, he may be found to have violated the statute.

Section 8 of the Clayton Act forbids interlocking directorships among firms competing in interstate commerce. Relatively little litigation has developed under this section, however.

Following is a summary of the major features of the Clayton Act.

THE CLAYTON ACT
HIGHLIGHTS AND MAJOR FEATURES

Importance

- It strengthens the Sherman Act.
- It excludes labor and nonprofit agricultural organizations from the scope of antitrust legislation.

Major Features

Section 2: Deals with price discrimination (see the Robinson-Patman Act).

Section 3: Forbids tying and requirements contracts.

Section 7: Restrains horizontal and vertical mergers which will lessen competition.

Section 8: Prohibits interlocking directorships.

Penalties

- Violations of Sections 2, 3, 7 and 8 are not made crimes, and the Act contains no sanction for forfeiture of property.
- The Justice Department can obtain injunctions to prevent violations of the Act.
- Injured parties can obtain injunctive relief and, in addition, are given the right to collect treble the damages plus court costs.
- The Federal Trade Commission (FTC) is also authorized to issue a cease-and-desist order subject to review by the Circuit Courts of Appeals.
- Section 14 imposes criminal liability on *directors* and *agents* of guilty corporations if they participate in prohibited activity.

The Federal Trade Commission Act

The Federal Trade Commission Act was passed in 1914 for the same general reasons that created the Clayton Act. The Act establishes the

Federal Trade Commission as an independent administrative agency and gives it investigating, prosecuting, legislating, and judicial powers.

Section 5 forbids unfair methods of competition and unfair or deceptive acts or practices. In recent years the courts have interpreted this legislation stringently. The effect has been to give the Commission broad legislative power to determine what practices fall within the vague category of being "unfair" on a case-by-case basis.

The Robinson-Patman Act

The Robinson-Patman Act is actually an amendment to Section 2 of the Clayton Act of 1914. It was adopted in 1936 and has been changed only slightly since that time. Both the original Section 2 of the Clayton Act and the Robinson-Patman Act deal with price discrimination practices. Since predatory price cutting to injure a competitor was made unlawful by Section 2 of the Sherman Act in 1890, it is clear that the Clayton Act and the Robinson-Patman Act go beyond predatory price cutting. The key words of subsection 2a of the Robinson-Patman Act are ". . . it shall be unlawful for any person engaged in commerce, in the course of such commerce, either directly or indirectly, to discriminate in price between different purchasers of commodities of like grade and quality . . . where the effect of such discrimination may be substantially to lessen competition or tend to create a monopoly in any line of commerce, or to injure, destroy, or prevent competition with any person who either grants or knowingly receives the benefit of such discrimination, or with customers of either of them." Three points should be made:

1. The statute refers to sales to purchasers. It is not violated by a refusal to sell, and the terms of leases are not within the Act. Likewise, there must be two simultaneous sales involved for discrimination to arise.

2. The Act deals only with the sale of commodities of like grade and quality.

3. The law is violated only if the effect of the discrimination is to lessen competition. The critical point to remember is that there are at least three levels at which such an injury may be inflicted. A price cut by a company may inflict an injury upon a rival manufacturer; this is known as injury at the primary level. The price cut may also injure a distributor of the product who competes with the favored customer; injury in this case is referred to as occurring in the secondary level of competition. Finally, a retailer or consumer may also be injured by the price reductions; in this case, the damages are said to be at the tertiary level.

There are three valid defenses:

1. The price differentials "make only due allowance for differences in the cost, other than brokerage, of manufacture, sale, or delivery resulting in the differing methods or quantities in which such commodities are to such purchasers sold or delivered."

2. The price differentials were "made in good faith to meet an equally low price of a competitor, or the services or facilities furnished by a competitor."

3. The lower price reflects changing conditions in the market, such as distress merchandise, close-out of model lines, and obsolescence of goods.

Following is a brief summary of the major provisions of the Act.

THE ROBINSON-PATMAN ACT
HIGHLIGHTS AND MAJOR FEATURES

Importance

This is probably the most important of the antitrust acts from the marketing point of view. It deals, in detail, with practices known as price discrimination.

Major Features

Section 2(a): Makes it unlawful to discriminate in price between different purchasers of commodities of like grade and quality, with certain exceptions.

Section 2(b): Places the burden of showing justification of price discrimination on the person charged with the violation.

Section 2(c), (d), (e): Prohibits various indirect price discriminations by making it unlawful to pay or receive a commission or discount on sales or purchases, except for actual services rendered; to pay a customer for any services or facilities he furnishes in connection with a transaction, unless such payment is available to all customers on equal terms; and to favor one purchaser of a commodity with facilities in connection with a sale which are not available to all purchasers on equal terms.

Penalties

• The final version of the Act applies criminal penalties for violation of its provisions.
• The Department of Justice has concurrent jurisdiction to enforce the amended provisions of the Clayton Act and also exclusive jurisdiction to enforce the criminal provisions added by the Robinson-Patman Act.

The Wheeler-Lea Amendment

The Wheeler-Lea Amendment of 1938 authorizes the Federal Trade Commission to take action to protect the public against unfair competition and deceptive practices; previously, the Commission took action only to protect the competition. The Amendment is administered by the Federal Trade Commission, which may levy fines of up to $5,000 per violation and may issue cease-and-desist orders.

State Laws

In order to eliminate predatory price cutting, many states have enacted unfair trade practices acts. These laws generally forbid the sale below invoice cost plus a specified markup percentage, normally about 6%.

The first state fair trade law was passed in 1931 by California. This law allowed manufacturers and wholesalers to establish retail prices with retailers who signed contracts with them agreeing to fix prices. The law was generally unsatisfactory since retailers who refused to sign the contracts were not bound. Accordingly, the law was amended in 1933 by the addition of a nonsigner clause. Under the terms of this law, an agreement between a manufacturer or wholesaler and a single retailer in the state became binding on all retailers in the state when they were informed of the contract and its terms. Since the state laws covered transactions only within the state, a federal law was required to legalize price-fixing agreements in interstate trade. These enabling agreements were the Miller-Tydings Act and the McGuire Act.

New York State and certain other states have affirmation laws, which prohibit a distiller from charging a higher price in, say, New York State than the lowest price charged elsewhere—except for cost differences in taxes and the actual cost of delivery.

Exhibit 60 shows the relationship of the statutes discussed in this chapter. (The Food and Drug Act and the Federal Food, Drug and Cosmetic Act were not included in the text because they are not pertinent to this discussion of marketing information systems. However, they are shown in Exhibit 60 for completeness.)

MARKETING INFORMATION REQUIREMENTS

Our purpose in discussing antitrust legislation is to provide the marketing executive with an indication of the pitfalls he must avoid, together with a basic understanding of the government's thinking.

Exhibit 60. History of antitrust legislation.

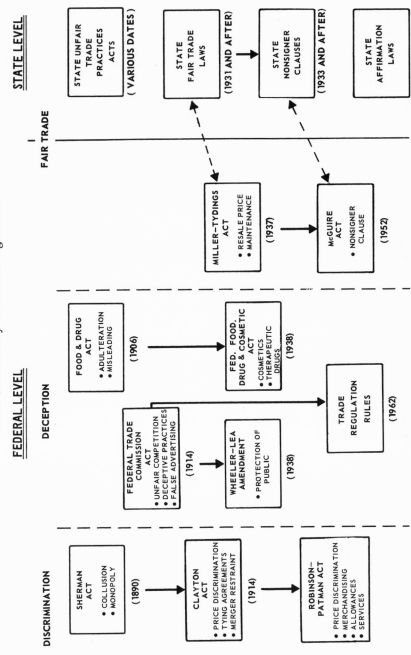

The marketing man's obvious next question is, "What can I do about it?" In other words, what steps should be taken to reduce the possibility that the government will intervene in response to marketing decisions made?

Marketing decisions, like those in other functional areas of business, are made, ideally, after a review of all pertinent information available. Thus, the key to a high batting average in decision making is the timely availability of pertinent information. This is particularly true with regard to pricing decisions.

It should be apparent at this point that marketing management needs two basic types of information for antitrust protection.

1. Information on competitive practices, such as prices for items of like grade and quality and market share data. In other words, he needs external information.

2. Information regarding the selling prices charged and services provided to customers, together with documentation of cost differences involved and actual reasons for specific price changes. This type of information could be called internal information.

We will discuss each of these information needs, showing illustrative examples of reporting required. Special emphasis, however, will be placed on the second point, which relates to the "cost justification" defense under the Robinson-Patman Act.

External Information

Besides making good business sense from a marketing point of view, the routine collection of competitive information has special importance with regard to antitrust matters. A company selling the same product at differing prices may legally defend its actions on the basis that the lower price was quoted in good faith to meet an equally low price of a competing seller. Thus, one of the more basic information systems required is simply a method for timely communication of pertinent competitive activity. Exhibit 61 shows a "flash report" submitted by field personnel as soon as the competitive activity becomes known. Experience indicates that if a company has some economic clout with its distributors, it can usually receive a report on competitive prices, promotional allowances, display allowances, and other services offered, such as illustrated in Exhibit 62.

Marketing management can use this type of information as documentation for those decisions involving a reduction in price in good faith, primarily to meet an equally low price of a competing seller.

Exhibit 61. Flash report on competitive activity.

Area _West_   Date _October 10, 19XX_

Brand _XYZ_   Product(s) _Soap Powder_

Market Area Covered by this Report _Los Angeles_

☒ NEW PRICES OR PRICE LIST (ATTACH COPY)

☐ NEW BRAND OR ITEM

☐ DISTRIBUTION CHANGE

☐ MERCHANDISING DEAL, CONTENTS OR PROMOTION (DETAILS ATTACHED)

    EFFECTIVE DATE OF DEAL _____ EXPIRATION DATE OF DEAL _____

    ADVERTISING: TV   MAGAZINE   POINT OF SALE

                    RADIO   NEWSPAPER   BILLBOARD   OTHER

Explanation:
ABC Corp. just reduced the price of its soap powder by 20¢/dozen in the Los Angeles market, effective 10/9/xx

        Submitted by _W. Smith_

Internal Information

Perhaps the more important type of information, from an antitrust point of view, is that information related to a company's own cost and prices—that is, internal information.

The marketing manager needs documentation of the actual selling price and services provided, by customer classification; cost differences relating to the different customer classifications; and the actual reason for changing a specific price on a given product.

This information is necessary in order to minimize the possibility of court action on a pricing decision. As discussed earlier, one of the key defenses against a Robinson-Patman Act violation is a definitive showing that the price discrimination among customers (or customer classes) can be justified by differentials in the costs involved.

Cost justification as a defense for an economically sound pricing schedule has often been misunderstood and not alway properly used. This has apparently happened because the record of success in court

Exhibit 62. Competitive price report.

AREA _West_   DATE __10/10/xx__

SUBMITTED BY: _Brown Brokerage Company_

	PRODUCT A	PRODUCT B
BASE PRICE	$6.95/DOZ.	$7.50/DOZ.
PROM. ALLOWANCE ⟋ TYPE ⟋	.50	.60
CO-OP		
COLOR		
NET PRICE	$6.45/DOZ.	$6.90/DOZ.
SALES SERVICE		
DISPLAY ALLOWANCE		
OTHER:		

SOURCE DOCUMENT:

PERIOD PRICE EFFECTIVE:

COMMENTS:_____

_____

_____

_____

ATTACH PRICE LIST OR OTHER DOCUMENTS WHEN AVAILABLE.

is mediocre and because the attorneys who handle antitrust matters often do not know or understand accounting adequately or fail to call on expert accountants. As a result, some attorneys and businessmen feel that cost justification is futile and should be used only as a last resort. This position does not consider the fact that successful cost defenses convince the Commission of the propriety of the pricing they support. Such cases, therefore, seldom get to court, get no publicity, and do not become a part of the public record.

The history of litigated cases shows that somewhat less than half the companies involved have been able to prove cost justification for even a part of their pricing policies. Some companies have acceded to the demands of the Federal Trade Commission and have made changes in their pricing policies because they believed that they could not cost justify the prices they were charging, or they believed that a satisfactory cost study would be too expensive or would be too unsure of success even though they believed their prices were cost justified. On the other hand, although there are no statistics available, many companies have consistently prevented complaints from going to court by showing that they have made studies before the fact to justify their pricing structures.

A cost study, made after a complaint is issued by the Federal Trade Commission or after a treble-damage action is brought by a customer or competitor, can be expensive because of the pressure of time and because the company now has to justify historical prices it has charged without having made due allowance for the related cost differentials. The company undoubtedly places itself in a difficult position because it did not establish procedures for justifying price schedules before they were issued.

In general, the proper time for a cost study is before major pricing decisions are made. There may be a need to prepare a new price schedule or to change pricing policies. There may be a need to quote lower prices to obtain business from larger purchasers or to raise prices to small-quantity purchasers where it appears that sales of this type are unprofitable. A definitive cost justification study made before the fact not only permits the seller to make a more informed decision but also defines the limits to which price differentials can be justified by differences in cost.

While the law and case history provide very few guidelines or precedents for a successful cost defense, experience and logic have developed certain ground rules which have general application.

LEGAL IMPLICATIONS

The cost proviso, while couched in accounting terms, is a legal concept. Therefore, although cost justification requires expert accounting determinations, the process is still one in which the attorney, competent and experienced in antitrust law, is the key figure. Particularly when litigation is involved or even anticipated, the attorney is the captain of the team. He is the one who must guide the effort and argue it effectively in court, but he may use other experts (engineers, accountants, and so on) in those areas where he does not have special competence. Cost justification in its technical phases is a joint effort of the attorney and the accountant: the accountant uses his special skills in compiling and analyzing data on prices and costs; the lawyer determines the legal implications of the results to be imputed to the data.

ACCOUNTING NATURE OF COST JUSTIFICATION

To be effective, the cost study must be soundly conceived in terms of accounting techniques, and its results should be clearly presented in accounting terms. The Commission has a competent staff of accountants who act as expert advisers to the Commission examiners, and the study must survive the critical scrutiny of this accounting staff. They are the persons who must be convinced that costs have been properly collected, analyzed, allocated, and presented. In many cases, complaints may be answered by presenting to the accounting staff cost data which show cost justification; such complaints never reach the trial stage.

In this connection, in the early stages of a cost study, it may on occasion be helpful to have preliminary discussions with the Commission staff to be sure that the basic premises are acceptable. The desirability of this procedure will depend on the circumstances, of course, and should always be the decision of the attorney.

Cost Allocation Concepts

Despite the lack of official pronouncements and reliable case precedent in cost justification, the Commission staff and courts have made it quite clear that costs cannot be determined on an incremental or marginal cost concept. On this basis, the additional sales volume of the large purchaser would be charged only with the additional out-of-pocket costs incurred and would be allocated none of the overhead costs. The courts have ruled that the per unit cost savings resulting from additional sales volume must be spread equitably to all customers and not allocated entirely to those customers who happen to generate the additional volume.

Another cost accounting technique which has been discredited almost since the beginning of Robinson-Patman cost justification is the "bootstrap" allocation, where the basis for the allocation creates an apparent cost differential which does not exist. The most common form is the allocation of a cost as a fixed percentage of dollar sales, which is seldom an appropriate basis in any event. Under this method, the customer paying the lowest unit price is automatically allocated less of the cost, which in turn may justify a lower price. For example, consider two buyers, one paying $1.00 per unit and the other $.90. If the cost of an operating function such as technical services was found to aggregate 10% of dollar sales, the first customer would be charged $.10 and the second only $.09, but the lower cost would result entirely from the lower selling price and would defeat the purpose of the cost study.

Use of Statistical Techniques

Experience has established that the proper use of sampling methods is permissible. In fact, sampling is almost mandatory since an examination of all the actual costs of any company in the detail required for a cost study would be extremely difficult, if not impossible. For this reason, the Commission accepts studies based on selective sampling of costs where it can be shown that such samples are representative of the aggregate costs (or "universe") from which they were selected. Whether such samples are in fact representative may involve a review of many factors, such as seasonal demand, weather, volume levels, employment conditions, nature of the market, and length of the operating cycle. As an example, one week or one month of a salesman's activity might be studied as representative of his activity over the entire year; or one regional warehouse operation might be studied as representative of all the company's regional warehouses. The results of the cost study should, however, include sufficient information to convince the Commission or the court that the samples used were selected with sound judgment and after a thorough investigation of their reasonableness.

Undoubtedly many cost studies, especially those involving complex and interrelated operating conditions, should also use more sophisticated mathematical techniques, such as correlation analysis and estimating equations. It should be borne in mind, however, that any litigation would eventually require that such techniques be supported by expert testimony. Since the Commission examiners, attorneys, and accounting staff are not expert in these areas, there is a practical problem of gaining legal acceptance for their use. For this reason, the final approval of this type of analysis should rest with the attorney.

Company Cost Accounting Records

It is a safe assumption that the data generated by a company's regular cost accounting system, no matter how sophisticated, will be inadequate for a definitive cost justification study. The courts have recognized that the expense of continuously and routinely providing such detailed information would be prohibitive and should not be expected in the normal course of business. Conversely, the company can proceed with a cost justification study secure in the knowledge that it will not have to defend any unfavorable methods or procedures it may use or have used for regular cost accounting purposes.

The Importance of Care and Soundness in the Cost Study

The company undertaking a cost study for Robinson-Patman purposes, whether it be prospective to support a new pricing schedule or retroactive in defense of a price-discrimination charge, should begin by recognizing that the traditional cost accounting methods and assumptions used in its regular accounting reports are probably inadequate. In the cost justification of price differentials, the rules of the game are demanding, the shortcuts are few, and the final product must be constructed soundly enough to weather the searching appraisal it may receive in court.

There is a tendency by nonaccountants to view cost accounting as an exact science, whereas, as accountants know, further progress is yet needed in its development. Cost studies cannot produce precise, unarguable conclusions but, at best, can only arrive at estimated costs subject to some reasonable margin of error. For this reason, it is essential that every item of cost be treated as soundly and precisely as possible to obtain maximum reliability in the final answer. In the event of litigation, every step in the cost analysis process may have to be exposed and justified in court, so that shortcut procedures, estimates, or allocations not supported by sound reasoning will be quickly spotted by the Commission staff and exposed for the court to see. Such exposures not only are embarrassing but, more important, may also cast doubt on the validity of other aspects of the work. Particularly in the area of allocating indirect costs, any attempt to use mere estimates or rules of thumb not supported by factual data will fail. Also, any allocation based on arbitrary assumptions (that every customer requires the same amount of technical service, that every sales call takes the same amount of time, and the like) is unacceptable.

The gathering and analysis of the cost information is a complicated process requiring numerous decisions. In making each decision, all the alternatives must be carefully weighed and tested to be sure that the one chosen is the most logical and defensible. Each step in the study may represent a foundation for all that follows, and one significant faulty decision can make the rest of the work invalid.

Internal Information and Customer Classes

We indicated earlier that marketing managers need documentation by customer classification of actual selling prices, services provided, and costs incurred. The term "customer classification" is important since without this provision a seller could be in the position of having to document all the pertinent data on every individual sale, and possibly of having to charge a different price on each.

The privilege of grouping customers in classes carries with it the obligation of defining these groups properly so that substantially all customers who purchase in the same manner and in similar quantities are placed in the same category. If the range of a classification is too broad, or if unlike purchasers are grouped together, then the process of averaging, inherent in this method, will produce distorted cost data for all buyers in the class. As an extreme example, if the cost of selling large-quantity orders to a department store were combined in one class with the cost of selling small orders to a neighborhood variety store, then the resulting average unit cost would be meaningless and would not be representative of the cost of serving either of the two.

In setting the limits of the classes into which buyers will be grouped for a cost study, it is important that all the buyers in a particular class be sufficiently similar to make averages meaningful. If properly done, the average unit cost of service for the class should reasonably approximate the cost of serving each member within the class.

In defining customer classes, the criterion may be quantities sold, but it may also be other factors, such as method of delivery, size of individual orders, or timing of orders. In addition, trade class (for example, jobbers, chains, distributors, or direct) is an important distinction for comparing price differentials by competing customers. In an attempt to show how the cost study team would go about properly stratifying customers for this purpose, the following example (much oversimplified) shows how the initial review of customer purchasing characteristics might be presented (see Exhibit 63). This shows graphically how 25 customers purchased in a hypothetical month, as to both method and quantities. Since three differing methods are involved (regular delivery, special delivery, and plant pickup), the customers are immediately segregated into three classes according to these methods.

The next problem is to segregate the buyers according to quantities of purchases. It is apparent at once that only two categories, separated at the midpoint of 500 units, result in classes that are too broad. On this basis, customer K with 520 units is averaged with customer M with 955 units, although it is quite unlikely that their cost characteristics would be similar. It would also put customer K (520 units) in a different class from customer Q (490 units) even though the two probably are similar in terms of cost. After further study of the data, it might be concluded that customers could logically be grouped without distortion in even multiples of 200 units. As a result, we might end up, for purposes of our cost study, with the problem of determining relative costs for

Exhibit 63. Customer purchasing characteristics for one month.

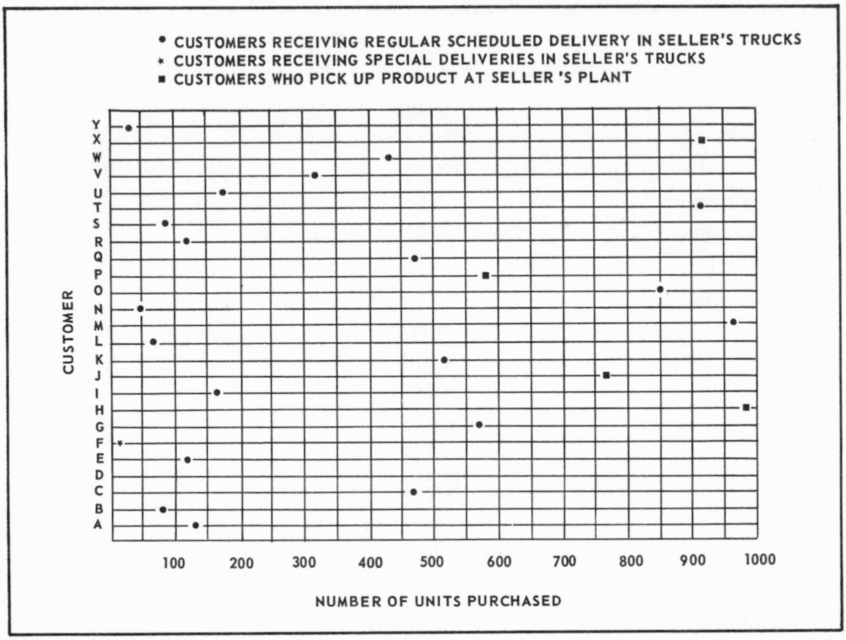

eight classes of customers who differ as to methods or quantities of purchase, as shown in Exhibit 64.

Once the customer classes are determined, it is important to document the actual prices charged to each class. We have included a number of illustrative reports that would provide important information to marketing managers. Exhibit 65 shows, on a historical basis, the actual selling prices for shipments of various sizes. These differentials must, under Robinson-Patman, be amenable to cost justification.

One method of insuring that proper documentation of all pricing decisions is maintained is to require the formal documentation and approval of each decision. Exhibit 66 shows an illustrative pricing recommendation report. Note that it requires documentation of current competitive information, as well as the primary reason for the price change recommendation.

APPROACHES TO A COST STUDY

Before we present a case study describing the details of a cost justification project, we will briefly discuss the basic approaches to such a cost study.

Exhibit 64. Division of customers into classes.

CLASS (BY QUANTITY)	METHOD OF DELIVERY			
	REGULAR	SPECIAL	PLANT PICKUP	TOTAL
0– 200	10	1	0	11
201– 400	1	0	0	1
401– 600	5	0	1	6
601– 800	0	0	1	1
801– 1,000	4	0	2	6
TOTAL	20	1	4	25

CLASS (BY DELIVERY METHOD)	NO. OF CUSTOMERS
REGULAR DELIVERY:	
200 UNITS OR LESS	10
201 – 400 UNITS	1
401 – 600 UNITS	5
801 – 1,000 UNITS	4
SPECIAL DELIVERY:	
200 UNITS OR LESS	1
PLANT PICKUP:	
401 – 600 UNITS	1
601 – 800 UNITS	1
801 –1,000 UNITS	2
TOTAL	25

Exhibit 65. Actual selling prices, 19XX (all figures are per-case averages).

	NO. OF CASES IN SHIPMENT			
	0 – 99	100 – 499	500 – 999	1,000+
GROSS SELLING PRICE	$ 12.50	$ 12.50	$ 12.50	$ 12.50
LESS ABSORBED FREIGHT	–	.50	.75	1.00
LESS VOLUME DISCOUNT	–	.50	.75	1.50
NET SELLING PRICE	$ 12.50	$ 11.50	$ 11.00	$ 10.00

Exhibit 66. Pricing recommendation.

TO _____ FROM _____ DATE _____

MARKET NAME _____ SALES AREA _____

ITEM _____ VARIETIES _____

YOUR RECOMMENDATION	REASON FOR RECOMMENDATION
T/L LIST $. _____	☐ COST JUSTIFIED (ATTACH DOCUMENTATION)
ALLOWANCE . _____	☐ TO MEET COMPETITOR'S PRICE
T/L NET . _____	☐ DISTRESS MERCHANDISE, CLOSE-OUT, ETC. (ATTACH DOC.)
DATES __ TO __	

SIGNATURE _____ DATE _____

CURRENT COMPETITIVE INFORMATION

	BRAND A	BRAND B	BRAND C	BRAND X
REGULAR T/L PRICE/DOZ.	$.	$.	$.	$.
PROMOTIONAL ALLOWANCE	.	.	.	.
NET T/L PRICE/DOZ.	$.	$.	$.	$.
EFFECTIVE DATE	__ TO __	__ TO __	__ TO __	__ TO __
ADDITIONAL ALLOWANCES				
RAIL CO-OP OTHER	CWT dz dz	CWT dz dz	CWT dz dz.	CWT dz dz

DECISION

☐ RECOMMENDATION APPROVED AS SUBMITTED   ☐ RECOMMENDATION CHANGED AS BELOW

T/L LIST $. _____	COMMENT
ALLOWANCE . _____	
T/L NET $. _____	
DATES __ TO __	SIGNATURE _____ DATE _____

Organization

In organizing the cost study team, it should be recognized that cost justification is a difficult task, and its success may have far-reaching effects on the company's methods of operation and its ability to earn a satisfactory profit. A cost study is a major effort which requires the best management and professional talent available.

The cost study team should include a nucleus of competent management personnel, together with the necessary staff to carry out the detailed information gathering and analysis procedures. Each management member should be well grounded in the nature of the company's operations, and one should be a skilled accountant who is involved at a reasonably high level in the controllership activities and who could participate virtually full time.

While competent outside professional assistance is important, a company should not normally look to its attorneys and outside accountants to deliver a completed package without company help. The consultants should, rather, be used to assist actively in the conceptual development of the study plan, to advise and counsel on significant decisions in its implementation, to participate in preparation of the reports on the results, to interpret the results, and to provide expert testimony in court. On the proper basis of participation, the outside professional can lend assurance to the company that the cost study has been soundly conceived and implemented. He can also provide substantial help in court proceedings where, as an unbiased expert with proven competence and responsibility, he can support the results of the study with sound reasoning and the weight of his professional opinion.

The reliability of a cost study usually depends on the way it starts out in life. Careful planning is essential, and it is here that the experience of the outside professional can be most useful. Once it has been properly conceived, the study can proceed with deliberate haste, but, in the best of conditions, several months are normally necessary to produce reliable conclusions.

Defining the Scope of the Study

The initial step in a cost study is the definition of the objectives. If being made in defense of a complaint, the study may be directed at a single product or product line. On the other hand, a study made in the ordinary course of business as a basis for a change in pricing policies may encompass several product lines or even a complete segment of the business. Even a broad study such as this, however, does not usually relate to an entire business, and therefore it is necessary to isolate costs applicable to the product lines under consideration.

In planning the study and accumulation of cost data, provision should be made to obtain such data on a basis consistent with the bases of pricing involved. For example, if the basis of pricing is a simple discount dependent entirely on the quantity in each individual shipment, then the cost study need develop only the relative differential costs of manufacturing, selling, and delivering shipments of varying quantities (regardless of the customers involved). A different problem arises if prices are based on an aggregate discount schedule whereby the percentage discount depends on the total quantities purchased over a given period. To justify such a pricing policy, it would obviously be necessary to determine the relative differential costs of serving customers, or classes of customers, whose aggregate purchases fall in the various discount brackets.

The language of the Robinson-Patman Act refers to "due allowance for the differences in the cost of manufacture, sale or delivery." This clause means that all differences resulting from varying methods or quantities of sale or delivery must be reviewed. There may be instances where a particular cost differential, such as that related to transportation costs, may alone justify a price differential, but all areas must be reviewed to determine that all negative cost differentials have been considered as possible offsets. The attorney and the accountant must, therefore, review in considerable detail the characteristics of all the company's operations which relate directly or indirectly to the product under study. They must probe into production policies, manufacturing processes, distribution patterns, and executive and administrative duties until they are satisfied that they have isolated all the functions whose cost may vary with differing methods or quantities of sale or delivery. The accountant then applies his special competence to the task of measuring these cost differentials.

Measuring Function Costs

For purposes of the cost study, company or division operating statements, standard costs, reports of expenses by natural categories, departmental and even product line cost reports, and other information routinely provided by the regular cost accounting system will have limited usefulness. This is particularly true because in one important area of cost justification (selling and delivery costs), the normal cost accounting system produces very little meaningful data. The overriding emphasis in justifying price differentials is the determination of the costs of the various functions carried out in the manufacture, sale, and delivery of the product to the customer. Thus, the process is essentially one of defining such functions and isolating the costs applicable to each.

Assigning costs to the various physical functions involved in operating the business can present complicated problems of allocation. A common problem is encountered when the cost study team finds that its investigation relating to the pricing of one product involves costs which are common to that product and several others. For example, if the seller's truck delivers several different products on the same trip to a buyer's place of business, costs must be reduced to a common denominator which takes into account the varying sizes and weights of the different products, requirements for special handling, and the like. Only a careful review of the delivery process and product characteristics will provide the most logical basis for measuring costs among the different products.

As the study progresses, certain direct costs will be relatively easy to determine. Simple techniques of counting, weighing, measuring, computing, or timing will reveal the cost of the time a salesman spends on a single call, the time a warehouseman spends loading a truck, or the time a driver spends at a customer's place of business. The cost of inserting one line item on an order or an invoice and the cost per line of a customer's billing statement can be measured rather simply.

Unfortunately, directly assignable costs are usually less than half the total, and the balance represents a conglomeration of activities which relate in some indirect way to the products under study. Initially, however, this relationship is vague. The cost analysis process must segregate these indirect costs in terms of the operating functions to which they relate so that the output of the functions can be measured as a cost per unit of product. As an example, a regional warehouse accounting department may be a single unit for regular cost accounting purposes. A functional analysis of its activities, however, may show that it handles the preparation of warehouse payrolls, keeps inventory records, handles incoming orders, prepares shipping documents, prepares billings to customers, maintains accounts receivable records, handles credit approvals and collections, and sends regular reports to the home office. For purposes of the study, the cost of each of these functions must be isolated and allocated to product lines and customers on some sound, realistic basis. For example, the cost of preparing shipping documents might be allocated on the basis of a line item (one order for one product, regardless of quantity) as being the best common unit of measuring the effort expended in relation to customers or classes of customers.

Another simple example of the problem of allocating indirect costs is the cost of operating a truck from which a seller makes deliveries. It is relatively easy to quantify these costs (gasoline, oil, licenses, maintenance, repairs). The problem arises in finding a common relationship between the trucking function and the product. An analysis of the characteristics of the trucking operation is necessary to determine whether the cost of this function is to be allocated to customers on the basis of driver time, number of units transported, number of customer stops, weight, a combination of weight and distance, or some other basis.

Exhibit 67. Comparison of price differentials on a per-shipment basis with differences in costs.

	BRACKET RANGE BY SIZE OF SHIPMENT (NO. OF UNITS)			
	0–100	100–499	500–999	$1,000+
PRICE PER UNIT FOR BRACKET RANGE	$ 12.50	$ 11.50	$ 11.00	$ 10.00
VARIABLE COSTS FOR SALES AND DELIVERY (per unit)	5.12	3.90	3.41	1.96
CUMULATIVE PRICE DIFFERENTIAL BASED ON LOWEST BRACKET RANGE	—	1.00	1.50	2.50
CUMULATIVE COST DIFFERENTIAL BASED ON LOWEST BRACKET RANGE	—	1.22	1.71	3.16
PRICE DIFFERENTIAL COMPARED WITH NEXT LOWER BRACKET RANGE	—	1.00	.50	1.00
COST DIFFERENTIAL COMPARED WITH NEXT LOWER BRACKET RANGE	—	1.22	.49	1.45

It can be seen that the differential in cost is greater than the differential in price in every instance except one (the price bracket at $11.00 per unit vs. the bracket at $11.50 per unit, difference of $.50 in price vs. $.49 in cost). In this instance the one "defect" may be considered as "de minimus" and the price schedule presented as cost-justified.

Results of the Study

The final results of the cost justification study should be presented in such a way as to clearly compare the differentials in price with the related differentials in cost. In the usual situation, such data represents the average cost differential for the sample period studied. The basis of comparison must necessarily relate to the pricing policies involved, but ordinarily it should show the relationship of each price or volume bracket to every other bracket. A much oversimplified example of the way in which such data might be presented in summary form is shown as Exhibit 67.

AN APPLICATION OF ANTITRUST CONCEPTS TO MARKETING

XYZ Distilling Company sells its products to wholesalers in all 50 states. It decided to embark on a cost justification study in order to document the company's belief that the cost of producing for and selling in New York State was one of the highest. This documentation would allow, under the law, either of the following two favorable marketing decisions: it could raise the New York price by the amount of the difference between New York and the lowest-cost state or, if the New York price of a particular brand was fixed by competitive pressure, it could lower the price in selected markets to attain market penetration.

The study itself consisted in determining the relative cost differences for a matrix of 22 brand/size combinations and 13 market areas. One of the determining factors for the choice of brands and market areas was that it represented a good cross section of the country and the company's product line. This included some "control" states, some open states, some states with affirmation laws and some states without affirmation laws. Brand choices included some that sold well in New York, some that sold poorly, and some average brands.

The Robinson-Patman Act allows cost justification for a broad range of costs, including manufacturing, selling, advertising, taxes, and delivery.

Content cost comprises the cost of bulk whiskey, the cost of the barrels, insurance, warehouse cost during aging, the cost of shipping grains, and, most importantly, the cost of evaporation during aging. Content cost differed by market area for two reasons. First, and most obvious, some market areas require a different age or proof than others, and cost varies directly with both age and proof. Second, different market areas are served by different plants, and no two plants operate exactly alike. Content cost is computed by each of its elements for each plant, then assigned the relevant market area.

Packaging supplies include the cost of the glass, cap, labels, cartons, and, with holiday boxes, the extra packaging labor. This cost element showed a major variation by market area, almost entirely because of holiday packaging cost. During the Christmas season, many of the brands are marketed in decanters with cartons or just in extra cartons. This costs from two to four times as much as regular packaging. In one case, more than 60% of the total cases sold in New York were sold in holiday packages. As a result, there were major variations in average cost per case between those states that allow holiday packaging and those that do not.

The bottling cost is a very complex element. It depends on the average run size in each plant (important because of set-up cost), the efficiency of machines used in the different plants, the shape of the bottle, the size of the bottle, and the application of state tax stamps. All these must be taken into account.

Shipping cost covers the cost of transferring the product from the end of the bottling line either to the trucks and trains or to the warehouse. There is usually no way to break this down by brand, short of a time study, and, since it is relatively minor, a reasonable approach is to use the average shipping cost per case by plant.

Among the distribution elements, advertising is by far the most costly. This cost element includes all aspects of advertising, such as newspaper, magazine, trade paper, and billboard. The magazine portion is allocated to market area by readership; that is, by the number of people in each market area who read the magazine. Very large variations in relative cost occurred here. Certain adjustments in data typically maintained by distilling companies must be made to insure the reasonableness of the final result.

1. Companies typically record this cost as a function of depletions (cases sold to retailers). This must be adjusted to reflect cost on the basis of cases sold to wholesalers (billings).

2. Spill-over advertising—that amount allocated on readership to areas where there was no real intent to advertise because of the small market for the particular product—must be adjusted.

3. Advertising discounts given by magazines must be reflected when determining the net cost by market area.

Sales promotion and merchandising go together. Sales promotion consists of the materials used for point-of-sale displays and some novelty items. Merchandising expense is defined as the labor element for the installation of sales promotion materials. These expenses were relatively simple to identify by brand and market area.

The costs involved in the sales accounting and credit section of the study involved billing, sales statistics, central order, inventory accounting, credit, accounts receivable, and the economic cost of carrying accounts receivable balances. All cost differences by brand and market, except the economic cost of carrying accounts receivable inventory, turned out to be immaterial on a per case basis.

The economic cost of carrying accounts receivable is determined by computing the average whiskey accounts receivable balance for each state and imputing an interest cost of, say, 6% to it. The cost per case is determined by dividing the imputed interest cost for each state by the total number of whiskey cases billed in that state during the study period.

Selling expense is the most difficult and time-consuming to run down. Company records typically show no cost breakdown by brand and market area. In order to allocate this huge expense, questionnaires must be designed and distributed to each salesman, state manager, regional manager, and division manager in the relevant market areas. (See Exhibits 68 and 69.) The basis of allocation chosen was time. The reasoning

Exhibit 68. Regional manager's questionnaire, state portion.

STATE	SALES CALLS		SPECIAL EFFORTS		OFFICE TIME	OTHER EFFORTS
	NO.	TIME	NO.	TIME		
1. MASSACHUSETTS	12	20%	5	15%	15%	10%
2. RHODE ISLAND	5	5	–	–	5	
3. CONNECTICUT	10	15	–	–	10	
4. UPPER NEW YORK	15	10	10	15	10	15
5. METRO. NEW YORK	20	20	15	40	15	35
6. NEW JERSEY	5	5	5	10	10	20
7. DELAWARE	3	10	–	–	15	–
8. MARYLAND	15	10	–	–	10	10
9. WASHINGTON, D.C.	15	5	10	20	10	10
	100	100%	45	100%	100%	100%
GROUP WEIGHT		30%		20%	20%	30%

Exhibit 69. Division manager's questionnaire, brand section (Kansas).

BRAND	SPECIAL EFFORTS		OFFICE TIME	OTHER
	NO.	PERCENT*		
1. A	7	60%	50%	
2. B	–	–	5	
3. C	2	10	10	
4. D	3	15	20	
5. E	1	5	10	
6. F	2	10	5	
7. G	–	–	–	
	15	100%	100%	
GROUP WEIGHT †		20%	40%	40%

* Include allocation of your time by brand if you feel that a straight weighting
  by the number of special efforts (projects, etc.) will not give a true picture.

† List the overall percentage of time spent on special efforts, office time, and
  "other," which is time attributable to all brands equally. For example,
  special efforts — 20%, office time — 30%, other — 50%.

Exhibit 70. XYZ Distilling Company, per-case cost summary.

Brand____A_____   Size___QUART_____   Period Covered _____19XX_____

Description:___86°, 8-YEAR____

	N.Y.	MASS.	N.J.	WASH. D.C.	KANSAS	MISS.
MANUFACTURING COST:						
CONTENT	2.76	2.76	2.76	2.76	2.77	2.77
PACKAGING SUPPLIES	1.84	1.90	2.06	1.75	1.54	1.54
BOTTLING	.84	.84	.84	.84	.97	.97
SHIPPING	.22	.22	.22	.22	.24	.24
TOTAL MANUFACTURING	5.66	5.72	5.88	5.57	5.52	5.52
DISTRIBUTION COST:						
ADVERTISING	2.81	1.44	2.73	1.30	—	—
SALES PROMOTION	.27	.35	.54	.23	.01	2.64
MERCHANDISING	.58	.45	.98	.36	.09	
SALES ACCOUNTING	.69	.89	.51	1.77	.61	.38
SELLING EXPENSES	.59	.70	1.16	.65	1.95	2.00
WAREHOUSING	—	—	—	—	—	—
TOTAL DISTRIBUTION	4.94	3.83	5.92	4.31	2.66	5.02
TOTAL RELEVANT COST	10.60	9.55	11.80	9.88	8.18	10.54
MEMO:						
CASES BILLED	164,281	79,491	65,106	4,794	1,590	2,500
THIS SIZE BRAND	99,370	49,778	33,980	922	43	435

is that, since the men were paid on the basis of time, if the time actually expended could be allocated to brand and market area, it would provide a reasonable method for spreading their cost. Major variations in this cost did occur.

Warehousing expense was the last cost element studied. Only public warehousing was included here since, for the most part, the company bottled to order, keeping very little finished goods inventory. The results indicated that only in "control" states with requirements for warehousing in state warehouses was this cost material.

The results of this cost justification study are summarized for each brand/size combination by market area in Exhibit 70, which shows that the cost per case varies considerably depending upon the state and the volume of business transacted in that state. Since price-discrimination law permits the adjustment of prices to reflect differentials in cost, this study provides management with additional flexibility that it might not otherwise have.

8

LINKAGE WITH
ELECTRONIC DATA PROCESSING

Marketing men often regard computers with a sense of frustration. Much has been written about this "great new tool"—there are many articles describing how computers have helped to pinpoint marketing opportunities, assign salesmen to territories, and analyze profitability of product lines. Unfortunately, many marketing men have not experienced these benefits and somehow feel an opportunity is passing them by.

Yet these marketing men have also heard the stories of missed deadlines, unfilled promises, and the huge expenditures associated with computer installations. They do not wish to be pioneers, yet they do not want to be outdone by their competition either. What, then, is the solution?

This chapter discusses the linkage of marketing with the data processing function. It reviews examples of routine and analytical marketing information applications, developments in the area of application packages that pertain to marketing, and the organization of coordination between marketing and data processing. As more and more companies use the computer as a tool to help in the decision-making process, competitive pressures mount on those who do not. We will describe how marketing management can reap some of these benefits by working with its data processing counterparts.

THE DATA PROCESSING VIEW

The chief characteristic of successful systems installations is the development of a well-defined objective, or goal, before any developmental activity is started. This characteristic applies to both large- and small-scale applications, and whether routine or analytical. Often an overall plan is developed so that individual systems tasks can be most effectively carried out. This approach provides a road map which management can use to plan capital expenditures and staffing levels, and to plan anticipated needs before they become emergencies.

Under this concept, projects are typically carried out by a task force. The task force reports to a steering committee, which guides the overall systems effort and is normally a senior management group. It may include the president, the marketing vice president, the treasurer, the manufacturing vice president, and others. The task force's responsibility is to analyze and evaluate the benefits of a specific project and report to the committee. This organizational approach will be covered in greater detail in Chapter 16.

Under an organized approach, a project normally passes through a series of phases from start to completion, beginning with an identification of needs and moving to actual conversion or installation. There are 12 steps in this process, as shown graphically in Exhibit 71. For marketing managers, prime concern is with the first two steps: project survey and general design. These are shown in greater detail in Exhibit 72.

Project Survey

The objective of the survey step is twofold. First, the survey must identify and categorize all existing information, and from that information define the scope and purpose of the proposed system. Second, it must develop a plan of implementation for the proposed system, based on the results of analyzing the problem.

In order to meet these two objectives, the survey team must thoroughly study and document the relevant information. The scope and objectives of the system must be defined in terms of functions, operations, and existing problems. The present system or method of performing (or not performing) the tasks that will be part of the proposed system must be identified and documented in detail. All economic factors, including cost, savings, and impact, must be identified and balanced against each other. The feasibility of the proposed system must be determined from a standpoint of cost, personnel, hardware, and ability to do the job, all of which are factors in deciding whether to continue or not. Finally, time schedules, personnel requirements, and a work program for the general design phase must be drawn by the survey team.

Exhibit 71. Project development steps.

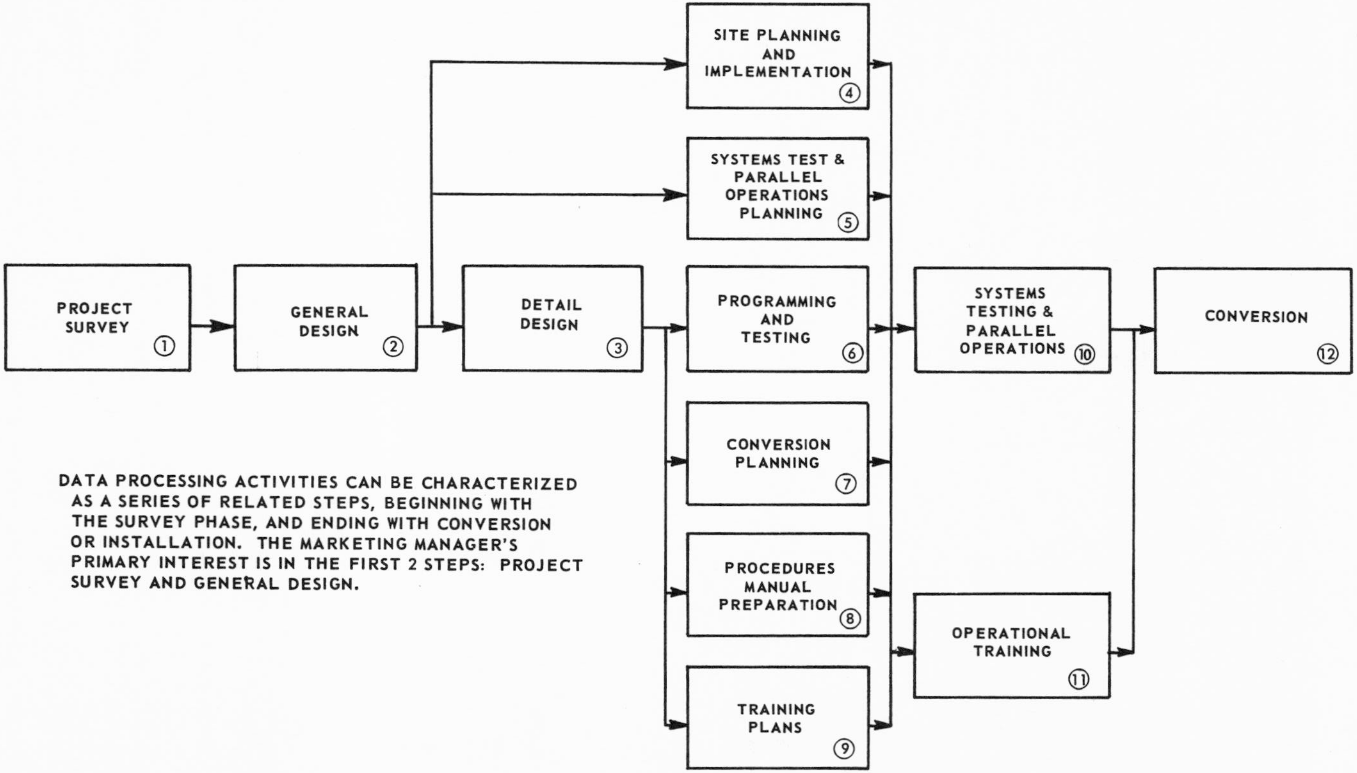

DATA PROCESSING ACTIVITIES CAN BE CHARACTERIZED
AS A SERIES OF RELATED STEPS, BEGINNING WITH
THE SURVEY PHASE, AND ENDING WITH CONVERSION
OR INSTALLATION. THE MARKETING MANAGER'S
PRIMARY INTEREST IS IN THE FIRST 2 STEPS: PROJECT
SURVEY AND GENERAL DESIGN.

Exhibit 72. Project survey and general design phases.

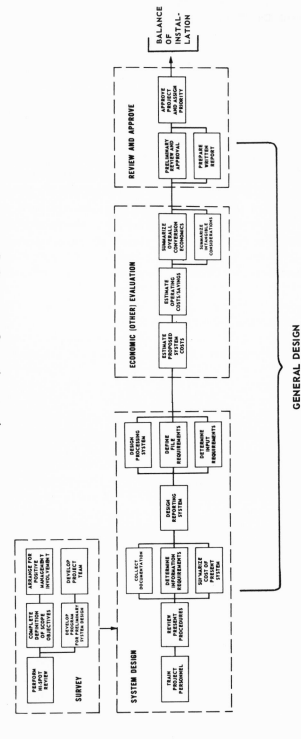

THE PROJECT SURVEY AND GENERAL DESIGN PHASES CAN BE EXPANDED TO SHOW MORE SPECIFIC
ACTIVITIES. THE WORK STEPS SHOWN HERE ARE PRIMARILY THOSE OF CONCERN TO MARKETING MANAGEMENT,
WHOSE INVOLVEMENT IS CRUCIAL TO SUCCESS.

General Design

Once the survey step has been completed and the conclusions and recommendations have been presented to management for a decision, one of two courses of action will result. Either the project will be judged unfeasible and further work will be terminated, or the project will be judged advantageous to the firm. If the latter, a priority will be assigned, an estimated starting date established, and resources allocated. The general design step will then begin.

On the basis of the approved scope and objectives of the project, the general design step will fully define the systems approach needed to develop a solution to the user's problem. Also, all systems concepts will be made final during this phase and will be primarily supported in the form of run-by-run flow charts. File specifications, control schemes, and timing estimates are key items that must also be supplied to provide assurance that the system meets its objectives. Hardware and software recommendations are made at this point to assist the firm in allocating its current resources and in planning its future needs.

(Although this discussion concerns electronic data processing, the same procedures would apply to manual systems.)

Marketing Involvement

The responsibility of the marketing manager in the design and development of a system is to define what is needed, how it is to be used, the frequency of the data, and the arrangement of the information. Terminology on the reports must be uniform from business area to business area (division to division, department to department), and this information must be tied into accounting reports and totals by department.

During the detail design and installation step, the marketing manager should be available for consultation. There may be technical problems which affect implementation of certain desired reports, or changes whose effects a systems or data processing analyst may not recognize as critical. It is the responsibility of the marketing manager to answer questions and help solve problems that may arise.

A data processing systems analyst should be included as an integral member of the project team during this entire process. His participation is initially limited because of the heavy input from marketing. He becomes more and more important in the course of the work, as installation time approaches. The analyst's involvement in all phases is important because familiarity with the initial thought processes will help him to implement the system.

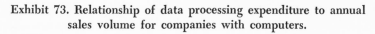

Exhibit 73. Relationship of data processing expenditure to annual
sales volume for companies with computers.

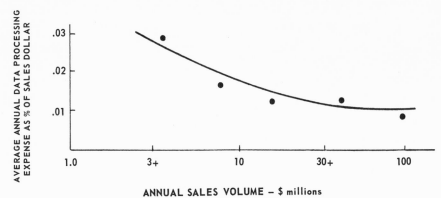

ANNUAL SALES VOLUME – $ millions

SOURCE: UNPUBLISHED REPORTS, MANAGEMENT SYSTEMS COMMITTEE OF THE
AMERICAN APPAREL MANUFACTURERS ASSOCIATION, JANUARY 1971

All this costs money, however. Computers and the required support
activities are expensive, particularly if they are not used well. But not
to use data processing equipment, considering the opportunities missed
and the lack of control of functions vital to marketing, is even more
expensive.

The American Apparel Manufacturers Association (AAMA) conducted a survey of its membership in the spring of 1970 to determine,
among other things, what a typical member company spends for data
processing activities. The results are shown in Exhibit 73. Expenditures
range from about $.03 per dollar of sales for companies with an annual
sales volume of $3 million down to $.01 per dollar of sales for companies
at the $100 million sales level.

Over the years, relative computer costs have been reduced significantly. An important result is the increased opportunity to perform more
analysis, in greater depth, at the same price. Experience indicates that
total expenditures on equipment may not drop, but much more can
be done for the same cost.

UNDERTAKING MARKETING SYSTEMS ACTIVITIES

Historically, data processing was first applied to clerically oriented
operations. Payroll, accounting, and billing activities are all in this category. As its initial success in terms of expense reduction and improved

Exhibit 74. Marketing systems development by phases of difficulty.

PHASE AND DESCRIPTION	ILLUSTRATIVE TYPES OF MARKETING INFORMATION
PHASE I	
THIS IS NORMALLY STRAIGHTFORWARD COMPILATION OF DATA, WITH TOTALS AND SUMMARIES FOR MANAGEMENT USE. LITTLE ANALYTICAL INFORMATION IS PRESENTED.	SALES REPORTING SALES ANALYSIS (INCLUDING RETURNS, ALLOWANCES) SALES INFORMATION BY MAJOR MARKET COMPARISON OF ACTUAL TO BUDGET/FORECAST
PHASE II	
HERE, THE INFORMATION SYSTEM WILL FEATURE EXCEPTION REPORTING AND ANALYTICAL DATA THAT CAN BE USED AS THE BASIS FOR PLANNING MARKETING OR SALES STRATEGIES.	CUSTOMER PROFILES INCREMENTAL FINANCIAL DATA MECHANIZED FORECASTING PROFIT & LOSS STATEMENTS BY MAJOR CUSTOMERS OR PRODUCTS ORDER ANALYSIS BY PRODUCT, SALESMAN, TERRITORY, ACCOUNT TRADE CHANNEL ANALYSIS
PHASE III	
THIS INFORMATION IS INTENDED FOR USE IN PLANNING. THE INFORMATION PROCESSING IS NORMALLY MECHANIZED, SO THAT ALTERNATIVE "WHAT IF" ASSUMPTIONS CAN BE EXPLORED RAPIDLY.	MARKETING MODELS INPUT/OUTPUT ANALYSIS

processing became apparent, applications were expanded to other areas of business, including marketing.

Marketing systems activities can be classified into phases, according to the difficulty of implementation and the complexity of data involved. Exhibit 74 lists various marketing systems activities according to their level of difficulty. Most marketing managers have the type of information available at phase I. However, it may not be in a good format, and clerical support is often needed to extract pertinent totals or to make useful comparisons.

Much work is currently under way to develop phase II type of information. Phase III is still on the drawing boards for most firms, but even here, notable examples of success have been recorded.

The Master Plan

The development of a master plan and timetable should be a first step to undertaking marketing systems activities. This enables any future development to be related to a master systems plan. Modifications to solve current problems or to produce major benefits with limited effort can then be given priority.

What are the steps leading to the development of such a master plan? A schematic is shown in Exhibit 75. Each of the steps is briefly described below.

Exhibit 75. Work steps in the development of an overall master plan.

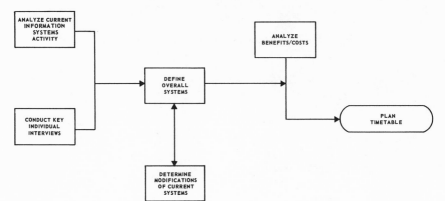

Analyze current systems. The task force must analyze the systems, procedures, and reports currently in use, as a basis for developing the master plan.

Conduct key interviews. Through interviews, the status and performance of the present information system is determined and needs not currently met are identified. These interviews are designed to cover only the major areas and to serve as a basis for the development of ideas.

Define overall systems. The systems concepts for the new system are defined in terms of the flow of principal transaction documents, controls, and information and planning reporting.

Determine modifications of current systems. The extent to which present systems should be integrated, combined, modified, or replaced to meet management needs effectively and economically is determined in this step.

Analyze benefits/costs. Here, expected benefits and both start-up and operating expenses associated with individual subsystems or systems features are specified. This includes a description of the number and type of personnel required to carry out the implementation and a schedule of the expenses.

Plan and timetable. In the final step, a plan and timetable for implementation is outlined, including priorities for implementing individual elements of the overall system.

The output is a master plan which will lead to the development of a management information system covering all areas of the company, as shown in Exhibit 76.

Review this schematic for a moment. All the major corporate func-

Exhibit 76. Management information system schematic (Part 1).

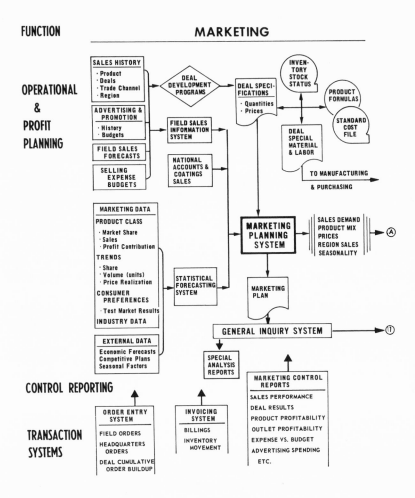

Exhibit 76. Management information system schematic (Part 2).

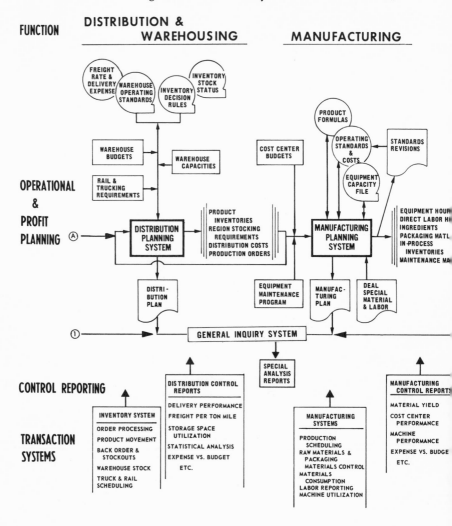

Exhibit 76. Management information system schematic (Part 3).

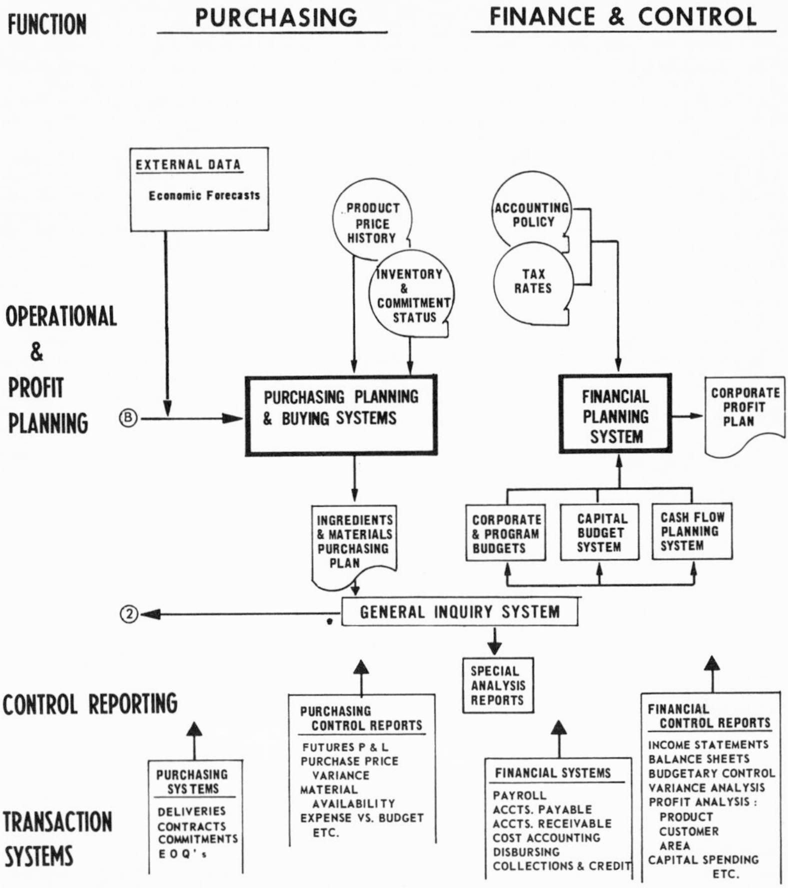

FUNCTION   <u>**PURCHASING**</u>   <u>**FINANCE & CONTROL**</u>

tions are included: marketing, distribution and warehousing, manufacturing, purchasing, finance and control. The activities performed for each of these functions are also shown: operational and profit planning, control reporting, and the transaction systems required to support these activities.

A system such as this necessarily requires a computer system for its operation. Master files are needed to store necessary data. Often an inquiry system will be included as part of such a master schedule. It is evident that strong data processing support must be provided to set up such a system properly.

As marketing men, our interest will naturally focus on the marketing function. The major components of the information system are shown, in terms of both the inputs required and their relationships to each other. The marketing planning system (center of diagram) represents the procedures that tie the pieces together to form a viable information system.

With such a master plan, activity can be undertaken to implement the system concepts, either in segments or in each area concurrently.

Development of the Marketing Information Systems Plan

Often the master plan approach as shown in Exhibit 76 is not possible. Marketing management may have urgent requirements for special procedures and information and may not be able to afford to wait until agreement has been achieved among all functional areas. It is certainly possible to develop only the marketing portion of the master plan. Unfortunately, certain advantages such as common data bases and integrated planning cannot be achieved. Review what would happen if the marketing system shown in Exhibit 76 had been developed independently. While some of the advantages would be missing, the subsystem would nevertheless satisfy the needs of the marketing manager in his everyday contact with the marketplace.

Exhibit 77 provides an illustration of the go-it-alone approach. Here, a subsidiary company had originally integrated its processing operations and reporting system with those of the parent company as part of a cost reduction move. Adverse customer reaction resulted—to an extent that caused loss of business—because the parent's processing system was unable to handle the special needs of the subsidiary's particular market. Since major systems changes would have been required in the much larger parent operation, marketing management decided to undertake those modifications that would meet its immediate marketing needs.

The results of this approach are shown in the modifications footnotes

Exhibit 77. Existing system used jointly by parent and subsidiary.

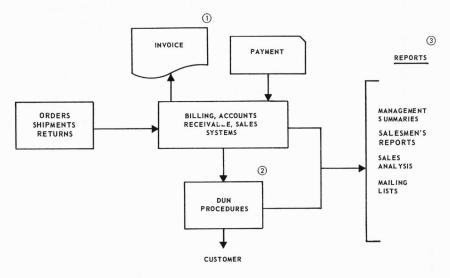

MODIFICATIONS FOR BENEFIT OF SUBSIDIARY:

① SEPARATE INVOICE PREPARED FOR SUBSIDIARY'S OPERATION.

② SPECIAL COLLECTION PROCEDURES ESTABLISHED TO MEET SPECIFIC NEEDS OF SUBSIDIARY.

③ REPORTS PREPARED TO MEET SPECIFIC NEEDS OF SUBSIDIARY'S MANAGEMENT.

of Exhibit 77. Some changes, such as use of a separate invoice, were relatively simple. Others, such as report changes, required considerable programming support. As part of this undertaking, an estimate of the costs and benefits, a schedule of priorities, and a timetable for completion was prepared. The system was subsequently installed and is now functioning as designed. In this situation, a marketing executive worked closely with a systems analyst. About four weeks of elapsed time was required to develop the concepts and the approach for a solution: one man-week for the marketing manager and four man-weeks for the analyst. In addition, about eight months of analyst and programmer time was required for installation. During this period, the marketing executive was on call to answer any questions or help with any unexpected problems.

Exhibit 78 provides a before-and-after summary of the modifications. The solutions are simply the application of good business procedures, developed through the joint efforts of a marketing executive and a data processing analyst.

Exhibit 78. Summary of modifications made to fulfill marketing needs of subsidiary.

AREA	BEFORE	AFTER
1. INVOICE	USE OF PARENT COMPANY INVOICE – DIFFICULT TO IDENTIFY NAME OF DIVISION ACTUALLY MAKING SALE.	PREPARATION OF SUBSIDIARY INVOICE REQUIRED REDESIGN OF INVOICE.
2. BILLING AND COLLECTION	PARENT COMPANY SYSTEM COULD ONLY DEAL WITH COMPANIES, NOT WITH INDIVIDUALS AS REQUIRED BY SUBSIDIARY.	SYSTEM MODIFIED TO BILL INDIVIDUALS. COLLECTION PROCEDURES DEVISED TO FOLLOW UP ON PERSONALIZED BASIS.
3. REPORTS: a. ORDER AND RETURN INFORMATION	DATA THAT WAS AVAILABLE WAS TABULATED MANUALLY.	BOTH ORDER DATA AND RETURN TALLY WERE PROVIDED MECHANICALLY.
b. SALES ANALYSIS	MASSIVE DATA BASE DESIGNED TO CAPTURE MOST POSSIBLE COMBINATIONS OF INFORMATION. NOT USED BECAUSE OF LACK OF ACCESSIBILITY AND FLEXIBILITY.	DATA BASE STRUCTURED TO MEET SPECIFIC NEEDS OF DIVISION. PREDETERMINED ON-REQUEST REPORTS DEVELOPED FOR MANAGEMENT USE.

ROUTINE VERSUS ANALYTICAL APPLICATIONS

It is important that the marketing manager and the data processing manager interact closely. The marketing man knows what information he needs for the decisions he must make, and in what time frame this data must be available. The data processing specialist then constructs the system to provide the information at lowest cost.

There is another important reason for this close coordination—the data processing specialist is familiar with consequences of certain information requests, such as volume reports, or the cost effect of certain types of systems decisions. The years the data processing analyst has spent learning his specialty can provide a valuable reservoir of suggestions and insights on the use and even the application of information.

The interaction between marketing manager and data processing varies depending on the complexity and nature of the application, as shown in Exhibit 79. Routine applications, such as billing and order entry, usually require the least coordination. In these situations, however, the marketing manager should review the proposed format for any advertising or esthetic appeal and to determine if it is in the best interests of the marketing effort. Since this is a processing application, almost everything else would normally be left to data processing to develop.

As the complexity increases, more of the marketing manager's time and thought will be required. In reporting applications, the manager must determine what information he needs, how he will use the data,

Exhibit 79. Interaction between marketing manager and data processing based on complexity of application.

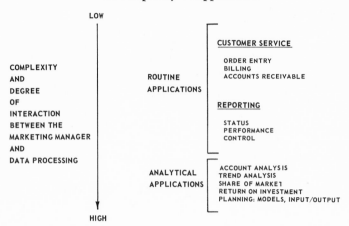

the format of the data, and the like. Data processing's role is one of helping to define these needs and of providing the information required.

Moving to the more analytical applications, even more of the marketing manager's time and thought will be required. At the planning end of the scale, it is evident that the marketing manager must fully understand the work and what went into the model if he is to have confidence in and understand how to use this new tool.

The Marketing Model

A marketing model should be viewed as little more than an extension of the marketing manager's thinking. As stated, the manager, to be most effective, must stay in close and continuous contact with both its construction and use.

The purpose of a model is to be able to analyze alternative marketing strategies quickly and effectively in terms of their financial consequences. To do this, the actual marketplace must be represented as realistically as possible. An illustrative model is shown in Exhibit 80.

In the exhibit, numerous relationships that may be representative of an actual situation are shown. As is evident, heavy user attention to detail is required. Information on relationships, such as number of salesmen to sales level and price-volume effects, can be developed by a data processing specialist using historical records, but realism can only be added by the manager directly concerned with the operation of factors under consideration.

Exhibit 80. A typical marketing model.

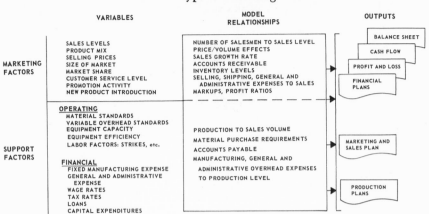

Reviewing Exhibit 80, the factors listed under variables are those that can be manipulated to answer different "what if" questions. For example, what if the sales level were to be increased by 5% (or $300,000), how many additional salesmen would be needed, and what would the effect on profit be? These are the kinds of questions the marketing manager will want to ask, since he is responsible for execution of the plans that are ultimately set for the marketing activity.

No model is complete without the support factors of the type that are also illustrated in Exhibit 80. These are the operating and financial relationships that are required to make the model meaningful and realistic.

Application Packages

The development of application packages to marketing situations is an area of increasing interest and importance to marketing managers. Much activity in this area is still in the pioneering stage; however, some very practical applications are coming into increasing use.

Application packages are intended to shortcut the process from development through implementation of a system. The benefits of their use are obvious: reduction in time required to obtain benefits and reduced cost of implementation. Packages are available from many sources, including specialty vendors, hardware manufacturers, and accounting firms.

At this point in their development, application packages can be grouped into four major categories.

1. *Data base systems.* Greatest use of packages by marketing man-

agers has been made in this area. The manager often requires performance information on his products compared to that of competitors, of actual to budget, and the like. Much of this is still done manually, but more and more is being mechanized.

2. *Sales forecasting.* A number of forecasting systems are available which use projection techniques based on historical data. Very useful for budgeting purposes, these systems provide a basis for preparing the annual plans.

3. *Sales reporting.* These packages provide sales analysis data. One is also available for controlling sales calls and providing follow-up information on salesmen's performance.

4. *Specialty.* This includes those packages which are generally experimental or pioneering efforts in specialized areas, such as facilities and location planning.

Here, the marketing manager's role is apparent. He should be familiar with the various packages available to him and how they could be of benefit. Once he has decided to use a package, it becomes the responsibility of the data processing function to install the system (or coordinate its installation in the event of a leased arrangement) and insure its proper operation.

This chapter has focused on the linkage between data processing and marketing. In many situations, there is a lack of coordination between the two, resulting in an information system not suited to the needs of the marketing manager. Data processing can turn out information in almost any combination conceivable, and all too often the reports tend to be listings of data that are at best difficult to use.

To have meaningful data, marketing managers must take the necessary time to define their information needs in terms of their operating requirements. It is up to the manager to take the lead in this area and to work with data processing. He is the user. No one else can make these decisions as effectively.

9

LINKAGE WITH OTHER AREAS OF OPERATION

THE CRITICAL POSITION OF MARKETING

It is no longer a surprise to many experienced executives to find the marketing function occupying most critical junctures between various parts of the management process. With the responsibility for forecasting volume, planning realized prices, executing substantial advertising and promotion budgets, and acting as a funnel for information concerning the marketplace, marketing personnel find themselves increasingly busy coordinating their activities with those of production, finance, distribution, and senior management.

The marketing information systems described throughout this book cannot be operated in a vacuum for the same reasons the marketing function cannot operate as a wholly contained, isolated unit. Most companies that embark upon significant information systems projects have in mind (or should have in mind) some overall management information system perspective. This concept necessarily requires that systems in one area feed or drive information systems in another area. The linkages between systems enable a company to maximize the value obtained from a given unit of data input, whether it be an order, an invoice, or a market research study, by using this information in a logical progression throughout all operations.

The clearest example of this linkage occurs when a sales forecast prepared by the marketing function becomes the major input to the production planning and scheduling process. The output from the marketing function can be a forecast for 10,000 units per month. The ultimate information required by the production function is an explosion of that single number to requirements for materials, labor, utilities, and even new plant and equipment.

MARKETING OUTPUTS AS INPUTS
TO OTHER AREAS: FORECASTS

Exhibit 81 shows a high-level view of the market planning process culminating in a sales and marketing profit plan. A well-organized planning system will provide monthly, or even weekly, volume forecasts as part of this plan. The plan will also include a great variety of detailed marketing strategies which influence activities in other parts of the organization. These strategies could include periodic short-term promotions requiring special packaging and inventory requirements, seasonal or trade channel pricing plans which have a direct bearing on cash flow, geographic sales coverage and sales volume strategies which must be supported by specific warehousing and inventory policies, and new product timetables which can require substantial changes in manufacturing processes and raw materials requirements.

The arrows on the right of the exhibit indicate that this system for preparing a marketing plan has direct links to other planning and operating systems. Drawing an arrow, however, will not make the linkage appear magically. The most common problem in establishing such linkages is the "people" problem. For example, all too often, product managers will struggle to generate an accurate sales forecast, in many cases using the computer to take advantage of an appropriate quantitative technique. The product manager fully expects that the plant manager will accept the forecast as is and use it as the starting point for production planning. Often, however, the production manager, having been excluded from the forecasting process, will not trust the resulting output and will instead rely upon his experience and some dog-eared schedules from last year. In this situation, there is constant organizational friction, which produces great heat when inventories of finished goods are either too high or too low and marketing and manufacturing each produces its own separate forecasts as justification for its position.

The breakdown in the linkages in this case has occurred because the designers of the forecasting system did not anticipate the need, first, to inform production management of the forecasting process and obtain its understanding and, second, to produce a forecast document in a format most useful to the production planning activity.

Exhibit 81.

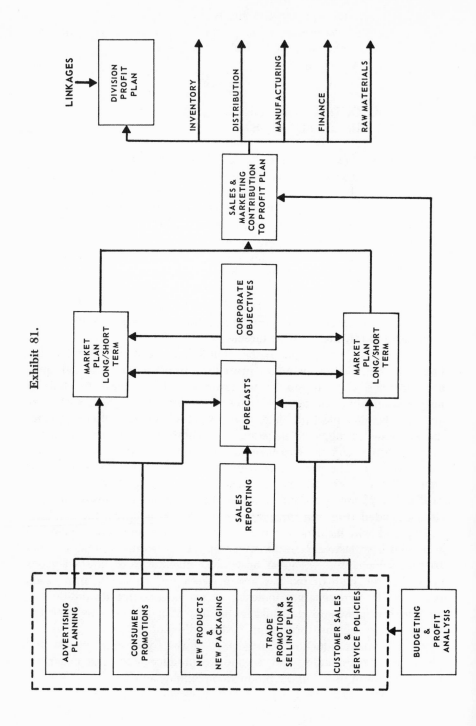

Exhibit 82.

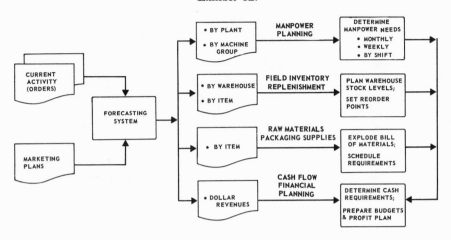

The forecast information contained in the annual marketing plan has a variety of uses, as illustrated in Exhibit 82. The initiators of forecasts within the marketing function should keep a few basic ideas in mind if the forecasts are to serve their intended purpose of triggering actions throughout the organization.

No forecasting system is perfect. If demonstrated results show large deviations from forecast over an extended period, face up to the task of modifying forecasting techniques before the information loses credibility among users.

Multiple projections of the same activity mean trouble. A single forecast (and well-defined responsibility for it) should be the rule. Sales quotas and territory objectives serve a different purpose and can differ from the forecast even though they may be based on the same assumptions.

*Date each forecast document—manual or computer-generated—*to avoid confusion about which is the most recent.

Documents containing forecast information should be designed for specific using groups, with such groups participating in the format decisions.

Work hard to obtain full understanding of the forecasting approaches and quantitative techniques. When changes in the forecasting system are contemplated, make sure that manufacturing and financial management are informed.

Another common communication problem with forecasts involves the need for both physical volume and dollar volume projections. These serve different purposes and both are necessary. In some organizations, the most convenient language for field sales personnel is retail dollar volume including markup; salesmen discuss how much a particular product will "do" for a customer. As long as resulting field forecasts are converted to *revenue* dollars, all will be well for internal planning purposes. In other cases, product managers project gross sales dollars at price levels that are largely fictional because of common trade discount policies or much lower prevailing market prices. The principle is the same here—clear designations of anticipated per unit prices and net revenue levels are required in the forecasts, regardless of references to published list prices.

Once the initial hurdle of deciding on forecasting procedures and responsibilities has been cleared, marketing management can stress the use of forecasts to signal the need for action. Exhibit 83 shows the general approach to this type of exception reporting. For any one of a number of objectives, such as physical volume, dollar volume, or margin dollars, management should lay out period-by-period objectives.

Equally important are action limits (Exhibit 83), which indicate acceptable levels of activity versus objectives. The action limits reflect a combination of possible forecast error and optimistic goals, and values between the objective and the action limit are considered to be within the scope of the original plan. Most forecasting techniques use the most recent actual performance as a critical input, and a forecast falling outside the action limit should be a clear signal for corrective action. Note that waiting for the "actual" line to breach the action limit means unnecessary and often dangerous delay. Action limit signals can trigger changes in manufacturing plans, sales-force campaigns, and pricing policies. Although the exhibit shows an action limit only on the low side

Exhibit 83. Action limits: early signals to management.

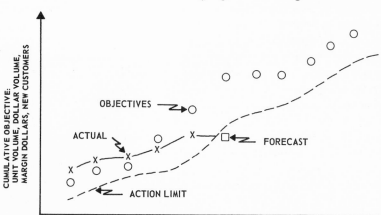

of the objectives, an upper limit is also possible, to indicate possible capacity problems or unusual trade channel inventory buildups. Like so many other forecasting procedures (as distinguished from quantitative techniques), action limits do not require the use of a computer. They do, however, require clear definitions of when and how they are to be used.

A logical step after the installation of the action limit concept is to draw up contingency plans covering the most likely circumstances under which the limits might be exceeded. With such plans in hand and basic contingency approvals obtained, action signals can trigger an orderly change in resource allocation rather than time-consuming replanning.

MARKETING OUTPUTS AS INPUTS
TO OTHER AREAS: BUDGETS

Exhibit 81 shows a budgetary input for each section of the marketing plan. These budgets, and their resulting summary marketing profit plan, serve three important purposes.

1. Budgets require product and sales force managers to carry the logic of marketing strategies through to projected financial consequences. Each portion of a large lump-sum marketing budget should be able to withstand careful, cost-conscious examination.

2. Budgets enable top management to better understand how middle managers advocate running the business for the coming year. Despite carefully written position descriptions, marketing managers usually have responsibility (particularly when things go wrong) but not authority. Top management rightfully reserves to itself the task of resolving conflicting demands for limited resources, with the budgetary process serving as the common thread and language for the allocation process.

3. The formal approval steps imbedded in the budgetary cycle lead to targets and limits against which progress can be monitored through reporting systems. While last year's spending levels can provide useful information for the preparation of next year's plans, few businesses can rely on history to measure current performance.

Although we all might agree that budgets are worthwhile, and perhaps even crucial, marketing managers often have difficulty establishing this link between themselves and financial and top management. The reasons for this problem usually arise from one or both of the following situations.

In company A, marketing resources (dollars and manpower) have been determined historically on a slush fund, or what's-left-over basis—what's left over after variable manufacturing costs, estimated fixed costs and overhead, and a profit objective. The remaining lump sum was turned over to the marketing function, with some reluctance, to do with what it would. This year, the president insists that marketing managers prepare detailed schedules showing what they propose to spend and why; he will then pass judgment on their budgets. He is stunned by the size of the proposed budget, and he is not satisfied with the reasoning behind spending requests. A difficult and time-consuming cycle of education and budget revision begins. Marketing personnel find it uncomfortable to be considered objects of microscopic examination rather than tolerated profit drains.

In company B's case, a very broad breakdown of marketing expenses has been part of the planning effort for some time—so much for advertising, so much for salesmen, so much for promotion. This year, profit responsibility will be decentralized to individual products and territories, and detailed budgets are required. The decentralization plans also include, for the first time, compensation related to performance versus objectives. Unfortunately, there is no appropriate historical data to rely on, and managers must estimate product and territory details. With its fingers crossed, the marketing department awaits the first set of responsibility reports, only to find that they are late, inaccurate, and incomplete. Everybody is confused.

In both these cases, the benefits of budgetary efforts were wasted because the necessary supporting data collection and planning systems were not carefully developed and tested. Company A might have had an easier time of it if budgets had been inaugurated gradually, with close attention to clearly stated assumptions. Company B's information system should have been revised according to requirements for timely and accurate reporting, because it could not handle the transition.

Our purpose in spelling out these examples of budget problems is to forewarn and, hopefully, forearm. Effective expenditure control must begin with thoughtful attention to communicating plans through budgets, and it cannot succeed without supporting information systems.

HOUSEHOLD PRODUCTS, INC.

As an example, the procedure for developing a marketing budget is given in the following illustrative case.

Background. The Utensils Division of Household Products, Inc., manufactures low-priced hardware items sold through variety, hardware,

Exhibit 84. Utensils Division, projected year-end 19X2 gross profit summary (000 omitted).

	PRODUCT A	PRODUCT B
GROSS SALES	$ 4,000	$ 7,000
TRADE DISCOUNTS	200	300
NET SALES	3,800	6,700
COST OF GOODS SOLD		
RAW MATERIALS	1,100	1,900
DIRECT LABOR	480	1,000
MANUFACTURING OVERHEAD	400	600
WAREHOUSING	100	220
FREIGHT	200	430
TOTAL	$ 2,280	$ 4,150
PERCENT OF NET SALES	60%	62%
GROSS PROFIT	$ 1,520	$ 2,550

9-4-X2

Exhibit 85. Utensils Division, projected year-end 19X2 net profit summary (000 omitted).

	PRODUCT A	PRODUCT B
GROSS PROFIT	$ 1,520	$ 2,550
MARKETING AND SALES		
SALES SALARIES*	330	330
SALES FORCE EXPENSES*	90	90
MEDIA ADVERTISING	250	370
RETAILER PROMOTION	170	400
CONSUMER PROMOTION	200	80
MARKETING OVERHEAD*	80	80
	$ 1,120	$ 1,350
CONTRIBUTION TO PROFIT AND GENERAL OVERHEAD	400	1,200
ALLOCATED OVERHEAD	480	480
NET PROFIT	$ (80)	$ 720
PERCENT OF NET SALES	(2.1%)	10.7%
* Allocated		

9-4-X2

supermarket, and institutional channels. Two major products, a line of kitchen utensils (A) and a line of cookware (B), account for most of the division's sales volume.

Historical performance. Arthur Russell, the Utensils Division marketing manager, is in the process of reviewing key statistics for products A and B (Exhibits 84 and 85) as part of his first pass at next year's marketing budget. Since it is only September, he has asked the division controller to project expense levels forward to cover the full year, and Russell has provided volume and price forecasts to fill out the year-end projections.

Russell notes that product A has not yet reached breakeven on a fully allocated basis, even though it is being promoted and advertised proportionally more than product B. He is not disappointed, however; his original plans for A included projected losses at this stage, and the product is almost breaking even. The summary reports, Russell is pleased to see, reflect the most recent changes in allocation procedures that he worked out with the division controller. For example, a study of sales-force effort showed about equal time devoted to A and B, so that sales salaries, expenses, and marketing overhead are divided equally for reporting purposes. New procedures for coding advertising invoices by product and for recording trade promotion discounts during the order entry process are also making the summary reports more accurate.

Product budgets. Russell's first task, he has decided, will be to prepare top-level budget estimates for product B. The product is well established in the marketplace, and thus planning for it should be straightforward. Naturally, market strategies are already under consideration to protect and improve B's market position and are reflected in Russell's preliminary forecast (Exhibit 86).

The total market is projected to grow by 5% next year. An overall strategy for product B is to increase its availability at retail. Russell's plan is to increase the current 65% market coverage to 70%. If the plan succeeds, product B will be available to a market whose total purchases are $57 million. In addition to increasing distribution, plans are also contemplated to increase market share by 1%, and thus next year's dollar forecast is shown as $8 million for product B. These dollars represent approximately 15% of the market that will be covered during the coming year.

The next step for Russell is to check on the manufacturing cost estimates for the coming year. Preliminary reports from the plant manager show a slight downward trend in per unit costs, to approximately 60% of net selling price. The division controller confirms the reasonableness of that figure for planning for next year (19X3), and also reports that general overhead expenses are expected to increase next year to the point where product B's share (assuming the same 50-50 split with A) will be about $550,000. These projections appear in the forecast column of Russell's budget worksheet (Exhibit 87) since he has very little control over them.

Product objectives. In view of last year's strong 10.7% profit level, Russell believes that his management will expect only a modest increase, and he budgets product B's net profit at 12.5% of net sales. The profit budget is thus $1,010,000, and, by difference, the preliminary marketing and sales budget is $1,680,000.

While the budget is $300,000 over the current year, Russell cannot relax—all his marketing strategies for product B will mean more dollars for salesmen, consumer promotions, and advertising. In fact, his past experience suggests that the additional $300,000 may not be enough to cover all the new or revised marketing programs he has in mind. He still has pricing decisions and unit forecasts to tackle, and he must begin detailed spadework with sales-force management before a consistent and dependable marketing and sales budget emerges.

INPUTS FROM OTHER AREAS TO MARKETING: ORDER PROCESSING

Just as marketing management supplies critical forecast and budget information to other areas of the organization, marketing is dependent

Exhibit 86. Utensils Division, planning base, product B, 19X3.

I. TOTAL MARKET ($000 OMITTED)

Factors: population, family formation, inflation
Method: regression analysis
Sources: trade associations, current industrial reports, internal
competitive intelligence files, U.S. Census Bureau

Actual market volume (this year) :	$ 77,000
Forecast market volume (next year):	$ 81,000
Percentage increase :	5%

II. SALES COVERAGE: Proportion of Total Market Served by Household Products' Accounts

Actual sales coverage (this year):	65% ($ 50,000)
Planned sales coverage (next year):	70% ($ 57,000)

Increased coverage will require addition to sales force

III. MARKET SHARE

SEGMENT	SEGMENT'S SHARE OF TOTAL MARKET	ACTUAL		PLANNED	
		PRODUCT B'S SHARE OF SEGMENT	PRODUCT B'S SHARE OF TOTAL MARKET	PRODUCT B'S SHARE OF SEGMENT	PRODUCT B'S SHARE OF TOTAL MARKET
Initial purchase	40%	7%	3%	10%	4%
Replacement & gift	40	20	8	20	8
Institutional	20	15	3	15	3
	100%		14%		15%

MARKET SHARE INCREASE OF 1% REQUIRES SUPPORT AND PROMOTION OF "INITIAL PURCHASE" SEGMENT, AND PROTECTIVE STRATEGIES FOR OTHER SEGMENTS.

IV. NEXT YEAR VOLUME PROJECTION: PRODUCT B

15% x $ 57,000,000 = $ 8,500,000

Exhibit 87. Budget worksheet, product B, 19X3 (000 omitted).

	PROJECTIONS FOR CURRENT YEAR-END	NEXT YEAR	
		FORECAST	BUDGET
GROSS SALES	$ 7,000		$ 8,500
NET SALES	6,700		8,100
COST OF GOODS	4,150		4,860
PERCENT OF NET	62%	60%	
GROSS PROFIT	2,550		3,240
MARKETING AND SALES	1,350		1,650
CONTRIBUTION TO PROFIT AND OVERHEAD	$ 1,200		$ 1,590
ALLOCATED OVERHEAD	480	$ 580	580
NET PROFIT	$ 720		$ 1,010
PERCENT OF NET SALES	10.7%		12.5%

upon other information systems for operating information. The order processing system is probably the most important of these, although financial reporting systems run a close second. At the time an order is received, the identification of customer, price, product, salesman, location, and quantity can be captured or lost forever. All these data find important applications for marketing managers, and many are described elsewhere in this book.

A highly useful offshoot from order entry data collection involves distribution monitoring. This concept is based on the purchasing habits of customers in large-volume industries, such as grocery products, proprietary drugs, and toilet articles. Most manufacturers in these industries present a broad product line to the market; it is not unusual for several hundred variations of package type, size, or price to appear within a multibrand product line. Success in marketing this large a variety of items is closely related to achieving wide distribution for each individual item. Ideally, a manufacturer would like each of his accounts to display and stock all the items on his price list. It would, however, be a rare supermarket or drug chain that could devote enough shelf space to one manufacturer to accomplish the full-line distribution objective. Thus millions of dollars are spent every year in attempts to muscle competing items off the shelves and replace them with new or existing varieties of other brands.

Distribution monitoring identifies those items that are not being purchased by key accounts as regularly as they should be. "As they should be" implies that the manufacturer can establish reasonable purchase frequency objectives for each type of account in his market. For example, a grocery products manufacturer might reasonably assume that any large supermarket buying office will place an order for fast-moving items at least once every two weeks. With this purchase frequency as the standard, incoming orders can be monitored to see whether specific accounts are purchasing regularly.

Exhibits 88, 89, and 90 show various control reports that a distribution monitoring system can provide. Exhibit 88 simply summarizes the number of accounts in each size classification that are purchasing a given item as regularly as the objective specified. Exhibit 89 shows the trend in distribution and has great benefit in tracking the effects of trade promotions. Exhibit 90 gets down to the account level and provides the salesmen with a powerful selling tool by identifying those items that have not been ordered during the most recent ordering cycle.

This use of the order processing system can also be combined with salesmen's call reports to monitor the effectiveness of merchandising programs in specific accounts or sales territories.

Exhibit 88. Distribution status.

- **ITEM** 633   JANUARY 19___
- **REGION** 6
- **KEY CHAIN DRUG ACCOUNTS**

	ACCOUNT CLASS		
	A	B	C
ORDER CYCLE OBJECTIVE (weeks)	4	6	8
NUMBER OF ACCOUNTS	40	135	260
% ORDERED	.67	.42	.42

DISTRIBUTION STATUS REPORTS MONITOR THE PURCHASE FREQUENCY OF SELECTED ITEMS BY KEY ACCOUNTS ACCORDING TO PREESTABLISHED ORDER CYCLE OBJECTIVES.

Exhibit 89. Item distribution status.

REGION 6   LAST 12 MONTHS

CHAIN DRUG

ITEM 633	A	B	C	WEIGHTED
JAN.	.67	.42	.42	.58
FEB.	.61	.36	.40	.52
MAR.	.73	.61	.45	.65
APR.	.70	.52	.33	.62
MAY	•	•	•	•
	•			

ITEM DISTRIBUTION STATUS REPORTS MONITOR KEY ACCOUNTS TO DETERMINE TRENDS FOR SELECTED ITEMS.

Exhibit 90. Key account distribution status.

REGION 6   DISTRICT 11   7X-09-01 to 7X-09-30

CHAIN DRUG

ACCOUNT	CLASS	633	533	534	098
REXALL – 01	A	X	X		X
REXALL – 02	A	X	X	X	
SUPER X	A		X		X
SAFEWAY	B	X		X	
BOB'S	B	X			X
•					

KEY ACCOUNT DISTRIBUTION STATUS REPORTS ENABLE SALES PERSONNEL TO QUICKLY IDENTIFY ITEMS THAT HAVE NOT BEEN ORDERED SO THAT THEY CAN DISCUSS INDIVIDUAL ITEMS WITH INDIVIDUAL ACCOUNTS.

INPUTS FROM OTHER AREAS TO
MARKETING: MANUFACTURING

In designing reporting systems, a good principle is to minimize the amount of information received by a manager who cannot act on that information. In many organizations, "everybody gets everything." In these situations, the sheer size of the in-basket each morning is enough to decrease efficiency noticeably. It is probably unnecessary for marketing managers to receive detailed inventory information daily, or manufacturing facility utilization reports, or even copies of salesmen's call reports. On the other hand, certain manufacturing statistics, in particular, can be very valuable to marketing managers where marketing has a strong voice in determining product characteristics.

A good example of this linkage between marketing and manufacturing is in the packaging materials area. Several kinds of action are possible based on the report illustrated in Exhibit 91. The report shows that packaging materials costs are out of line with standard costs established by the engineering department. Corrective steps could involve

Exhibit 91. Marketing summary item cost sheet.

ITEM	2060	BILLING UNIT	CASE	STANDARD QUANTITY	100 CASES
BRAND	04	SHIPPING UNIT	CASE	STANDARD EFFECTIVE	6/1/X2
SALES GROUP	12/24	PRICE EFFECTIVE	4/30/X2	DATE LAST CHANGED	12/1/X1

	STANDARD	3-MONTH AVERAGE AS OF 8/1/X2	VARIANCE	ACTION SIGNAL
RAW MATERIALS & CONVERSION	$ 2975	$ 3085	$ + 110	*
LABOR	430	450	+ 20	
PACKAGING				
LABELS	295	345	+ 50	*
PLATFORMS	60	65	+ 5	
DIVIDERS/INSULATION	97	110	+ 13	*
TOPS/BOTTOMS	341	330	− 11	
CASES	204	217	+ 13	
NET PACKAGING	$ 997	$ 1067	$ + 70	
OVERHEAD	655	655	−0−	
STANDARD COST	$ 5057	$ 5257	$ + 200	

SHIPPING UNIT PRICE	$ 84.50
GROSS MARGIN	38.9 %
PREVIOUS MARGIN	40.1 %

obtaining new bids on label supplies, changing the label, or redesigning the package completely to reduce total packaging costs.

It is even possible that continued increases in packaging costs could lead to a price increase. Marketing, and specifically product development and design personnel, should have had a major influence on the type, and thus the cost, of packaging materials. For this reason, they require continuous information on the quality of their decisions in this area so they can revise their recommendations if appropriate.

This example of cost analysis and corrective action illustrates the close liaison that marketing management must maintain with both manufacturing and the financial and accounting functions.

INPUTS FROM OTHER AREAS TO MARKETING: INVENTORY AND DISTRIBUTION

Finished goods inventory planning and control responsibilities often float around an organization without a secure home. From company to company within an industry, these responsibilities can be found in the marketing area in one case, in the manufacturing area in another case, and in a separate distribution function in still a third case. We will not dwell here on the problems that can be caused by poor definition of responsibility for inventory control; in too many cases, senior management gets the job of monitoring inventory positions because no lower level of responsibility has been identified. Regardless of official job definition, product managers must establish an information link with the distribution function. It is marketing, after all, that should be initiating recommendations for product line deletions, price changes, and special promotional packaging—all of which have an immediate and substantial effect on inventory policy.

A basic type of inventory report, shown in Exhibit 92, relates current levels to months' supply. Note that this example includes both raw materials and finished goods. While an effective materials procurement planning system will minimize stocks of ingredients and supplies, product managers should be alert to failures in this system so that they can anticipate pressures to reduce raw materials stocks. In the exhibit, items have been separated into planning categories, which identify both planning responsibility and importance; an A item may have more volatile demand swings than a B item and thus require closer attention for planning and control of inventory. Significant changes in period turnover identify potential problems with excessive or depleted inventories.

Exhibit 92. Period inventory performance report.

PLANNING CATEGORY	STOCKKEEPING UNIT NUMBER	DESCRIPTION	PERIOD-END UNSOLD BALANCE	THIS PERIOD SHIPMENTS	THIS PERIOD TURNOVER	LAST 3 PERIODS TURNOVER	PERIOD'S SUPPLY
FINISHED GOODS			CASES				
A	0200	12 BOX LG.	2450	2206	0.90	1.02	1.0
A	0210	24 BOX LG.	1100	1258	1.13	1.21	.8
A	0300	24 BOX SM.	3473	2815	0.81	0.80	1.3
B	0401	PREPAK –10	575	482	0.84	0.68	1.2
B	0402	PREPAK –50	303	109	0.36	0.42	2.8
RAW MATERIALS			USAGE (lb.)				
A	1200	GEL	4710	2500	0.53	0.47	1.8
A	1300	ACTIVE	1250	420	0.32	0.40	2.1
B	1063	DYE	185	40	0.22	0.28	4.2
B	1100	INERT	7470	3900	0.52	0.66	1.9

Exhibit 93. Inventory performance report.

PLANNING CATEGORY	STOCKKEEPING UNIT NUMBER	NET INVENTORY POSITION	PERIOD'S SUPPLY	NORMAL REPLENISH. LEVEL	SEASONAL REPLENISH. LEVEL	ACTION SIGNAL
FINISHED GOODS		CASES			CASES	
A	0200	2450	1.0	2000	3500	•
A	0210	1100	0.8	1400	1800	•
A	0300	3473	1.3	2450	3000	
B	0401	575	1.2	400	480	
B	0402	303	2.8	100	130	
B	0502	625	1.0	500	700	•
RAW MATERIALS		USAGE (Lb.)			USAGE (Lb.)	
A	1200	4710	1.8	4000	6000	•
A	1300	1250	2.1	900	1100	
B	1063	185	4.2	50	75	
B	1100	7470	1.9	6000	9000	•

In Exhibit 92, for example, item 0200 slipped below a once-a-period inventory turnover, while item 0401 showed a faster turnover than usual.

Few businesses operate on such a regular monthly demand pattern that "months' supply" is a completely reliable measure of inventory levels. Exhibit 93 shows another approach, which involves planned inventory levels that increase and decrease according to forecasted seasonal demand variations.

Below are some of the marketing decisions that depend at least in part on current and forecasted inventory levels.

1. Consumer or trade promotions that can be expected to generate substantial increases in short-term sales volume.
2. Product line changes that could result in stocks of finished goods which cannot be moved without substantial price reductions.
3. New customer solicitation programs which could generate demand on limited warehouse facilities.
4. Special package promotions which require stocks of wrappers, labels, or display materials.
5. Changes in customer service policies regarding cut orders and back orders which could revise inventory record-keeping requirements. For example, inauguration of a no-back-order policy could create confusion among warehouse personnel if back-ordered items continue to be included as demands on existing stocks.

COMMUNICATION THROUGH CODING SYSTEMS

As was mentioned earlier in this chapter, the vital links between marketing and other functional areas and information systems will not materialize automatically from flow charts, or even from sincere policy statements and coordination meetings. Those kinds of steps are, of course, important ones which need to be accomplished and publicized in order to consolidate a feeling of mutual cooperation throughout the organization. On a much more fundamental level, however, the communication links in practice must rely upon a set of common languages that everybody can understand and use. These languages are usually a series of codes which economically identify the pigeonholes into which operating data must be placed in order for it to become useful information.

Basic Coding Requirements

Codes are usually required for three types of information: products, customers, and production facilities. While specialized coding requirements for employees, vehicles, dealers, and the like are also required in many organizations, it is impossible to get away from the needs for product, customer, and facility identification as the means to efficiently process information.

The schematic diagram in Exhibit 94 shows some of the uses of these kinds of codes. On the left side of the diagram are the detailed codes for products, customers, and facilities. The product codes might logically be assembled in a catalog where each entry would specify

Exhibit 94. Basic coding structures.

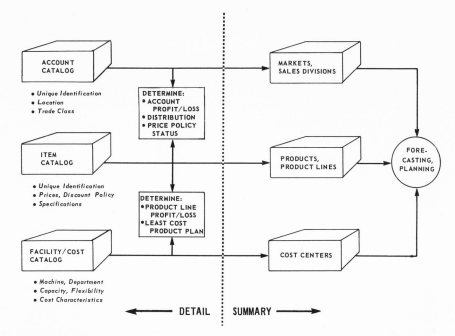

the product variation, its characteristics, and basic prices, and perhaps its raw material requirements. The catalog thus provides a unique identification for every manufactured item and not coincidentally provides the basis for coding raw materials and intermediate products as well.

A catalog of accounts or customers can look the same as a product catalog; that is, each page of the account file contains information on a specific customer, including his trade class, his location, and his approximate size. The account coding then begins to generate useful information on the geographic distribution of accounts, the number of customers active in various trade classes, and the size breakdown of the customer list.

A catalog of production facilities is also required to identify individual machines, departments, or entire plants. With the three detailed catalogs in hand, it becomes possible to combine data elements from any two of them to produce valuable control information. For example, the combination of product identification and account identification produces trade class profitability data based on the mix of products sold. In the same way, the combination of process or facility identification with product identification produces comparisons of group profit for items manufactured in more than one location.

The right side of the exhibit indicates the uses of summarized catalog information. Groups of accounts can be coded to produce summaries by market, by trade class, or by sales division. Groups of items can be coded to summarize an entire product group or product line. In the same way, groups of machines can be summarized into cost center categories. The ability to summarize detailed information is one of the most important benefits of a coding structure. The lack of appropriate summaries is a common complaint about many information systems that are otherwise well designed.

Exhibit 94 also illustrates the primary purpose of summarized information: the planning and forecasting process required to allocate effort and resources.

Common Coding Problems

The inability to summarize is only one symptom of coding system problems. There are other common difficulties.

1. *Multiple definitions for the same basic item.* For example, if the special holiday package is called the "holiday pac" by product management, item 206-H in the warehouse, and item 206 in the plant, serious difficulties will eventually arise when attempts are made to monitor the activity of that item. All three functions must have a common name for this unique item, and the name itself should be assigned by a manager responsible for coding systems and not for manufacturing, marketing, or warehousing.

2. *Inflexible codes.* Once an overhaul of a coding system has been accomplished, it should not be necessary to repeat the exercise more than once in the next five to ten years. In order to maintain the usefulness of a coding structure over that period of time, it is necessary to allow room for expansion. If the present product line has 20 items, it might seem reasonable to allow a three-digit product code which could accommodate 999 items. If growth is rapid, however, it will probably be necessary to subdivide several hundred products into groups for easy summarization, in which case only 10 groups with a maximum of 99 products in each group can be accommodated with three digits. The initial cost of providing additional space on manual forms and computer files is small compared to the costs of revising all such forms.

3. *Lack of documentation and control.* A coding supervisor who has responsibility for maintaining and updating all codes was mentioned earlier. This function can pay for itself many times over if unnecessary codes are kept out of the catalogs and files, if obsolete codes are deleted promptly, and if clear definitions of codes are developed and observed.

Requests for additional codes should be processed with care and objectivity; establishing dozens of new codes for prospective products or one-shot special variations will inflate the code catalog without any accompanying benefits.

4. *Failure to minimize error probability.* Some types of codes are designed with the expectation that people will automatically relate the code to the item it describes (mnemonic codes are the best example). As long as such codes are limited to 10 or 15 catalog items, the expectation is reasonable. With a greater number of items, however, the process of looking up a cross-reference, entering the correct cross-reference, and avoiding reliance on memory is highly prone to error.

5. *Reinventing standard codes.* A number of coding structures have already been organized for multi-industry use. There is thus no need for expending valuable man-months of effort redefining the same things. In fact, the use of preestablished codes can have substantial benefits in tying internal data on customers, products, and territories to external data published by governments, trade associations, and syndicated data suppliers. As examples:

- *S.I.C. codes* define manufacturing, mining service, and financial businesses in minute detail and are widely used in governmental and trade association data.
- *Geographic codes* for states, counties, cities, zip code areas, and even city blocks are available from computer manufacturers and software suppliers.
- *Customer codes* that identify individual business organizations are available (for a price) from Dun & Bradstreet.
- *Trading area codes* for specific industries are common where a well-established industry trade association is active.

10

MARKETING AND
OPERATIONS RESEARCH

The supporting information systems for marketing activities must deal with a set of interacting variables that are constantly changing; new factors are entering and old ones are frequently disappearing. These information systems encompass information flows both within the company and between the company and its marketing environment, information elements with very dissimilar characteristics (for example, actual sales of a new product to a customer group versus measurement of a consumer's qualitative response to the new product), and information flows in diverse time frames (for example, the cumulative impact of an advertising campaign versus the short-term influence of a price change).

These considerations point to the complex, yet essential, requirements for continuous market measurements, evaluation of information, and revision of decisions. Consequently, marketing management has frequent and urgent needs to address the information system with requests for information that are structured and interpreted in terms of a particular decision. It is to this end that operations research, using tools such as models, may be incorporated as an ingredient of a marketing information system.

DESCRIPTIVE MODELS

One class of models, commonly referred to as descriptive models, is directed toward providing a meaningful representation of a given marketing situation. For example, a model might describe how consumers behave or are expected to behave when a price change is put into effect. A model of such behavior may be used to transform test market data into estimates of brand loyalty characteristics of consumers. The transformed data may indicate a lack of adequate information and lead to subsequent research and data collection. Testing may suggest that the model is an inadequate description of consumer behavior and lead to alternative formulations of an appropriate model.

This type of testing helps the decision maker gain further insight into the problem area and provides a framework for identifying the variables that are significant and need to be measured. As new values of these variables are estimated and input into the model, the output of the model will be a forecast of future consumer behavior. Here again, if the forecasts are unreasonable, this points the way toward a revision in the descriptive model or in the method of estimating inputs. All these uses of a descriptive model are related to improving the problem-solving capability of the user since they focus on better problem definition and quantification of the marketing environment.

OPTIMIZATION MODELS

A second class of models deals with a definitive specification of how a problem should be solved if some criterion established by the decision maker is to be optimized. These optimization models, combined with an appropriate solution technique, are powerful tools.

Developing such a model forces a formal structuring of subjective factors. For example, in order to determine a product price which will maximize profits over the long run, the model must be able to incorporate the empirical information that management has relating to consumer and competitive reaction and the associated risks of such reaction occurring. The solution obtained will, of course, be subject to the limitations of the model's assumptions. Nevertheless, the total implications of the course of action (for example, to increase prices by 20%) will be depicted. The model will also enable the manager to establish the sensitivity of the solution to changes in particular variables or controlling parameters. In this respect, as part of an ongoing information system, optimization models can be used to update decisions and serve as a timely and consistent control function whenever relevant factors in the marketing environment change.

The diversity of marketing problems and the related applicability of both descriptive and optimization models in advertising, pricing, distribution, selling, and new product decision areas could fill several volumes. The specific role of models, however, can be illustrated by a given marketing situation. Consequently, the balance of this chapter will be devoted to a discussion of two cases of significant marketing decisions; namely, determining the length of a product line and determining where to allocate personal selling effort. In both instances we will see how the information system needed to support these decisions is enhanced by the introduction of a model.

LENGTH OF THE PRODUCT LINE

Effective marketing of consumer goods generally calls for development of a line or lines of products, each comprising a variety in style, color, or other aspects not related to the functional use of the product. Since this variety is believed to be a major factor in determining market share, management places considerable emphasis on decisions concerning changes in the line. Such changes include removal of marginal or slow-moving items, addition of new items, replacement of removed items, and concurrent removal, replacement, and new additions.

The decision to add or delete an item from the product line depends on the incremental effect on the cost of company operations and on the market impact in terms of sales. Of these two factors, the effect on costs can usually be measured with some degree of precision and reliability. The effect on sales is likely to be a more subjective judgment on the part of marketing management. The information output from a model to guide this decision must nevertheless deal with both of these elements.

Consider the question of increasing the product line, which brings with it changes in several elements of cost, such as:

Design, product planning, and engineering and research costs that are directly associated with the introduction of new items and not with maintenance of production or cost reduction on existing items.

Promotional costs associated with the announcement of specific items, including samples, which are generally nonrecoverable.

Inventory costs, including the normal carrying costs for the additional inventory investment, obsolescence costs, and write-down losses arising over the life cycle of an item.

Additional scheduling costs resulting from increased variety, including production planning and control effort, paperwork, and equipment changeovers.

To incorporate the joint impact on costs and sales, the criterion for deciding on the number of items to be carried in the line is the recovery, through additional sales, of the costs of adding a new item.

In this case study, the management of a textile company was considering a product line with 200 items and examining the decision to add 50 more items (color and pattern variations). The total cost of introducing each item was determined to be $3,800, and the expected life of each item was three years. Economic justification for including these additional 50 items therefore required that the expanded product line of 250 items would return a gross profit in three years of at least $3,800 × 50, or $190,000, above that of the current line of 200 items.

The predictability of the product line unit sales with added items still remained the most elusive factor. Marketing management generally recognized that adding an item to the product line did not necessarily bring a proportionate increase in sales. In fact, part of its sales might be obtained at the expense of other items as a result of the substitutability of one item for another within a given product line.

Interestingly enough, it is precisely this behavior of a product line that could be modeled and used effectively to provide a basis for a product line decision. The necessary data for the model was developed by analyzing the product line as follows.

1. For each of six separate product lines for each of the past five years, items were arrayed in descending order of unit sales, and the percentages of total sales for each item were calculated.

2. Using the percentages, curves were plotted (see Exhibit 95 for one product line for one year) showing cumulatively the percentage of items accounting for a given percentage of total unit sales.

3. From the cumulative ranked distribution of sales percentages (plotted in 2) for each of the five years, the ratio of sales of the lowest-selling or marginal item to the average item was estimated. These 30 individual ratios were plotted against the number of items in the line that year (see Exhibit 96). A curve was fit through the points and extended beyond the 200 items.

Exhibit 96 indicates, for example, that with a line of 50 items, the sales of the marginal (50th) item would represent about 0.5 times those of the average item. Since the average item would sell 1/50, or 2%, of the total, the marginal item would sell half of that, or 1%.

Similarly, for a line of 200 items, the marginal item would sell about 0.33 times the average item or 0.17% of the total.

A general mathematical equation can be written for the curve shown in Exhibit 95 and represents, in fact, a descriptive model of the way total annual unit sales are proportioned among all items constituting the line. The specific equation related to the curve in Exhibit 96 reflects

Exhibit 95. Cumulative ranked distribution of annual unit sales.

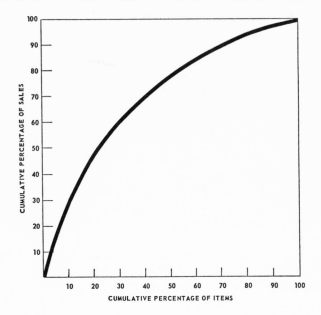

Exhibit 96. Unit sales ratio of marginal to average item for product lines of varying length.

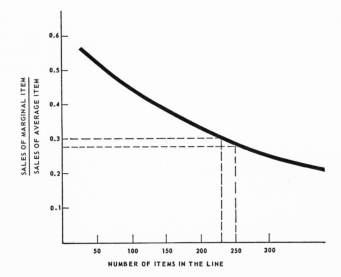

the proportional relationship between the marginal and average item, irrespective of the individual items involved.

How, then, are these relationships applied to a specific product line decision? To determine the volume of sales needed to recover $3,800 expense per item, the unit gross margin first had to be estimated for the new line. The gross margin was determined to be $2.20 per thousand yard unit based on budgeted margin percentages applied to existing selling prices, averaged for all items in the line.

With a $2.20 unit gross margin, a minimum of approximately 1,720 units of a new item would have to be sold over its three-year life cycle in order to offset the $3,800 cost of adding the item. While it was difficult for marketing management to predict the sales of a particular new item, it was clear that the *average new* item should have minimum sales of 1,720 units.

Next, from Exhibit 96, the expected ratio of sales of the marginal item to sales of the average item for a planned product line of 250 items was established at 0.285. If the marginal item in the resulting product line is to sell 1,720 units, then the overall average item's unit sales should be maintained at 6,020 units (1,720 ÷ 0.285) for a 250-item product line.

As previously indicated, this particular product line turns over approximately once every three years, and sales goals had to be predicated on a three-year life cycle. An initial three-year forecast of 1,320,000 units for the entire product line indicated that a 250-item line could not be economically justified because the sales of the average item would be roughly 5,300 (1,320,000 ÷ 250), some 700 units short of the 6,020 required to achieve 1,720 units for the marginal item. Through trial-and-error calculations it is found that in fact the 1,320,000-unit forecast would support a 230-item line, with the resulting average item's sales at 5,730 units. With a ratio of 0.300 (marginal to average item, corresponding to 230 items) a minimum of 5,730 × 0.300, or 1,720, units for the lowest-selling item would be maintained, thus providing an even chance that, with 230 items in the line, the cost of adding each new item would be recovered.

Thus, once the curve (Exhibit 96) has been derived (the ratio as a function of the number of items), the breakeven sales volume has been determined (in this case, 1,720 units), and the total unit forecast for the line has been made the number of items to carry can be calculated.

It should be recognized that the model serves to indicate the approximate level of the product line that could be profitably maintained, but is not intended to establish conclusively the exact length of the product line for the next year. Other judgmental considerations, such as competitors' offerings, need to be taken into account.

In this case, a plan was put into effect to control changes to the product line so that, unless the total volume forecast increased, the supportable limit of 230 items would be maintained. The model could then be used to reassess this limit based on changing cost factors and new market conditions that might lead to revised requirements for the product line.

The development of a cumulative distribution of sales among items in rank order for a product line (Exhibit 95) was further expanded to establish a standard of performance for items in the various product lines. From the curve, the percentage of total sales accounted for by the best five items as a function of the total number of items in the line and the total unit sales for the line was taken. The selection of five as the number of best items for which to determine this general relationship was a marketing management decision based on the assumption that total line performance is significantly influenced by these items.

The general model was used to estimate the standard percentage of sales to be accounted for by the best five items. This standard was compared with actual sales in each product line and the degree of variations was reported in the information system, thereby directing management's attention—on an exception basis—to those product lines needing further consideration and analysis.

The latest evaluation of existing product lines showed four lines which deviated significantly from the standard (see Exhibit 97). In two of these (lines 7 and 6), the best five items accounted for 78% and 66%, respectively, of the total line sales, which is significantly more than the standard percentage for the best five items. After further con-

Exhibit 97. Sales performance of product lines against standard.

LINE NO.	NO. OF ITEMS	TOTAL SALES (000)	STANDARD PERCENT OF TOTAL SALES OF BEST 5 ITEMS	ACTUAL PERCENT OF TOTAL SALES OF BEST 5 ITEMS	STANDARD LESS ACTUAL
9	120	$100	73%	68%	+ 5%
3	140	110	71	80	− 9
7	190	130	65	78	−13
5	230	140	63	65	− 2
1	290	180	59	41	+18
2	300	183	57	42	+15
4	300	185	57	56	+ 1
6	370	194	50	66	−16
8	410	198	45	41	+ 4

sideration, management concluded that these lines were exhibiting a fashion trend and possessed a few unusually attractive items. Management felt that a fashion line needed a larger number of items to make the complete line marketable; without them the few attractive items and the total line would not sell as well. Consequently, action was taken to enhance these lines with new items, while removing the weak items.

Two other product lines (lines 1 and 2) had a much smaller proportion of sales concentrated in its best five items. Management considered these to be rather stable lines and decided to perform the economic evaluation previously described to determine whether some items in these lines should be removed, or replaced less frequently.

This particular case illustrates how the use of a single model can, by application of an analytical technique, indicate a possible optimum solution (namely, the number of items to be carried in a line to meet a given profit/cost objective) and serve as a basis for an exception reporting system to monitor the performance of a product line.

ALLOCATING SALES EFFORT

Sales control and the allocation of sales effort depend, in principle, on customer response (in terms of sales) to varying levels and types of sales effort. The difficulty in developing quantitative measures of this response for effective sales planning are obvious. However, a company usually has a prodigious amount of data relating to the sales function which can be organized to guide a specific set of sales planning decisions. We report here a case study involving (1) the development of a model of the interrelationship between sales and customer activity, (2) the use of measures derived from the model for estimating future sales, and (3) the integration of the resulting estimates into a sales plan for establishing sales targets. This approach has become the basis for a continuing information system supporting sales management decisions on the total sales effort to be applied in terms of the number of customers to be called on, how this effort should be allocated among different types of customers, and the timing of calls to customers. The company is a textile manufacturer with a product line characterized by style features.

The sales data analyzed consisted of the sales by product line for each customer during each of five consecutive selling seasons (spring 19X0, fall 19X0, spring 19X1, fall 19X1 and spring 19X2). Selling seasons were selected as the appropriate time period since sales effort is replanned twice a year when a specific (and often new) line of merchandise is shown to customers. The sales volume data were processed by season and summarized by selected customer classifications. These classifications characterized a customer according to sales potential, method of operation (retailer, jobber, manufacturer), type of application (including product line, price, and end use), and markets served by the customer. Discussion of the approach to the problem and subsequent analysis will be in terms of manufacturers, the single largest classification of customers.

A preliminary investigation of sales data showed that the total number of active customers in the manufacturer class had remained relatively constant from season to season. However, the individual customers making up these totals were not the same from season to season. In fact, in each succeeding season a substantial number of customers who had purchased goods in the previous season were lost. Further, many customers who did not purchase in the previous season were acquired each season.

It was literally impossible for members of the sales organization to recall the factors which contributed to such instability in customer composition from season to season. Because of this instability, however, further investigation of the continuity of an individual customer's frequency and quantity of purchases was undertaken. Continuity of purchases was measured in terms of the "age" of a customer at the end of a given season, where "age" was defined as the number of consecutive seasons in which the customer purchased goods.

The number of new customers in each of the five selling seasons was established. It should be reemphasized that customers were considered new if they did not purchase goods in the previous selling season and, consequently, the same customer was considered new if he purchased again after having broken a consecutive sequence of purchases in prior seasons.

By tracing each customer's purchase through five selling seasons it was possible to establish the total number of customers who made repeat purchases for two, three, four, and five consecutive seasons. A summary of the results is shown in Exhibit 98. It can be seen that, regardless of the season in which the customers were defined as being new, the retention of customers from one season to the next followed a similar pattern.

Similarly, the quantity of goods purchased by these customers was determined for each season and traced through consecutive seasons. Exhibit 99 indicates that the average new customer purchased, over the historical period considered, 50 units in its first season. Where customers were retained from season to season, they tended to purchase

Exhibit 98. Pattern of customer retention (manufacturers).

FIRST SEASON	NUMBER (PERCENT) OF CUSTOMERS RETAINED FROM PREVIOUS SEASON				
	SPRING 19X1	FALL 19X1	SPRING 19X2	FALL 19X2	SPRING 19X3
SPRING 19X1	226	79(35)	56(71)	39(70)	32(83)
FALL 19X1		161	52(30)	38(73)	30(79)
SPRING 19X2			115	36(31)	24(67)
FALL 19X2				143	49(34)
SPRING 19X3					127

Exhibit 99. Pattern of sales development (manufacturers).

FIRST SEASON	AVERAGE UNIT SALES PER CUSTOMER AND RATE OF CHANGE FROM PREVIOUS SEASON									
	SPRING 19X1		FALL 19X1		SPRING 19X2		FALL 19X2		SPRING 19X3	
	UNITS	CHANGE	UNITS	CHANGE	UNITS	CHANGE	UNITS	CHANGE	UNITS	CHANGE
SPRING 19X1	53	–	110	2.1	173	1.6	231	1.3	276	1.2
FALL 19X1			49	–	103	2.1	156	1.5	208	1.3
SPRING 19X2					46	–	97	2.1	142	1.5
FALL 19X2							51	–	105	2.1
SPRING 19X3									51	

greater quantities in each succeeding season. Although the data for this analysis did not cover a sufficient span to show it, management felt that purchases per customer would level off after a certain number of consecutive seasons of repeat business.

The relative stability of these customer-retention and sales-development patterns over the historical period considered provided the basis for establishing a general relationship (model) which helped the sales manager develop a sales plan for a forthcoming selling season. The basis of this sales plan was (1) an estimate of the number of customers expected to be retained from the previous season, (2) calculation of the anticipated volume of purchases from retained customers, and (3) determination of the number of new customers required to attain a specified level of activity.

An example of the development of a sales plan for one class of customers (manufacturers) is shown in Exhibit 100 for the coming fall

Exhibit 100. Sales plan for fall 19X3 season.

ESTIMATED NUMBER OF CUSTOMERS TO BE RETAINED

	SPRING 19X3		FALL 19X3
AGE GROUP	NUMBER OF CUSTOMERS	RETENTION RATE	ESTIMATED NUMBER RETAINED
1	127	.33	42
2	49	.70	34
3	24	.74	18
4	30	.83	25
5+	32	.84	27
	262		146

DETERMINATION OF NUMBER OF NEW CUSTOMERS TO BE OBTAINED

	SPRING 19X3	FALL 19X3 – (ANTICIPATED)		
AGE GROUP	TOTAL QUANTITY PURCHASED	CUSTOMERS RETAINED	AVERAGE PURCHASES	TOTAL PURCHASES
1	6,477	42	102	4,284
2	5,145	34	158	5,372
3	3,408	18	185	3,330
4	6,240	25	250	6,250
5+	8,832	27	304	8,208
	30,102	146		27,444

ANTICIPATED VOLUME FROM RETAINED CUSTOMERS

	SPRING 19X3		FALL 19X3
AGE GROUP	AVERAGE QUANTITY PURCHASED	SALES RATE	ANTICIPATED AVERAGE PURCHASES
1	51	2.0	102
2	105	1.5	158
3	142	1.3	185
4	208	1.2	250
5+	276	1.1	304

NEW CUSTOMERS REQUIRED

$$= \frac{\text{Total Purchases (Spring 19X3)} - \text{Expected Purchases (Fall 19X3)}}{\text{Average Purchase for New Customer (Past 3 Seasons)}}$$

$$= \frac{30,102 - 27,444}{49} = 54$$

season. At the close of the preceding spring season, customers were classified by "age" (that is, by the number of consecutive seasons of repeat business up to and including the spring season). By applying the last five years' average customer retention rates, the number of customers expected to be retained in the fall season was established by age group. Similarly, the average quantity purchased by customers in each age category was determined at the close of the preceding spring season. The expected sales to these customers in the fall season was calculated by multiplying the actual sales in the spring season by the sales growth rate for each age group.

The sum of the product of the expected number of customers to be retained and the estimated average purchase for each customer, by age group, gave the total expected purchases for retained customers in the fall season of 27,444 units. As a minimum objective, management wanted to attain a sales level at least equivalent to that of the previous season. Assuming that new customers acquired in the fall season would purchase, on average, 49 units per customer (average of last three seasons), it was determined that 54 new customers must be sold to reach a sales level equivalent to the preceding spring season.

The resulting sales plan provided target figures for customers and quantities to be met in the new season. Obviously, the strategy for sales management was not limited to acquiring new customers; other factors also have an influence on aggregate sales in a given season. To illustrate, the use of the general model permitted determination of the sensitivity of new customer requirements to an improvement in the historical pattern for other customer behavior factors for the fall season, as depicted in Exhibit 101. The magnitude of the effect shown is for the fall season only, and in each case only a single factor is assumed to change at any one time. What action is required to achieve these changes is a question always confronting the marketing organization and involves consideration of product line, price, service, competition, and the like. The purpose of the analysis illustrated here is only to suggest where action could be most productive.

Whatever management decisions are made to align customer and quantity targets with a current sales program, control over the attainment of these targets is best realized through a system of information feedback. In this case study, management control was exercised through a system of call reports dealing with the allocation of sales effort to calls on new customers and with repeat calls on customers who had purchased in the previous season. These reports were consolidated weekly into a control report depicting progress toward meeting customer retention targets, progress toward attaining the target rate of acquisition

Exhibit 101. Sensitivity of new customer requirements to changes in other variables.

FACTOR	IMPROVEMENT OVER HISTORICAL PATTERN	RESULTING CHANGE IN NEW CUSTOMER REQUIREMENTS FALL 19X3
AVERAGE SALES TO NEW CUSTOMERS	Increase 10%	Reduces by 8%
	Increase 50%	Reduces by 33%
	Increase 100%	Reduces by 50%
CUSTOMER LOSS RATES	Decrease 10%	Reduces by 59%
	Decrease 50%	Reduces by 100%
SALES DEVELOPMENT RATES	Increase 10%	Reduces by 100%

Exhibit 102. Example of progress report on sales effort.

Season: FALL 19X3
Week ending: 9/25

AGE GROUP	SPRING 19X3 ACTUAL CUSTOMERS	ACTUAL VOLUME	CUSTOMERS-FALL 19X3 ANTICIPATED	ACTUAL	VOLUME-FALL 19X3 ANTICIPATED TOTAL	ANTICIPATED TO DATE	ACTUAL TO DATE
1	127	6,477	42	26	4,284	3,427	2,652
2	49	5,145	34	34	5,372	4,298	4,810
3	24	3,408	18	6	3,330	2,664	1,195
4	30	6,240	25	27	6,250	5,000	6,750
5+	32	8,832	27	20	8,208	6,634	5,766
NEW	—	—	61	48	2,989	2,391	2,120
	262	30,102	207	161	30,433	24,414	23,293

of new customers, and quantities sold to retained and new customers compared against the target levels to be attained (following a historical seasonal sales buildup). Exhibit 102 is an example of such a report.

This type of summary control report highlights the customer groups where the sales organization is failing to attain the season's target levels at a rate consistent with the seasonal buildup pattern (in this example 80% by the end of September). Redirection of the direct sales effort can be made accordingly. However, it should not be assumed that a single factor is controlling—namely, that the customer merely requires more direct calls. To support this report, the salesmen were required to indicate, where possible, the primary reason for loss of a customer and for purchases significantly below anticipated quantities. These reports permitted a more complete appraisal which included factors of price, product quality, delivery, and credit.

In summary, the structuring of selected data into a model reflecting the interrelationships of customer behavior (attrition, retention, and cumulative impact of repeat business) provided (1) greater understanding of how these key behavioral patterns influence the attainment of sales goals, (2) a basis for developing a sales plan at the beginning of a season which quantitatively specifies the degree to which selling effort should be allocated to different customers depending on whether they are new or old, manufacturer, jobber, or other classification, and (3) a basis for monitoring week-to-week progress toward the sales plan objectives and a means for reevaluating the impact of variances in one or more customer behavior factors from the general pattern reflected in the model.

The two case studies in this chapter show that the complex influences of marketing factors on overall company performance can be isolated through quantitative analysis and incorporated in a representation (model) of the particular problem area involved. Once this is achieved, the model provides a framework for gaining further insight into the interplay of the identified variables as a guide for marketing management in its decision-making process. Where a quantitative criterion of performance is defined by management, the model can be employed to give direction to the course of action to be taken, for example, the number of items to be carried or the number of new customers to be obtained. In both instances; the inclusion of the model as an integral part of the ongoing information system enabled marketing management to estimate future performance based on a carry-forward of historical patterns and on changes in assumptions and values of the variables. These estimates were also used effectively to monitor performance and to identify the requirement for additional investigation or revised action—on a true exception basis.

11

AN INTEGRATED
MARKETING INFORMATION SYSTEM
FOR A CONSUMER
PRODUCTS MANUFACTURER

This chapter presents a case study of the experiences of a major national food processing and distribution company which, over a three-year period, undertook the design and installation of a comprehensive marketing information system. The company's experience illustrates the practical application of many of the systems concepts described in earlier chapters as they relate to the marketing of consumer products. The importance of the clear identification of systems needs at the outset, the approach taken in organizing the systems effort, and the benefits which resulted from installation and operation of the system are stressed. While all the planning and control concepts, sample reports, and data are based on the actual system, they have been altered as required to protect the firm's identity.

THE MARKET

The Biscuit Company is a manufacturer and marketer of a broad line of high-volume, low-margin snack food products. A general definition of the company's particular market includes baking products, candy, chewing gum, and other snacks, all of which are, in turn, a part of the packaged foods business. These products are made available to the consumer through a wide variety of distribution channels, including chain and independent food stores, syndicate, drug, and variety stores, vending machine operations, and other retail outlets supplied by specialty wholesalers and jobbers. More than half the industry's sales are through food outlets; vending and other wholesalers account for most of the remainder. In recent years the industry has placed increasing emphasis on sales through supermarkets, supported by heavy expenditures in advertising and promotion.

The industry structure is such that about 75% of the market is now handled by a few major national firms, like Biscuit Company. The remainder of the market is fragmented among many small local and regional manufacturers. Their presence makes the market extremely price conscious and subject to wide geographic variations in the distribution of market share.

As an early entrant into the market, Biscuit Company developed an impressive historical sales record, achieving a 25% market share and enjoying a strong consumer franchise. Until recently, company sales increases kept pace with the general growth of retail packaged food sales. While the company has a broad product line, the major portion of its sales comes from a few key, well-established brands. Its sales force of 400 men services a stable group of 11,000 customers.

The company's organization, as depicted on the chart in Exhibit 103, is characteristic of firms operating in the consumer products market.

Business Problems

In recent years, Biscuit Company sales growth and market share had been declining. Competitors made substantial inroads into its markets with the introduction of a number of highly successful new products. Large national consumer goods companies moved aggressively into the snack market, often through the acquisition of local and regional manufacturers. Competition increased drastically, and competitors supported their new product introductions and other marketing programs with heavy expenditures in advertising and promotion. Their sales forces were comparable in size to, and sometimes more aggressive than, Biscuit Company's in servicing the same basic group of customers.

Biscuit Company's reaction to these changing market conditions and increased competition was a more aggressive marketing effort with higher levels of advertising and promotional expenditures, the introduction of a significant number of new products, and extensive changes

Exhibit 103. Biscuit Company organization chart.

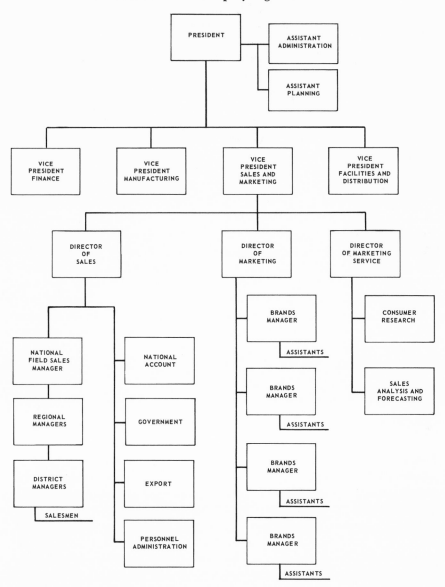

in the packaging and composition of existing products. In spite of these actions, market share and sales growth continued to decline, and profit levels were further eroded by high introduction costs for new products, higher advertising, increased promotional and selling expenses, and higher manufacturing and distribution costs.

The strain imposed on the organization by the new marketing programs was apparent. The expanded product line increased the difficulties of production scheduling—inventories of some products expanded while others were continuously short. Customer service suffered and dissatisfaction increased. The morale of the field sales force declined as salesmen felt subjected to pressure to get sales but were given little direction on how best to direct their efforts. In all, competitive pressures were causing a deterioration of communications and impairing the coordination of activities between functions.

The company's management recognized that the problems facing it could be dealt with effectively only by restructuring the entire planning and control process. It recognized, too, that while many of its problems were marketing related, a program for improvement had to be sufficiently comprehensive to deal with communications between marketing and all the major functions. However, high priority was placed on the development of an improved system for marketing planning and control, since Biscuit Company management considered the marketing operation the forefront of the company's planning and control process. In its view, effective, detailed marketing plans and forecasts were required for establishing production, inventory, distribution, and other operating plans and budgets. In addition, facilities planning and other capital expenditure programs required accurate long-term projections of the snack foods market and the company's position in it. Increasing competitive pressures and ever higher levels of marketing and selling expense added further weights to management's decision to begin its efforts with the development of a marketing information system.

DOCUMENTING THE EXISTING SYSTEMS

The first step undertaken in the development of Biscuit Company's marketing information system was the collection and documentation of all information sources and planning and control procedures used in the company's marketing activities. These included marketing planning (short- and long-range), sales and profitability reporting, product planning, marketing and sales operating policies and controls, advertising, market research, and marketing coordination with related areas such as customer service (warehousing and distribution), production, and data processing.

In each area reviewed, questions were asked in the following areas.

Planning. To what extent are plans developed in necessary detail, using prescribed formats with an adequate timetable and clear definitions of responsibility?

Information. Is information adequate as required for planning, analysis and reporting? Is the information base complete, correct, sufficiently detailed, and manageable? Are the individual data elements within the base consistent, comparable, integrated, and summarized?

Coordination. To what degree are information, plans, or reports generated in one area available as required for use in other areas?

Performance reporting. Do reports provide for the matching of actual performance results with plans and objectives according to area of responsibility?

Findings of the Documentation Phase

This documentation step provided more specific evidence of deficiency in the existing marketing information system. Much of the marketing operation exhibited a lack of specific performance goals, with unclear definition of responsibility and few uniform, comprehensive procedures applied to the marketing and sales planning process. It revealed the following.

1. While there were a number of areas within the marketing organization where sales, market, or competitive data existed, there were no procedures for collecting and organizing such information uniformly and regularly. Much time and effort was expended by managers in finding, assembling, and evaluating both internal and external data.

2. The marketing department made little effort to monitor the effects of volume and mix on profitability. Cost information relating to selling and marketing was maintained only in the most summarized forms.

3. Although sales statistics were available in some detail for individual sales areas by salesmen or customers, no effective means had been developed to accurately monitor productivity and profitability. Planning of the selling effort was not carried out regularly or consistently.

4. Although considerable amounts of money were spent on promotions and advertising, no formal procedures existed for planning such projects or for evaluating their effects. In most instances, the goal of a particular campaign or promotion was not clearly stated.

5. There was little coordination in the development and use of sales

forecasts between the marketing, warehousing and distribution, and production areas.

6. Comprehensive plans outlining both long- and short-term marketing strategy were often not developed in detail or with sufficient quantification to be used to monitor performance. In those areas where plans were developed, they were usually not consistently implemented or monitored through all levels of the organization.

At the conclusion of the documentation phase, a listing was prepared both of the deficiencies of the current system and of additional or improved information requirements. This served as a basis for the conceptual design of each of the major elements in the system.

OVERVIEW OF THE MARKETING SYSTEM

A conceptual overview of the system ultimately developed is shown in Exhibit 104. It indicates the four basic elements within the system which provide, in a continuing cycle, data collection, planning, development of performance goals, and the reporting of actual performance against plans.

The basic job of collecting and reporting internal sales statistics in a format and level of detail required by the market planner is fully computerized. Sales are identified by customer, trade class, product type, and pack type and are related to basic geographic units, including customers, counties, and standard metropolitan statistical areas (S.M.S.A.'s). External market and competitive information and data on distribution levels and salesmen's coverage of customers are also maintained in compatible levels of detail for comparison and combination with internal sales data. By establishing standardized evaluation procedures which identify problem accounts, areas, and products, the system generates a series of key reports for use by sales and marketing management in controlling current performance and revising marketing strategies. Some specific regular performance reports generated by the system include:

1. Sales volume performance against plan and potential.
2. Salesmen's productivity and coverage performance.
3. Advertising performance.
4. Promotion effectiveness.
5. Customer order pattern analysis.
6. Forecast effectiveness.
7. Budget performance and sales variance analysis.

Exhibit 104. Overview of Biscuit Company marketing information system.

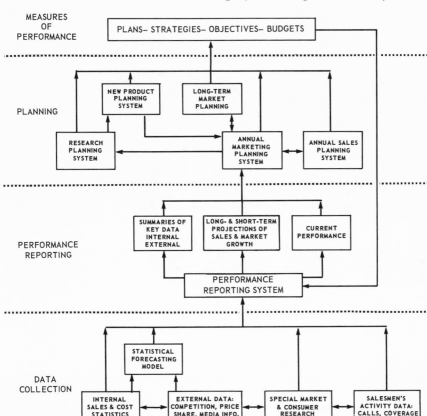

These and other performance reports incorporate both summary and exception techniques in the presentation of information. In addition to the regular reporting of performance against plans, the system, through the accessibility of the data base, allows preparation of summary reports which consolidate and integrate key performance statistics and for projections of future trends. Customer purchase profiles, product and brand profiles, competitive activity summaries, and market environment projections are prepared to provide a uniform base for the start of planning and, at the same time, relieve the market planner of the burden of data collection.

The heart of Biscuit Company's marketing information system is the planning process. In all, five individual planning subsystems are included:

Long-range planning.
New product planning.
Marketing planning.
Sales planning.
Research project planning.

Each of the planning subsystems is supported by information collection and performance reporting. Plans developed throughout the system include specific objectives, stated in quantified and measurable terms, as well as the primary and secondary strategies employed in achieving those objectives.

The integration of each of the basic planning and reporting elements of the system is best illustrated by the company's annual marketing planning and reporting calendar shown in Exhibit 105. The left side of the calendar indicates the timing required of each of the basic plans; the right side shows the frequency of review and evaluation.

For example, the five-year plan is prepared early in the first quarter, as soon as the results of the previous year's operation have been analyzed. The plan is reviewed and updated annually. A detailed annual marketing plan is prepared in the third quarter and is evaluated monthly as it is implemented together with sales plans, research plans, and budgets. Forecasts of performance are prepared at various points in the planning cycle, with a final month-by-month forecast of performance

Exhibit 105. Biscuit Company planning time frame.

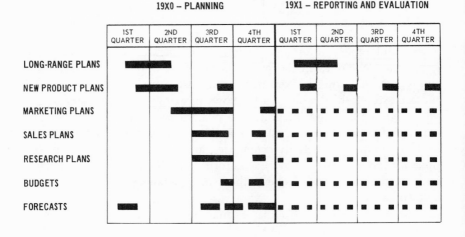

included as a part of the marketing plan. Once planned volumes have been established, forecasts are updated monthly.

In the following sections, each of the major planning systems components will be described more fully.

THE LONG-RANGE PLAN

The starting point for the development of the company's annual long-range plan is the preparation of a market projection for each of the company's major market segments. These projections are based on the application of statistical analysis and marketing judgment on data consolidated in an environmental summary. The summary includes the following.

1. *Consumer data:* current consumer demographics, including age, income, location, expenditure patterns, and projections of population trend.
2. *Trade data:* current and future trends in trade channel structure, distribution patterns, and government regulations.
3. *Economic data:* evaluations of inflationary trends, raw materials prices, and other general economic indicators.
4. *Competitive data:* summaries, by major competitor, of sales growth, market share, new product introductions, price changes, and marketing strategies.

In addition to market trends, the system also provides Biscuit Company market planners with an analysis of past company sales performance by major product line and a projection of future sales at current growth rates. With this information, the planners then evaluate current rates of growth and profit contribution against long-term company objectives and develop basic statements of marketing strategy for current products and, for new products, a schedule of volume and profit contribution to be generated. Plans also include estimated levels of selling and marketing expenses associated with various alternative strategies.

An example of the final summary output of the long-range marketing planning process is shown in Exhibit 106. The overall level of sales volume and gross contribution year by year is projected on the basis of current rates of growth for present products and anticipated volume from new products and new marketing and sales strategies. The costs associated with current and future marketing and selling programs are also indicated. Estimated increases in distribution and overhead expense are provided by financial management. The combination of projected

Exhibit 106. Long-range marketing plan summary ($ millions).

	CURRENT YEAR 1972	PLAN 1973	1974	1975	1976	1977	FIVE-YEAR INCREASE OVER CURRENT YEAR TOTAL
Sales							
Current rate	300.0	315.0	320.8	336.0	352.8	370.4	195.0
New strategies	–	13.0	20.1	25.2	32.2	34.8	125.3
New products	–	–	7.2	14.0	21.0	30.0	72.2
Subtotal	–	13.0	27.3	39.2	53.2	64.8	197.5
Total Sales	300.0	328.0	348.1	375.2	406.0	435.2	392.5
Gross Profit							
Current rate	100.0	105.0	107.0	112.0	117.0	123.5	64.5
New strategies	–	4.3	6.7	8.4	11.4	11.6	42.4
New products	–	–	3.6	7.0	10.5	15.0	36.1
Subtotal	–	4.3	10.3	15.4	21.9	26.6	78.5
Total Gross Profit	100.0	109.3	117.3	127.4	138.9	150.1	143.0
Marketing Expense							
Current rate	25.6	27.1	28.7	30.4	32.2	34.1	24.5
New products and strategies	–	3.5	4.1	5.0	6.5	7.0	26.1
Total Marketing Expense	25.6	30.6	32.8	35.4	38.7	41.1	50.6
Marketing Contribution							
Current rate	74.4	77.9	78.3	81.8	84.8	89.4	40.2
New products and strategies	–	.8	6.2	10.4	15.4	19.6	52.4
Total Marketing Contribution	74.4	78.7	84.5	92.2	100.2	109.0	92.6
Contribution Objective	74.4	78.0	84.5	91.6	99.3	107.8	89.2
Estimated Overhead	32.2	31.8	33.7	35.7	37.8	40.1	18.1
Pretax Profit Goal	42.2	46.2	50.8	55.9	61.5	67.7	71.1

increases in gross profit and marketing expense (defined as marketing contribution) is evaluated in terms of its ability to cover projected overhead costs and meet management's net pretax profit objectives. In the example, the long-range marketing plan calls for an increase above the current level of gross profit contribution (over the next five years) of $143.0 million with projected increases in marketing and selling expenses of $50.6 million. After marketing and selling expenses are deducted from the projected increased gross profit, the plan provides an increase in marketing contribution of $92.4 million, compared with management's contributing objective of $89.2 million. About 55% ($52.4 million) of increased marketing contribution is to be the result of planned new products and strategies while the remaining 45% ($40.0 million) is based on the current rate of growth for present products.

NEW PRODUCT PLANNING

The design of the new product planning segment of Biscuit Company's marketing information system includes provisions for evaluating new product ideas and controlling their cost from development through introduction. The initial phase of the new product development process is the formalization of new product objectives in the annual long-range plan. This includes a statement of the sales volume and profit contribution to be generated by new products and the basic criteria by which new products can be evaluated in comparison with key market segments, price ranges, and product types established on a basis compatible with existing products.

The second phase of the process includes search, identification, and screening. To centralize this process, the company established the position of new products manager under the director of marketing. This provides a focal point for submission of new product ideas from a wide number of sources, including salesmen, advertising agencies, other brand managers, competitive activity reports, and product and market research, as well as aggressive searching by the new product manager. New product ideas are screened by the new product manager who develops preliminary definitions of target markets, price levels, and volume levels for the products. Product ideas which are found to have potential are subjected to a more formal and intensive economic analysis, and basic product strategies, in terms of target markets and product characteristics (price, weight, packaging, and the like), are formulated. The new product manager, together with the research and development department, establishes budgets and project schedules for the new product development program. Each project is again evaluated at the prototype stage to determine, in more detail, the profit potential of the new product. At this point, a detailed manufacturing and marketing plan is developed which includes the specific selling and manufacturing requirements for the product. A program and budget for test marketing is also established. Upon approval of this phase, the product is made available in volume for store and market tests. Test market results are evaluated and, if appropriate, product and market strategies are modified. At this point, the product is ready for national introduction, and specific budgets, volume levels, and required sales force support are included in the annual marketing plan.

ANNUAL MARKET PLANNING

The system established by Biscuit Company for the development of detailed marketing plans and objectives is outlined in Exhibit 107. This flow chart illustrates the process by which the marketing managers, early in the second quarter of each year, analyze industry and environmental information and historical product performance to formulate detailed marketing strategies and goals for the coming year. It consists of six major phases.

1. Identification and collection of key marketing information to be used in the planning process.

2. Comparative evaluation of brand performance in terms of long-range plans and company objectives. These objectives are specified each year in a management letter prepared by the chief executive after review of the long-range plan.

3. Formulation of preliminary brand plans and budgets and sales volume, market share, distribution, and profit contribution levels together with a preliminary outline of major strategies.

4. Compilation of brand plans into a preliminary marketing plan for review by marketing and sales management. This review allows for a coordination of strategies between various brands and provides the basis for initiating the detailed planning of sales force activities.

5. Preparation of detailed statements of objectives and strategies for each brand, specifying the level of marketing activity and brand expenditures. Performance goals, including detailed monthly forecast of individual products within the brand, and schedules of major advertising and promotional programs are also established.

6. Submission of the marketing plan to top management. The acceptance of the marketing plan becomes the starting point for development of the company's annual profit plan, with anticipated levels of activity in all other areas responsive to sales levels specified in the marketing plan.

Since sales promotions represent a major category of marketing expense for Biscuit Company, it is of some value to look at the process by which promotions are planned and evaluated. The sales data base segregates promotional and nonpromotional sales at the customer level to provide a historical record of past performance. Such information is available to the brand manager on request. On the basis of his evaluation of the need for some promotional effort and his review of past promotion performance, the brand manager specifies alternative promotional strategies. A simple analysis provides information on the required breakeven volume for each alternative promotion. This volume level

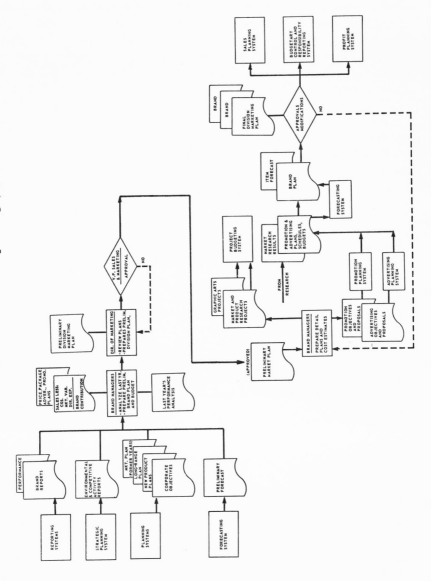

Exhibit 107. Annual market planning system.

Exhibit 108. Promotion planning and evaluation.

ITEM _274 -24 CT CHOC CK_   PROMOTION TYPE _Trade STD case allowance_

AREAS _National_

DATES _Nov. 1 - 30_

DEVELOPMENT AND GRAPHICS BUDGET _$12,000_

CURRENT FORECAST _40,000 CS_   PRICE _$10.00/CS_

BREAKEVEN SCHEDULE

	STD ALLOWANCE	REQUIRED FOR BREAKEVEN
1	1.25	24,800 cs
2	1.00	18,900 cs
3	.75	14,000 cs
4	.50	9,800 cs

ALTERNATIVE 2   PROMOTION ALLOWANCE ___$ 1/CS___

	CASES	DOLLARS	GROSS PROFIT CONTRIBUTIONS
TOTAL FORECAST SALES	70,000	$700,000	$262,500
FORECAST - UNPROMOTED	40,000		
GROSS GAIN FROM PROMOTION	25,000		
SALES LOSS - PRECEDING MONTH	–		
SALES LOSS-SUBSEQUENT MONTHS	5,000		
NET GAIN FROM PROMOTION	20,000	200,000	85,000
TOTAL VARIABLE PROMO. EXPENSE			70,000
TOTAL FIXED PROMO. EXPENSE			12,000
			2,000

ALTERNATIVE 3   PROMOTION ALLOWANCE ___$ .75/CS___

can be compared with the most recent forecast of sales for the period to determine the probable contribution of the promotion. A detailed promotional program (see, for example, Exhibit 108) is then prepared. It includes goals of the promotion, forecast sales without promotion, forecast sales with the promotion, subsequent loss prior to or after the promotion (based on past history), net volume gain from the promotion, cost of the promotion, and planned profit contribution. Actual costs and volume related to the promotion are then monitored against such plans, and the results of the comparison are provided to the brand manager.

Procedures have also been established for developing advertising plans on the same systematic basis and in the same level of detail. Sales, demographics, market, and competitive data on a regional basis, together with past advertising media performance, are available to brand managers in a summary report. This allows each manager to establish both the specific audience he is trying to reach and the amount of advertising money to be spent to best satisfy the requirements of a particular area.

SALES PLANNING SYSTEM

The sales volume and marketing contribution objectives, with their supporting advertising, pricing and promotion strategies, specified in the Biscuit Company marketing plan are translated into an action plan at the district and customer level through the sales planning system. The system provides sales management with the information needed to establish the most profitable and realistic level of selling activities for the year, including:

1. Assignment of sales volume objectives for each selling area and major account.
2. Determination of call and coverage standards for various types of current and prospective customers.
3. Establishment of required manpower levels needed to support volume and coverage goals.
4. Allocation of sales manpower to territories on the basis of maximizing potential profit contribution.
5. Assignment of specific promotion and merchandising goals best suited to particular groups of customers in coordination with scheduled advertising and promotion programs.

One of the first steps undertaken in the development of the Biscuit

Company sales planning system was the identification and collection of information on all accounts, both active and inactive, serviced by the company's sales force and then classified by potential sales volume.

An analysis of the distribution of sales volume among Biscuit Company customers showed the following when customers were ranked by size:

Percent of Customers	Cumulative Percent of Customers	Percent of Sales	Cumulative Percent of Sales
2	2	21	21
3	5	19	40
10	15	25	65
25	40	15	80
60	100	20	100

As would be expected, about 15%, or 1,700, customers were generating almost two-thirds of company sales volume. One result of the analysis was the application of a key customer concept in sales planning and customer performance reporting. Sales classification levels were established based on potential volume, and customer information was coded accordingly. Detailed information is maintained and monitored weekly for key customers, while less detail and lower reporting frequencies are provided for various other classes of customers.

In addition, statistics were collected on the type and number of calls made on the various classes of accounts, and these were analyzed in terms of frequency, cost, and resultant profit contribution level. Information was also collected on competitive coverage practices.

Sales coverage levels are established annually for various types of accounts to be serviced by Biscuit Company. After reviewing marketing program and historical company and competitive call performance, sales management establishes, on judgment, a minimum number of calls required for each class of customer within each distribution channel. For example, calls on chain buying offices are more frequent and require more time than those for vending operations. While it was not possible to measure the specific relationship between the level of sales effort and the resultant increases in sales, it was felt that sales management's experience and judgment were the best possible indicators of this relationship.

Once minimum coverage levels are developed for each type and class of account, they are combined with anticipated cost and sales potential estimates. A simple calculation is carried out to determine the cost of coverage for all account types and the anticipated contribution for each dollar of selling effort. An example of the output of this process is shown in Exhibit 109. In this particular case it was decided that account classes 7 and 8 had a level of contribution which would not support direct regular coverage. Sales plans for the year instead called for salesmen to direct large jobbing accounts to service the requirements of these smaller customers. While this plan eliminated the need for direct coverage of 6,000 accounts, it was anticipated that little,

Exhibit 109. Projected contribution and coverage levels, direct accounts 197X.

CLASS	ACCOUNT SIZE (SALES POTENTIAL)*	NUMBER OF ACCOUNTS	ESTIMATED CONTRIBUTION ($000)	ESTIMATED CONTRIBUTION PER ACCOUNT ($000)	PLANNED ANNUAL MINIMUM CALL HOURS HEAD-QUARTERS	RETAIL SUPPORT	TOTAL	ESTIMATED SELLING COST ($000)	CONTRIBUTION PER DOLLAR OF SELLING EFFORT
1	$250,000–	240	17,100	71.2	48,000	70,000	118,000	1,298	$13.17
2	120,000–250,000	350	16,300	46.8	35,000	85,000	120,000	1,320	12.35
3	75,000–120,000	710	18,900	26.6	35,500	124,000	159,500	1,754	10.07
4	40,000– 75,000	970	13,400	13.8	24,250	90,000	114,250	1,156	11.58
5	15,000– 40,000	1,400	8,900	6.4	35,000	55,000	90,000	1,100	8.09
6	7,500– 15,000	1,650	4,100	2.5	24,750	28,000	52,750	580	7.07
	SUBTOTAL	5,320	78,700	–	202,500	452,000	654,500	7,208	–
7 †	3,000– 7,500	1,800	3,400	1.8	31,600	31,000	62,600	688	4.93
8 †	below 3,000	4,200	2,900	.6	25,000	25,000	50,000	552	5.27
	TOTAL	11,320	85,000	–	259,100	508,000	767,100	8,448	–

*ACCOUNT SALES POTENTIAL ESTIMATE AT 25% MARKET SHARE.
†NOT INCLUDED FOR REGULAR COVERAGE.

Exhibit 110. Coverage and personnel summary.

DISTRICT 12 – BOSTON

ACCT. CLASS	# OF ACCTS.	CALLS LAST YEAR TOTAL	AV/MO/AC	STD. CALLS MO/AC	CALL OBJ. MO/AC	PLANNED CALLS	AVG. MAN-DAYS/CALL	MAN-DAYS REQUIRED
DIRECT								
1	10	240	2	3	2	240		
2	20	240	1	2	2	480		
4	30	270	0.8	1	1	360		
6	60	360	0.5	1	0.5	360		
TOTAL	120	1,110				1,440	.5	720
RETAIL								
A	80	480	0.5	0.5	0.5	480		
OTHER	100	300	0.3	0.5	0.5	600		
TOTAL	180	780				1,080	.2	504
TOTAL	300	1,890				2,520		1,224

STAFF

	ACTUAL		PLANNED	
	DIST. MGR.	1	DIST. MGR.	1
	SALESMEN	4	SALESMEN	5
	TOTAL	5	TOTAL	6

if any, sales volume would be lost. Small accounts would be retained as Biscuit Company customers through intensive jobber coverage.

Coverage levels, once established as national standards, are used to calculate manpower and staffing requirements for each sales district. A sample report (Exhibit 110) for District 12 shows the number of accounts by classification and the total number of calls made per month compared with both the national standard and the district's objective. Since available manpower or particular customer requirements differ for each district, the coverage objective may differ from the standard. The report also shows the total number of calls required for the district and the total estimate of required manpower. As indicated, one additional salesman would be assigned to the district.

Once overall manpower and coverage levels have been established, the sales planning system then establishes the specific sales volume objectives to be assigned to each district territory and major account. A principal input to this process is the marketing plan, which includes the overall national objectives for each brand.

Area objectives for new products are established on the basis of the new product introduction schedule included in the marketing plan. The introduction schedule identifies, for each target area, the anticipated new product sales volume levels—based primarily on the area's demographic characteristics, particularly age and income. Consideration is also given to the special support programs, such as advertising and promotion, planned for the new product in a given region.

Area objectives for current products are determined in two phases. First, each district is assigned a share of the marketing plan objective using an index of potential developed by the market research department which incorporates *Sales Management's* "Buying Power Index" and other key demographic factors. The second step is the adjustment of these preliminary area objectives on the basis of:

1. Account potential and unusual changes in account activities (such as opening or closing a major warehouse or strikes).
2. Anticipated sales coverage levels for each type of account.
3. Special promotion and advertising program scheduled for the area.
4. Planned changes in district staffing levels.
5. Area budgets.

Once area objectives are established, a special report for each major account is prepared including such information as historical sales performance, products not carried, estimated potential, and a recommended account objective. The district manager works with his salesmen to prepare a selling program for each account outlining plans for the year. The recommended objectives assigned to an account may be modified according to the salesman's knowledge of and plans for an account. However, the total district objective must remain unchanged. Each account objective in terms of sales volume, retail support, and product placement is fed back to the system and is used in generating periodic performance reports.

RESEARCH PLANNING

The research planning component of the Biscuit Company marketing information system is the process by which the market research department develops plans for undertaking and controlling in-depth research efforts required to satisfy the special information needs established in the marketing and sales plans. Research projects required to support the strategic information needs of the planning systems are of three types.

1. *Product research:* conducting internal product tests (such as taste tests and image tests) and external research (such as store tests).
2. *Market research:* collecting and analyzing specific performance data by trade channel or customer group and geographic or demographic segment.
3. *Competition activity research:* collecting and analyzing special competitive information, such as promotional policies, price changes, or new product activities.

All such efforts undertaken by the research department are organized on a project basis. A brand manager or sales manager requests a project, defining his requirements. The research department develops a specific proposal and budget for each project. Projects are then reviewed with the initiator, and a decision is made to have the work completed either by the Biscuit Company research department or by an outside research organization with the company's research personnel serving as coordinators. In both cases, all the costs of the project are charged to the originating responsibility area. Summary information for all research projects is coded and cross-referenced by product, type of application, area, and so on, and filed in a readily accessible form for use in the planning process.

SALES FORECASTING

A major undertaking during the installation of the system was the development of a statistical forecasting model. The company's forecasting system has two major components: a computerized statistical forecasting model, which produces a preliminary projection of sales volume by product for each month, and a formal review of the model forecast by marketing analysts and brand managers. The forecast system operates to produce a dynamic estimate of future sales since the model, in addition to projecting a historical trend, considers the estimated effects of planned promotions and price changes. The estimated effects of these variables are carefully reviewed and updated periodically to insure forecast accuracy.

The forecasts are monitored internally against a set of action limits, and marketing and selling programs are reviewed when a forecast of product performance is substantially out of line with original goals. This process gives Biscuit Company planners better advanced warning than simple comparisons of *actual* current results against plans, and at the same time it highlights only significant deviations from plan.

RESPONSIBILITY REPORTING

A basic approach in developing the performance reporting system was the integration of the responsibility reporting concept; that is, the organization of performance information to parallel the organizational structure. This concept assumes that specific individuals are held accountable for different elements of cost and revenue performance and that performance for each cost element is reported in detail only to the individuals who exercise control.

The integration of this concept into the marketing information system required Biscuit Company management to define, in much clearer terms than it had in the past, the responsibilities of various individuals in the marketing organization. This effort resulted in considerable revisions in job descriptions and eliminations of substantial functional overlaps. It also required a reclassification of expense data into controllable and noncontrollable categories.

A typical brand manager responsibility report is shown in Exhibit 111. The report shows brand manager responsibility, including sales and standard gross profit. Controllable marketing expenses are reported down to the level of brand contribution. The report also provides an explanation of the components of actual variance from planned per-

Exhibit 111. Biscuit Company sample district report.

RESP. AREA: Sweet Chips		
RESP. OF: J. R. Smith	**BISCUIT COMPANY**	
COST CENTER NO.: 0120		

| REPORT NAME: Brand Contribution |
| REPORT NO.: 12 A |
| MONTH: March 197X |

CURRENT MONTH			($ 000)	YEAR TO DATE		
BUDGET	ACTUAL	BETTER (WORSE) PLAN		BETTER (WORSE) PLAN	ACTUAL	BUDGET
2,415	2,604	189	GROSS SALES	733	6,014	5,281
1,634	1,690	56	STANDARD COST OF SALES	117	3,957	3,840
781	914	133	GROSS PROFIT	616	2,057	1,441
			DIRECT BRAND EXPENSES			
48	45	3	Consumer Promotion Expense	(4)	104	100
80	85	(5)	Trade Promotion Expense	(15)	200	185
100	102	(2)	Consumer Advertising Expense	10	290	300
15	15	-	Trade Advertising Expense	3	25	28
21	20	1	Graphics Expense	8	53	60
12	10	2	Market Research Expense	(5)	20	15
276	277	1	TOTAL DIRECT BRAND EXPENSE	(4)	692	688
505	637	132	BRAND CONTRIBUTION	612	1,365	763

	EXPLANATION OF VARIANCE	
28	Price	76
90	Volume	340
13	Mix	200
1	Spending	(4)
132	TOTAL VARIANCE	612
	KEY PERFORMANCE STATISTICS	
.21	Market Share	.25
.82	Retail Distribution Level	.86
.94	Wholesale Distribution Level	.89
	CONTRIBUTION PERCENT OF ANNUAL PLAN	24%
	MARKETING EXPENSE PERCENT OF ANNUAL PLAN	20%

formance in terms of price, volume, mix, and product spending. Other indicators of performance against marketing goals, such as distribution levels and market share, are reported under key performance statistics.

PERFORMANCE REPORTING

The interrelationship of various types of marketing information and their integration is outlined in Exhibit 112. It shows the various types of information maintained in the system and the specific performance reports generated from it.

Sales data and customer information are maintained at a low level of detail and can be combined with research data, cost information, media performance statistics (supplied by the company's advertising agency), and retail market data from syndicated services such as Sales Areas Marketing Inc. (SAMI) and Nielsen.

Exhibit 112. Performance reporting systems.

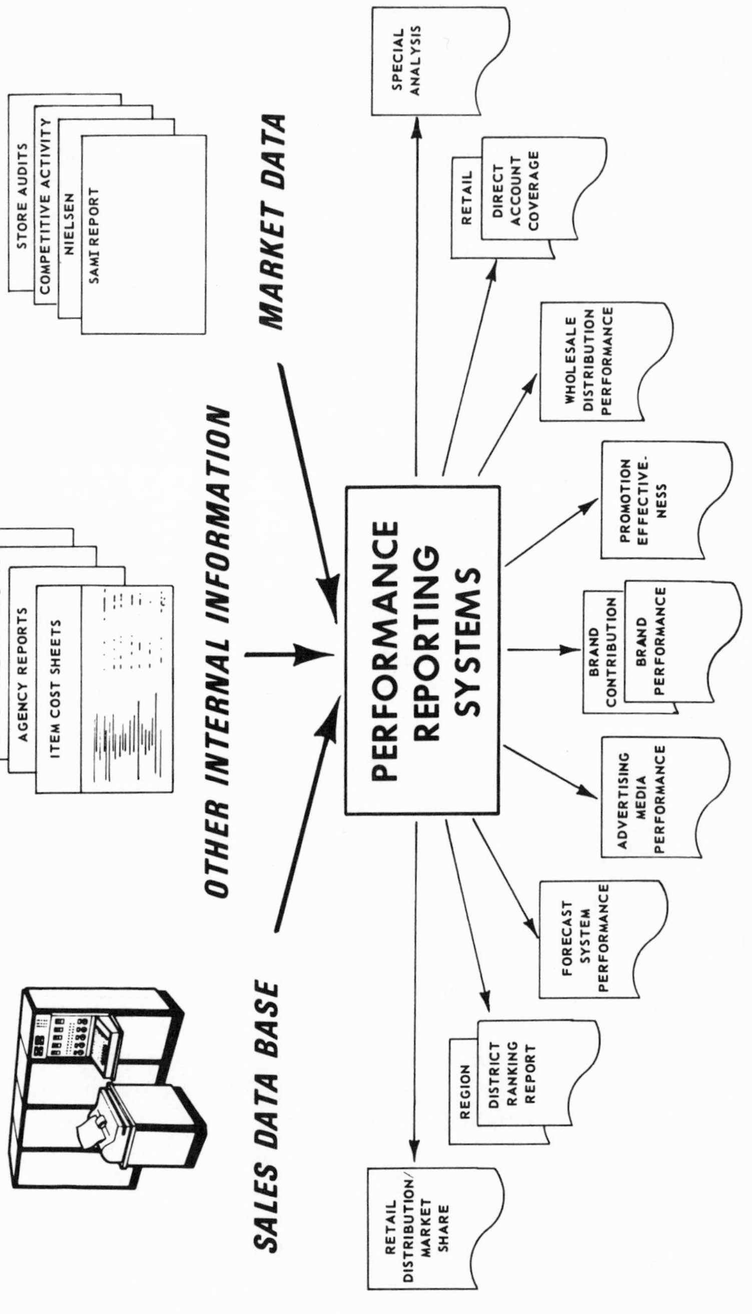

DATA PROCESSING

A considerable portion of the information included in the Biscuit Company system is maintained in a computerized data base. However, by using criteria of selectivity, such as key customer details and key product details, the amount of storage capacity required by the system is kept at a manageable level. A significant amount of work was required in establishing meaningful coding schemes for all the data entering the systems and a series of procedures for validation of new information.

Data is not maintained on-line; generally, updating of performance data is done weekly. This decision was reached in the course of designing the system after marketing management recognized that few, if any, of the corrective marketing actions available could be undertaken with less than a few weeks lead time. Day-to-day fluctuations in sales performance are not monitored by the system since they are too erratic to be meaningful.

The company's system uses both internal data processing and time-shared facilities. The bulk of the system, the data base, performance and responsibility reports, and the forecasting model are operated internally, while the manpower planning model, sales volume objective allocation model, and promotion breakeven analysis model use an outside time-sharing service.

RELATION TO OTHER AREAS

Biscuit Company's marketing information system cannot be viewed solely in terms of its service to the marketing operation. It is directly related to the planning and performance of other areas of the company. For example:

1. The overall level of sales volume and gross profit used in the company's profit plan is established by the marketing plan.
2. The marketing forecasts, broken down by product and area, are used to establish factory and warehouse inventory levels.
3. The new product planning system provides the primary control over the research and development effort of the basic research group.
4. Customer profit contribution information is used to establish customer service levels for inventory and distribution planning.
5. Facilities expansion plans and other capital projects are guided by the sales levels established in the long-range marketing plan.

In addition to these, the basic concept of responsibility reporting established in the marketing information system was applied to all areas of the company.

ORGANIZING THE SYSTEMS EFFORTS

The total magnitude of the effort required in analyzing the company's marketing information needs and in designing and installing an effective, broadly accepted system was difficult to gauge at the outset. It was clearly recognized, however, that it would be a major effort involving several man-years of both systems and marketing personnel time. In addition, it would require coordination among different groups within marketing and also between marketing and other areas of operation.

Accordingly, senior management took four steps which proved critical to the project's ultimate success. First, a steering committee was established. It was composed of senior management personnel (division heads or deputies) representing finance, data processing, marketing, production, and distribution under the chairmanship of the company's chief financial officer, reporting to the president.

Next, a marketing task force was organized under the guidance of the steering committee to carry out the project. The task force was composed of a basic complement of two full-time analysts, one with marketing background and the other with systems and data processing experience. Part-time assistance was also provided as needed by cost accounting, production planning, and other specialists. During the implementation phase, full-time programming support was added.

The responsibility for success of the project and for direct supervision of the marketing information systems task force was assigned to the director of marketing services, a position reporting to the vice president for sales and marketing. This assignment clearly demonstrated the priority of the project.

Finally, an outside consulting organization was engaged to give guidance and also to provide supplementary manpower at critical stages in the project.

The primary purpose of the steering committee was to assure complete coordination among all areas of the company. It assisted in identifying major operating problems, in establishing priorities and timetables for systems development, and in identifying individuals for assignment to the task force in conjunction with specific projects.

It was also the steering committee's function to oversee progress and to provide management approval for each major element in the systems design. It performed a similar guiding function with respect to other task forces which were working—in part concurrently—on the development of improved information controls and systems in the areas of accounting, inventory control, and distribution.

Work Program

A key element in the administration and control of the marketing information systems task force was a work program whose preparation constituted its first major task. The work program specifies in some detail each step to be performed, including scheduled start and completion dates and identification of individual task force members responsible for that particular step. Time estimates for each task were provided by the task force member most familiar with the particular area. Exhibit 113 illustrates the format of this work program, showing the work assigned to two task force members in the documentation of the existing information system.

While the work program controlled overall progress during the design and installation of the system, it was recognized early that a continuing effort would be required for the maintenance, refinement, and improvement of the system once it became operative. Consequently, the position of manager of marketing information systems was established, reporting to the director of marketing services, with responsibility for continuing system maintenance and development. Considerable thought was given to organizational location, and it was concluded that it was best placed within the marketing area, with the explicit requirement to coordinate closely with the corporate systems and data processing departments. This arrangement appeared best because much of the system is geared to facilitating the planning carried out within the marketing areas and must respond quickly to changing information needs in support of the planning process.

COSTS AND BENEFITS

The total effort required to develop the system and make it operational ultimately represented approximately 3,600 man-days of work on the part of the marketing information systems task force and the company's programming staff. Approximately 30% of this effort represents the design phase, including definition of all reporting requirements, input requirements, and general processing logic. The remaining 70% of the effort applied to installation, testing, and conversion of the system and, most importantly, to the training of sales and marketing personnel in

Exhibit 113. Marketing information system, task force work program.

DESCRIPTION	RESPONSIBILITY OF	MAN-DAYS			DATES		MAN-DAYS		DATES	
		TOTAL	Jones	Smith	START	FINISH	Jones	Smith	START	FINISH

A. Document current information systems
  1. Obtain copies of all reports, source documents, manuals, procedures
  2. Document information flow
    a. Determine sources for all data items
    b. Determine purpose and responsibility for preparing each document noting:
      Level of Detail
      Decisions Made/Information Purposes
      Manipulations Performed
    c. Data Classification
    d. Geographic area, brand, salesman, trade channel, etc.
    e. Measures of Performance
  3. Note all files, frequency of reports, distribution, timeliness, etc.
  4. Interview individuals for additional information requirements on an "as needed" basis
	JONES SMITH	26	9	17	4/28	5/19	9	17	4/28	5/21

B. Develop narratives for manual & EDP elements in each system & area 1. Indicate similarities, if any, between reports & operations, & cross-reference like items. If same function is performed in several locations, see that all differences are reconciled.		9	4	5	5/12	5/26	5	5	5/12	5/24

its use. Throughout the project, strong reliance was placed on establishing user orientation. Each proposed report and design concept was reviewed and approved by operating managers at the appropriate stage of development. While this approach placed a burden on the time of operating personnel, it proved highly effective in getting sales and marketing people to accept the system more readily and made the job of training them in the use of the system significantly easier.

Considerable thought was given at the outset, and at various stages in the course of this project, to the evaluation of its potential benefits and to assuring that effort and expense applied were clearly justified. It was concluded that these benefits could be found in six areas (see below). The dollar magnitude of benefits is, of course, extremely difficult to establish. In this case, rough order of magnitude figures were developed along the following lines.

1. *Sales coverage*. By identifying the potential associated with different individual accounts or categories of accounts, and concentrating sales coverage appropriately on those with higher potential, it was estimated that an additional sales volume representing $3 million per year in contribution to profit (after selling and marketing expense) could be generated. District sales objectives were set so as to call for increases of only about 20% of this added potential, and these were consistently met and exceeded.

2. *Sales effort*. By reducing the application of sales effort on marginal or unproductive accounts, a potential saving in selling expense within the first year of operation of over $400,000 was identified.

3. *Promotion effort*. Through improved procedures for promotion planning and detailed evaluation and analysis of trade and consumer promotions, a number of promotional programs were eliminated with no observable impact on the sales growth of the brands affected. In the first year of operation, this represented savings estimated at $350,000.

4. *Advertising effort*. Similar improvements in the effective allocation of advertising expenditures were identified, but it was not possible to associate a specific dollar figure with these.

5. *Forecasting and inventory control*. Through an improved forecasting system and its integration with production planning and inventory control procedures, substantial reductions were achieved in plant and warehouse inventories. The estimate of savings in carrying costs on an annual basis is $325,000.

6. *Clerical and analytical effort*. While the information system led to some increases in data processing costs, these were offset by reductions in clerical and managerial time in data collection and preparation of manual reports and analyses.

The company's objective in undertaking this systems development work was primarily one of achieving improvements in its marketing operations. It was concluded that these were achieved beyond initial expectations, and that the total costs of systems development and implementation were easily recovered in a half year of operations once the system became fully effective. Of even greater importance was the system's capacity to respond quickly and effectively to continuing changes in highly competitive markets and to set realizable objectives of increased share within these markets.

12

AN INTEGRATED
MARKETING INFORMATION SYSTEM
FOR AN INDUSTRIAL
PRODUCTS MANUFACTURER

This chapter describes a case study of the experience of a manufacturer of industrial products which, over a period of two years, developed and installed an integrated system to serve the company's planning and reporting requirements in support of its marketing activities. The names of the company, its products, and its customers, as well as some of the numerical information, have been altered to protect the company's identity.

COMPANY BACKGROUND

Dobbs manufactures and sells industrial refractories for use in the steel, aluminum, rubber, and glass industries; some 20% of its sales go to American Processing, the parent company, which also serves some of these same customer industries. The Dobbs Division has a net sales volume of $20 million and after-tax profits of $650,000; its growth rate has been slight over some three years, while the parent company's sales have been growing 10% per year with substantially higher growth in profits.

The organizational structure of the Dobbs Division marketing functions is shown in Exhibit 114. The company sales force serves customers

Exhibit 114. Organizational structure, Dobbs Division.

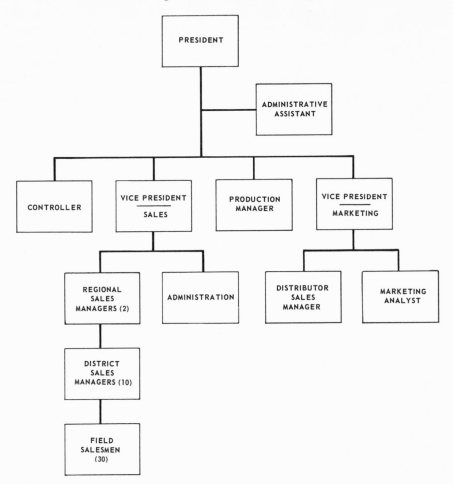

in the eastern two-thirds of the United States, while the remainder of the country is handled by distributors. Dobbs operates three plants and six warehouses. There are approximately 2,000 direct customers (not including 70 distributors) of which 200 account for 70% of the total sales volume.

Each of 40 salesmen and district managers handles an average of five major customers, each of which they normally call on once in a week. In most of the major customer operations, several departments must be covered. The salesmen are technically trained and are expected to spend time with plant foremen and department supervisors as well as with purchasing agents. Because of the highly technical nature of the product line and the customers' processes, salesmen are frequently involved in service problems. They are able to call on a small group of home office customer service personnel for help where necessary.

General product acceptability, pricing, and delivery terms are negotiated with customer purchasing departments; Dobbs salesmen have some discretion in setting final prices. Actual week-to-week ordering is normally done by plant foremen, usually in truckload quantities. Both the price and performance of Dobbs products are believed to be on par with those of its major competitors.

While the division has had no major new product introduction of its own during the past three years, it has been able to match product modifications introduced by competitors on short notice. The particular segment of the industry in which Dobbs operates has not been generally characterized by major product innovation.

START OF THE SYSTEMS EFFORT

The president of Dobbs Division had passed the earlier years of his professional career in the sales and marketing operations of a major chemical company, through whose ranks he had risen to the vice presidential level. He viewed complete and up-to-date knowledge of customer operations and close contact with both purchasing and engineering personnel of customer organizations as critical in light of the dispersion of specifying authority in industrial purchasing organizations, and of the technical character of selling operations.

He arrived at his decision to overhaul the Dobbs Division marketing information system soon after assuming the presidency. At Dobbs, he found information on markets, customer operations, and personnel largely incomplete, unorganized, and, to a substantial degree, unrecorded. Not only customer information but also internal company reports were deficient in many significant areas, particularly in regard to background information and specific costs of doing business with individual customers on individual products or product lines. Available information was not manageable because summaries of sales and expense data necessary for periodic analysis were not regularly or consistently prepared.

DEFINITION OF MARKETING APPROACH

Dobbs Division's eventual success in implementing the system described here was to a large degree the result of recognizing at the outset that information needs are closely tied to the marketing approach the division wished to take. Some care was taken to define this approach, with the understanding that this initial, somewhat idealized definition would be modified as development progressed. The following principal elements were established at the start of the marketing information systems project.

1. *Establish the appropriate method of providing sales coverage by area or region.* Depending on the size and location of potential customers and their concentration within an area, the costs of direct selling versus use of distributors or sales representatives need to be periodically weighed against the potential sales volume.

2. *Differentiate between major and minor customers* in areas served by company sales personnel. A limited number of customers in each territory, and in total, represent the major portion of sales, and the attention and effort of the company sales force should be focused on them. For smaller accounts a minimum level of selling effort must be established.

3. *Identify key and major accounts, markets, or industries,* not only on the basis of sales they produce currently but also on their potential over three to five years. Potential should be defined in terms of products currently bought as well as other products the division makes or sells, but which the particular customer is not buying currently.

4. *Set a range of objectives for two to three years for each major customer.* The base or lower end of the range represents, essentially, maintenance of the division's present share of his business. The upper end of the range represents a development objective for expansion of sales on products he already buys or introduction of other products currently in the line which he uses but buys from others.

5. *Identify specific sales programs needed to achieve maintenance objectives and then development objectives.* Estimate the man-days required by field sales and supervisory personnel for sales planning and for sales calls. Examine sales assignments and balance out the load by territory and the equity of individual salesman's compensation.

6. *Provide a follow-up monitoring procedure* which will regularly report performance relative to objectives using summary and exception reporting principles.

In addition to meeting the information needs for the management of selling operations, the needs for product line management information were also identified (leaving aside technological aspects of product and process performance, which are outside the scope of this description). Product management requirements include (1) definition of markets in terms of groups of industries, customers, and product categories within which the company is currently operating or for which it has technological capability and (2) collection of statistics on the total usage and company sales of specific products in specific markets (customer industries or geographic areas). Where market statistics come from different sources of varying reliability, there must be a means of comparing and reconciling different estimates; both historical data and future projections are needed.

This information is necessary to identify weaknesses or opportunities for increased market penetration in specific product categories, user industry categories, or geographic areas. These may then lead to improvement in product, pricing, or customer service efforts or in redirection of sales operations through the existing sales force or through assignment of specialists to carry out specific developmental objectives. Here the product line area merges with sales planning and control.

ELEMENTS OF THE MARKETING INFORMATION SYSTEM

The marketing information system eventually implemented comprises a series of planning procedures through which the company explores and tests alternative lines of action and establishes objectives, and implements a series of reporting and monitoring systems which track performance relative to these objectives. The four principal planning systems are as follows.

1. *The long-range planning system* covers a span of five years, with emphasis on the first three years and complete detail on the first year. The first-year section represents the basic marketing plan; it defines product development and introduction to be carried out by market segment, specifies required changes in method of sales coverage or alignment of sales assignments, and projects the company's growth objectives for sales volume, market share, and earnings.

2. *The annual sales plan* covers both sales activity and sales volume objectives for major customers individually and for territories.

3. *The order backlog and inventory plan* is keyed to sales objectives and updated through a monthly forecasting procedure. This provides the basis for coordinating the planning of sales, manufacturing activities, and cash requirements.

4. *The budgetary plan* is keyed to established profit objectives and covers all elements of sales and marketing expense, including price adjustments, freight allowances, advertising, promotion, and marketing overheads.

On the performance side, a corresponding set of monitoring reports compares actual performance with objectives in the areas of product and market segment sales and profitability, sales territory and major customer sales performance and sales activity, shipment, back-order performance, and inventory turnover, and an analysis of expense against budgets, with an explanation of variances.

The following sections describe only the major distinctive features of this system, since many of the reports are, of course, quite conventional.

OVERVIEW OF THE SYSTEM

An overview of the marketing information system is illustrated in Exhibit 115. It shows the relationship between the planning and reporting systems. The planning systems derive their basic input from three primary sources.

1. The company's sales, expense, and profit history compiled from internal accounting records for individual products, customers, or areas and coded to facilitate analysis and summarization of related items and customer groupings.

2. Comprehensive data on individual major customers, collected by customer profiles prepared by sales personnel, with the help of marketing analysts. These profiles cover company data, but, more importantly, provide background information about the customer's operations and personnel and his total needs in quantitative form in areas of interest to the division. Also covered are competitive manufacturers with whom he does business, and competitive factors which influence his buying decision.

3. Market and industry statistics from published sources (government, trade associations, trade publications) or special research studies.

Because these data come from different sources, and are often incomplete, they are validated to the degree feasible before they enter the planning process. If this were not done, and different elements of the marketing plans were based on different source data, the result would be inconsistent and consequently confusing. Complete validation is, of course, not always possible, but a procedure is provided which is partly mechanical (preparing subtotals or ratios which can be matched or compared) and partly judgmental. In some cases, one set of numbers can be adjusted to relate logically to another—internal sales statistics normally being the fixed reference point. Where discrepancies are large and no reasonable method of reconciliation is available, the probable

Exhibit 115. Overview of marketing information system, Dobbs Division.

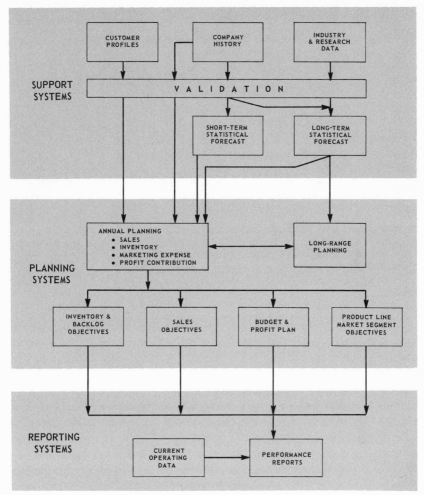

range of error is estimated, and this estimate is made part of subsequent planning schedules. The emphasis on validation of planning data from different sources is a distinctive feature of the Dobbs marketing information system.

In addition to the validation procedures, the planning systems are supported by a long-range (up to five years, by year) and a short-range (up to 18 months, by month) forecasting system. Each of the two forecasting procedures is again partly mechanical—involving statistical projection methods—and partly judgmental. The forecasts produced by the two procedures are periodically reconciled by comparison of the one-year forecasts with which they must agree.

CUSTOMER PROFILES

Because the customer profile is a key element in the company's marketing approach, it will be given special attention here. The customer profile sheets illustrated in Exhibits 116 and 117 relate to a line of refractories supplied in quantity to basic steel producers. A similar format applies to other customer categories. In this instance, an individual steel mill represents not a single customer but several since each of some ten departments in the mill may use Dobbs products and order them independently. The illustration covers information that was collected for the blast furnace department of American Steel's South Chicago plant.

The profile describes the facilities in use or under construction and provides basic operating statistics which define the tonnage of steel processed. It identifies the operations where company products are used or may be used. The second sheet of the profile, Exhibit 116, lists data obtained from the company's technical staff or estimated by the salesman regarding the quantity by department of each refractory required per ton of steel. Subsequent sections present estimates of current and projected steel tonnage levels and summaries of planned changes in facilities or technology, to the extent the salesman can learn about these. A final section lists major competitors and their estimated shares for each product category.

The preparation of the customer profile in the formal manner required, is, without doubt, a time-consuming job. The president and his sales management took the position, however, that the information called for in the profiles is essential to the salesman's proper performance, that the effort applied in obtaining it will also serve to put him in closer contact with customer personnel who have specifying influence, and that the effort is feasible since the average salesman deals with only five major customers for whom this analysis will be required. Obviously, not all the information can be readily obtained in every instance, and sales personnel are cautioned not to press for information where the customer resists. As a practical matter, however, most of the information was normally known to the salesman or was willingly supplied by the customer.

Exhibit 116. Example of customer profile.

	PAGE 1
CUSTOMER PROFILE	

CUSTOMER NAME *American Steel* LOCATION *South Chicago* DEPT. *Blast Furnace*
PERSONS CONTACTED *Charles Jones (Supervisor), Frank Brown (Purchasing Agent)* DATE PREPARED *5/6/7X*
NUMBER AND DIAMETER OF FURNACES *Two (#11, #12) #11-30' #12- 29'2" at Bosh*
CAST CYCLE *#11-8.16, #12-7.12* HRS.   CAST SIZE *#11-510, #12-495* TONS
19X9 PRODUCTION *#11-349-7 #12-315-3* 000 TONS; 19X0 PLANS *#11-361-0, #12-328-0* 000 TONS 19X1 FORECAST
#11-360-0, #12-330-0 000 TONS

PRODUCT USAGE

ROW	PRODUCT LINE	HEARTH	HEARTH WALLS	BOSH	STACK	STOVES	TRANSFER LADLES
1	SELAG I	#11,#12	#11,#12	#11,#12			
13	FLUXITE						#11,#12

TRANSFER LADLE TYPE *Pugh* LADLE LIFE *150,000* TONS HAULED
LADLE MAINTENANCE DESCRIPTION: *Scanned by crew after each heat; reviewed by foreman weekly; minor maintenance every 100 casts; major overhaul at 600 casts*
INSTALLATION _____ LB./TON PRODUCED; MAINTENANCE *.0012* LB./TON PRODUCED; TOTAL *.0124* LB./TON
COMMENTS (ANTICIPATED PRACTICE CHANGES THROUGH 19X5): *Will phase Blast Furnace #12 (built 1941) out in 19X3. Replacement not determined.*
COMPETITORS *Maxwell Chemical, Inter-American;*
REASONS *Nearby warehouse and faster delivery*

Exhibit 117. Example of customer profile, department detail.

DEPARTMENT *Blast Furnace*	PAGE 2

ROW	PRODUCT	$ OF CHEMICALS USED PER TON PRODUCED
1	SELAG I	.0040
2	SELAG – CASTABLE	
3	CLAY CASTABLE	.0387
4	H. T. FIRE CLAY – BRICK	.0775
39	HIGH ALUMINA	
	DEPARTMENT TOTAL REFRACTORIES CONSUMPTION *.0124* $/TON	

MARKET SHARE ANALYSIS

An important byproduct of the customer profile system is the ability to prepare market share analyses on individual customers. The resulting reports are used in long-range planning and by salesmen in preparing their territory plans. Exhibit 118 shows an example of a market share report.

The mechanics of developing market share information in this degree of detail are straightforward. For major customers, the customer profile form calls for estimated usage of Dobbs product lines by customer department. Actual sales of individual product lines to each customer by Dobbs are posted from internal sales reports. These product sales are allocated by the salesman to the individual department or operation. This procedure has proven particularly useful in identifying weak spots in sales performance and in correcting these through assignment of technical specialists.

LONG-RANGE PLANNING SYSTEM

The long-range marketing planning system developed for the division is especially concerned with those environmental factors which are beyond the immediate control of the marketing and sales department. The long-range marketing plan focuses on the organization of the division, the resources available for its use, the economic environment in which the division exists, and the products manufactured and sold by it as they relate to the objectives of the company as a whole.

An important element of the long-range planning system is the use of industry input-output analysis. Many industrial companies have used the tables prepared by the Department of Commerce, which group the economy into 370 industries. Dobbs, however, found it necessary to make a special study of census data, breaking the two industry classifications in which the division participates into 30 product lines, not all of which the division now sells. Similarly, the six customer industries identified in the Commerce Department input-output tables were subdivided into 20. A portion of the Dobbs input-output table is given in Exhibit 119. The coefficients of this table are developed from two sources: the customer profiles and independent data provided by the research and engineering staff based on laboratory and pilot tests.

The long-range planning system uses one input-output table for the current year and another, modified, input-output table for five years in the future. The differences in the coefficients between the tables represent expected technological changes. For some customer industries, the

Exhibit 118. Example of market share reporting.

CUSTOMER NAME *American Steel*   LOCATION *South Chicago*

ACTUAL SALES/ESTIMATED USAGE

PRODUCT LINE	OPEN HEARTH FURNACE		SOAKING PIT		REHEAT FURNACE		IRON LADLES AND MIXERS		TOTAL FOR PRODUCT LINE	
	00 LBS.	SHARE	00 LBS.	SHARE	00 LBS.	SHARE	00 LBS.	SHARE	00 LBS.	SHARE
SELAG I							30-30	100%	30-30	100%
SELAG – CASTABLE			91-130	70%	12-26	46%			103-156	66%
TOTAL SELAG			91-130	70%	22-36	61%	30-30	100%	143-195	78%
CLAYS	3-48	6%							3-48	6%
TOTAL CLAYS	3-48	6%							3-48	6%
TOTAL REFRACTORIES	3-48	6%	91-130	70%	22-36	61%	30-30	100%	146-243	60%

Exhibit 119. Example of input-output table.

REFRACTORIES MARKETS

(LBS. OF REFRACTORIES PER UNIT OF CUSTOMER INDUSTRY OUTPUT)

PRODUCT LINE	BLAST FURNACES	OPEN HEARTH	ELECTRIC	CEMENT
SELAG I	1.56	1.00	2.13	.84
SELAG – CASTABLE	1.73	1.21	2.56	.65
CLAYS	.79	.63	—	.17
HIGH ALUMINA	.07	.03	.11	.01

coefficients may change significantly, while for others, where little technological change is occurring, the coefficients remain unchanged.

Using customer industry forecasts for the next five years, an estimate is made of the total market for each product line by customer industry. This information guides the long-range capital budgeting effort and is of particular use for planning research and development efforts and new product development.

When completed, the long-range marketing plan includes the following.

1. A discussion of the nature of the marketplace and the marketing trends during the next five years, with emphasis on those elements having a critical bearing on the division's marketing methods.

2. Total market potential estimates for present and planned product

lines with detailed estimates for market segments of significance.

3. A forecast of market share by major competitor.

4. The nature of the product:

    a. Discussion of the nature of the product lines which the division plans to market for the next five years.

    b. Identification of customer services which may be required or are to be provided as normal supporting effort.

5. A quantitative statement of objectives in terms of growth rate percentages, profit objective percentages, and number of customers.

6. A statement of the assumptions on which the marketing and sales programs are based (these assumptions relate principally to elements beyond the control of marketing and sales management).

7. Forecasts of total sales supported by detailed estimates for each product line of significant size.

8. Principal marketing plans and strategies which will be used in meeting the objectives of the division.

9. A summary of all manpower requirements for the next five years. This summary, by program and type of personnel, is used for recruiting, training and budgeting.

10. A discussion and charts of the organization for the next five years.

ANNUAL PLANNING SYSTEM

The annual planning system at Dobbs has as primary inputs the division long-range plan, including a new product plan, the customer profiles, historical sales information, and product profitability information. The output is an annual marketing and sales plan, with associated forecasts and objectives, which in turn are input for the profit plan and the performance reporting system. As a first step, the input-output table prepared in the long-range plan is used, with economic forecasts for customer industries and technological trends, to develop an estimate of total industry sales. A statistical forecast of division sales is made at the same time. These data are compared with customer profile summary information in arriving at overall objectives, which are then translated into estimates of expected division sales by product line, customer industry, and region. Strategic objectives such as the addition of new distributors are also outlined at this time.

The final step is the development of territory plans, illustrated in Exhibit 120. Initial regional and territory objectives for each major line as established in the marketing plan are forwarded to all salesmen and district managers, who are responsible for developing specific per-

Exhibit 120. Annual planning system, territory plan.

PRODUCT LINE ___Clays___   TERRITORY __Detroit__   OBJECTIVE _286,600_ LBS.

ACCOUNT	TOTAL DOBBS $ SALES	SALES OF THIS LINE (lbs.)	ESTIMATED TOTAL USAGE—19X1 (lbs.)	PLANNED SALES (lbs.)
PRESENT CUSTOMERS – LINE				
Althouse Furnace	80,900	37,100	131,000	40,500
Toro Manufacturing	45,000	28,100	99,100	30,800
J. & L.	123,700	12,500	60,500	12,600
-				
-				
	2,334,000	203,000	1,007,500	227,800
PRESENT CUSTOMERS – COMPANY				
Detroit Steel	76,800	-	87,600	
Blake & Stone	16,900		113,000	
-				
-				
	1,779,800	-0-	565,500	56,600
POTENTIAL CUSTOMERS				
Garden Manufacturing	-	-	17,600	
Mercury Corporation	-	-	4,700	
-				
-				
	-0-	-0-	73,700	2,200
TOTAL				286,600

formance objectives. Each salesman receives a territory planning form which lists the past year's actual Dobbs sales of each product line, by customer, sorted into three categories: (1) customers currently buying the product line from Dobbs, (2) customers buying some Dobbs product but not buying the particular line, and (3) customers in the area who use the product but buy nothing from Dobbs.

The salesman establishes a specific objective for each of these customers based on his personal knowledge of its operation and his estimated success in selling. Objectives established for each product line are aggregated by customer and included in the performance reporting system. The salesman then receives a monthly series of reports by customer indicating his performance against objective in each line.

SHORT-TERM FORECASTING SYSTEM

The short-term forecasting system provides monthly updating of product demand forecasts for use in inventory control and production planning. Initial overall inventory plans, production plans, and raw materials purchase requirements are computed from the annual marketing plan and its sales objectives. The short-term forecasting system is used to adjust these base plans as necessary.

The mechanics of the system are relatively simple. They consist of a series of exponential smoothing forecasting models on a time-sharing computer. The major problems the division had in defining the forecasting system were (1) determining the frequency of forecasts, (2) determining the number of periods into the future to forecast, and (3) determining the degree of detail to which products should be forecast.

At Dobbs, a forecast is prepared quarterly for each product group for twelve months into the future. These annual product forecasts are reviewed and revised semiannually, as are all of the marketing plans.

Additionally, forecasts for one quarter into the future are prepared for each product within the product group for inventory and production planning. Quarterly product forecasts are aggregated to the product group and monitored against the annual plan. When major discrepancies occur, they are brought to the attention of marketing management, where the differences are reconciled or plans are modified as warranted by market conditions.

PRODUCT PROFITABILITY

One of the critical inputs into the annual planning system at Dobbs is product profitability information. The accounting department provides marketing and sales management with such information as average selling prices, marginal income, and profit contribution after all allocable expenses. In addition to receiving this information quarterly for actual sales, management also obtains estimates of marginal income and profit contributions for future periods. These estimates, when compared with overall division objectives, help to identify the need to change selling prices and to determine the effect of individual price changes on overall profitability. Additionally, by using the profitability information on individual products, it is possible to determine the profitability of different customer groups. This information is used in arriving at the amount of sales effort (call frequency and support) required for various customer groups.

NEW PRODUCTS

The marketing information system project included procedures for the development of new products at Dobbs. Revised systems were developed for:

1. Screening and evaluation of new product concepts.
2. Scheduling and control of new product development.
3. Budgetary control of new product development projects.
4. Planning and reporting of product performance.
5. Planning and reporting of field tests of new products.

These systems concepts are discussed in some detail in Chapter 6.

COSTS AND BENEFITS

The development and installation of an effective system takes time and effort, and the costs of implementation, as well as the continuing annual costs of maintaining the system in operation, should be clearly justified by improvements in overall profitability and market position.

To consider the benefits first, it was recognized from the outset that these should be looked for not in cost savings but in increased sales and profits. Systems, of course, do not sell—only salesmen do. But the system is specifically designed to identify sales potential which may otherwise not be recognized. In the Dobbs situation, this previously unidentified potential represented roughly 10% of the market, or $2,000,000 a year, on which the company felt it had an above average chance of making a sale once it knew of the customer's need, or understood better the reasons for failure to secure his business in the past. While this additional incremental sales potential is identified as a direct consequence of customer profile analysis, it must be recognized that not all of it could be translated into sales, and that some portion would eventually have been brought to the company's attention by the customers themselves. The true sales increment can, therefore, only be guessed at. Company consensus, however, placed the net effect of the information system on overall profit safely in excess of $100,000 a year.

Costs of system development, including the equivalent of roughly two man-years of time on the part of company personnel, plus outside services for consultants and data processing assistance, were well within this figure. Continuing annual costs are limited to part-time involvement of a sales planning analyst and a market research analyst. The time spent by sales personnel themselves in collecting and recording information is judged to be an essential and integral part of their normal customer service relationship.

The cost-benefit relationship was further enhanced in the case of Dobbs because the system installed in this division represented a prototype which could be subsequently extended to other divisions of the parent company at relatively lower costs insofar as many of the basic concepts and report formats could be readily adapted with little or no development effort.

The single most important element in the success of this project could, in retrospect, be identified as the careful planning which went into the initial organization of the project effort. Overall responsibility for development and installation of the marketing information system was assigned to a senior sales executive who was detached from his regular administrative functions for approximately six months to devote himself to the systems project during the key phases of development. He headed the systems task force, which included two members of the corporate systems staff and a market research specialist assigned by the Dobbs division. Thus, the task force incorporated in a close working relationship the necessary combination of sales, marketing, and systems know-how. It also had the support of outside consulting assistance.

The task force reported to a steering committee composed of the top marketing, sales, and accounting officers of the Dobbs Division and the corporate director of systems development. This steering committee established an initial charter for the task force, endorsed its work programs, and reviewed progress in monthly meetings. Necessary demands on the time of company personnel, particularly in the sales and marketing departments, were readily cleared through the respective department heads, who were fully informed on objectives and progress by virtue of their membership on the steering committee.

The enhanced understanding of mutual problems and a greater facility for focusing on customer needs and for communicating as a management group carried through into day-to-day operations beyond the conclusion of the marketing information systems project. The system also proved an excellent vehicle for training and developing younger sales and marketing personnel since it embodies and continually enforces the application of a sound marketing approach. With the information the system provides, it continues to be easier to make the right moves and more difficult to make the wrong ones.

The Dobbs marketing information system is one of the few comprehensive systems implemented in an industrial environment. The key elements of this system—customer profiles, input-output analysis, and long-range and annual planning—have been described in marketing literature for some time. The distinctive feature in the Dobbs experience is the integration of these diverse elements into an overall approach for meeting the information needs of marketing management.

13

MARKETING INFORMATION SYSTEMS IN RETAILING

The success of retailing organizations is dependent in roughly equal measure on the selection of store sites; the selection, display, and promotion of merchandise; the recruitment, training, and motivation of sales and merchandising personnel; and the financial management of inventory turnover, credit, and receivables. Marketing information systems approaches to date have found application primarily in the areas of product line evaluation and selection and merchandise inventory management; consequently, attention will be focused here on these areas.

The principal objectives in merchandise management systems are the maintenance of high volume, high turnover, and high margin or maintained markup. The principal action alternatives are addition or deletion of items, allocation of display space, initial stocking, reordering, pricing, promotions, and markdowns.

The particular systems approaches used vary, of course, depending on the type of store and the merchandise involved. Of particular interest is the area of fashion merchandising, because on first glance it seems least amenable to systems approaches; yet there are highly effective systems now in use by major retailers which incorporate some of the most advanced information and control concepts. To explain their operation, some general background information is necessary.

Many advances have been made in the past ten years in the general field of fashion inventory control, including such major technological breakthroughs as point-of-sale recorders and print-punch price tags for capturing data and electronic accounting and calculating devices to sort, analyze, and present such data to management in the form of various types of reports and records.

Another phenomenon of the past few decades has been the development of department store branches. Multiple selling outlets have introduced many complexities into the department store structure, particularly in the field of fashion inventory management.

The combination of these three factors: (1) point-of-sale recording devices, (2) the virtually unlimited sorting and printing capacity of modern electronic equipment, and (3) the rapid increase in the number of locations (branches) in which merchandise is stored and sold and, therefore, must be controlled has resulted in the production of a vast quantity of reports and records, which burden buyers with a mass of facts and figures far beyond their abilities to use effectively. What was needed was the development of techniques which would capture matters of significance contained in the vast quantities of data being processed and highlight these for the prompt attention of management.

CHARACTERISTICS OF FASHION MERCHANDISING

A system which proposes to reduce the clerical load of the ready-to-wear buyer must be tailored to the step-by-step logic of the fashion business. Based on the buyer's initial judgment of a style's salability, new, untested styles are purchased, brought into the store, and placed on the floor to sample test customer demand. If the sales response is especially good or bad on a particular style, the buyer must detect the condition quickly and mark the item down or reorder it, as appropriate. In the larger chain or multiple-unit store, this requires a great deal of report analysis, since it is impossible to "eyeball" the operations under such circumstances. Spotting the winners is critical, because they must be reordered to develop profits to offset the losers in the initial-order guessing game. The slow-moving styles also must be spotted quickly and moved out through price markdowns action to free cash and space for reorders and fresher merchandise.

A system to routinize the numerical portion of the buyer's work must assist in detecting exceptionally good and exceptionally bad sales performances. The buyer conventionally does this through daily review and evaluation of the sales performance of individual styles as shown on sales reports and checkout sheets. The system described below flags the reorder and markdown items daily by comparing their actual sales performance with a predetermined standard or norm.

Style Life

The operation of the system revolves about the determination of this standard style life against which the sales activity of individual styles is measured. The system has been dubbed "Style Life Inventory Management," or SLIM. Basically, style life is defined as the length of time a style is expected to sell actively. Where different garment types sold in the same department have different life expectancies, they must be categorized accordingly before analysis.

Style life is initially determined by a study of the actual rate of sale experienced by many individual styles in the department in which the system is to be installed. Upon analysis, sales patterns such as are shown in Exhibit 121 develop.

By eliminating the exceptionally slow sellers and those hot sellers on which sufficient stock was not available to support a full selling life, a sales pattern is developed for the so-called routine sellers. This sales pattern has certain very significant characteristics:

1. The rate of sale remains relatively constant for an initial period, after which it tails off.
2. The initial period (style life) remains relatively constant regardless of the quantity purchased.

This sales life pattern is the composite result of merchandise char-

Exhibit 121. Characteristic inventory sell-off patterns.

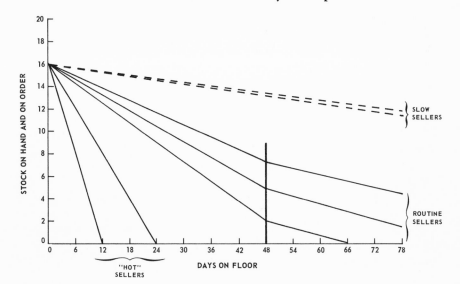

acteristics, customer habits, store image and character, store turnover objectives, markdown policies, and other factors. The key fact is that most styles for a given department and price line have a limited number of selling days within a season, after which they fail to generate active customer response. This sales life may be arbitrarily set on the basis of policy in some cases, but more often is tailored to the situation by analyzing past history of sales of styles in the department. The practical use of style life in the system is to set a par for normal sales performance from which exceptions can be determined for the buyers' attention.

Conversion of Style Life Into an Action Tool

The system is designed to highlight any style selling at a rate which would cause it to be sold out before the end of its style life. If, for example, the initial order quantity were 16 units and the style life 8 weeks, the indicated rate of sale would be two per week. If the item began selling at a rate faster than two per week, a reorder should be considered—if less than two a week, a markdown. The question is one of degree. For example, an item may start fast and tail off, or it may start slow and pick up. Many combinations are possible. This is shown graphically in Exhibit 122.

As in most decision-making processes, the question is one of risk. Certainly it is riskier to reorder an item selling at a rate of two times

Exhibit 122. Variations in sales pattern for reorderable styles.

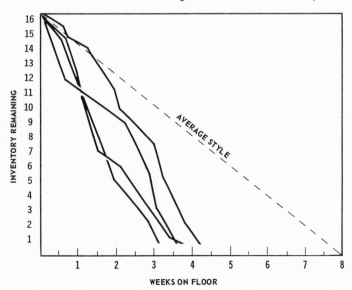

the average than one selling at a rate of five times the average, and it is riskier to reorder a large than a small quantity.

Based on trials with different risk levels, reorder signals have been set here so that they will show items selling at a rate of 150% of average in an average of nine days. Experience in operation of the system has indicated that the reliability of the signal is excellent.

Markdown (slow seller) flags have been set up using the same concepts, except that the signal appears on an 18-day average.

OPERATION OF SYSTEM

The system can operate manually or it can be automated on electronic data processing equipment. In the interests of simplicity, the manual system is described here first.

Garment tags are stubbed, sorted, and entered in the checkout book in the normal manner. No reports of any kind are prepared at this point. As checkout sheets are entered, a simple graph printed on the face of the checkout sheet is plotted, as shown in Exhibit 123. This graph is set up with the inventory commitment (on hand plus on order) on the vertical axis and selling days on the horizontal axis. A standard sell-off line is preprinted for the initial order quantity (in this case, 36), based on a 9-week or 54-day style life. On either side of the sell-off line are the action signals. The lower line is the reorder signal and the upper line is the markdown signal. These lines have been placed at such distances from the sell-off line as to reflect appropriate reorder and markdown odds.

The data in Exhibit 123 illustrate a reorderable item. On the seventh selling day, the balance on hand dropped (through sales) from 28 to 25, and the plot line crossed the bottom (reorder) guideline. This means that, based on the rate of sale attained at the end of the seventh selling day (11 units in seven days or an average of 9.4 per week), chances are better than 80% that a sales rate of at least 150% of average (in this case, 36 items in nine weeks, or four per week) will be maintained over the balance of the nine-week style life.

The buyer, after reviewing the item, placed a reorder to bring stock up to where it would have been had 150% of 36, or 54 units, been ordered initially. To determine this reorder quantity, a new sell-off line is drawn on the graph on the basis of 54 units initial stock (Exhibit 124). This line indicates a desired inventory at the seventh selling day of 46. Accordingly, the order is placed for 21 units (46 desired stock position minus 25 units actually on hand). For the remainder of the

Exhibit 123. Style life inventory management.

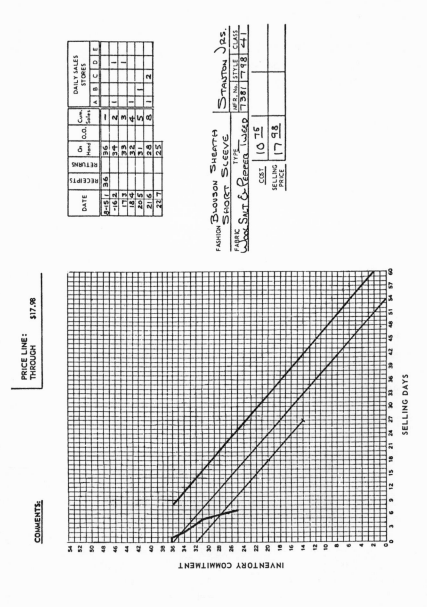

Exhibit 124. Style life inventory management.

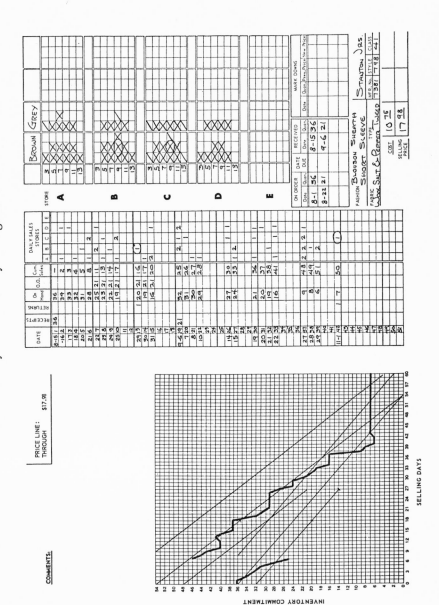

selling period, further plotting does not reveal any action lines being crossed. However, reorder action lines stop after 27 days to prevent reorder when there is no longer sufficient time within the style life period for reorders to be received and sold. Exhibit 124 illustrates the complete record, including a tally of individual branch store movement.

Additional examples of filled-in checkout sheets are shown in Exhibits 125 and 126. Exhibit 125 is illustrative of a slow-moving style which, lacking sufficient sales velocity, triggers a markdown signal after 21 days. A markdown from \$17.98 to \$13.99 is taken at that point (dated 8-25), and sales pick up substantially. However, the markdown line is crossed again on the 39th day, and a further markdown is taken a week later to \$9.90. This brought the price below cost of \$10.75, but the buyer felt the action was justified to avoid getting stuck with the remaining 16 units, which had shown no sales activity for five days.

Exhibit 126 illustrates the average style, which closely follows the standard 9-week sell-off pattern and requires neither reorder nor markdown.

Reports

Daily summary listings are prepared of items which have crossed either the reorder or markdown action lines. Exhibit 127 shows a sample reorder report.

In addition, periodic reports are prepared—usually every two to three months—summarizing overall system performance. Examples of these are shown in Exhibits 128 and 129, dealing with junior dress departments in two different stores. The first is a specialty store. The report points up the substantially higher gross profit—in percent of sales and, even more dramatically, in dollars per style—realized on reordered dresses. Comparison of successive reports over a period of time will show whether the buyer is successful in maintaining a high level of reorders.

The second example shown, dealing with an eight-store group of department stores, indicates less effective reorder performance (less than a third of the styles signaled for reorder is actually reordered), and suggests room for improvement.

In both cases, the system always signaled action (reorder or markdown) earlier than the buyer would have, and earlier than action was actually taken.

The manual system described here is no more (and may be less) costly to maintain than a typical "black book" system in that the time spent in plotting the graphs and preparing the exception reports is more

(*Text continues on page 268*)

Exhibit 125. Style life inventory management.

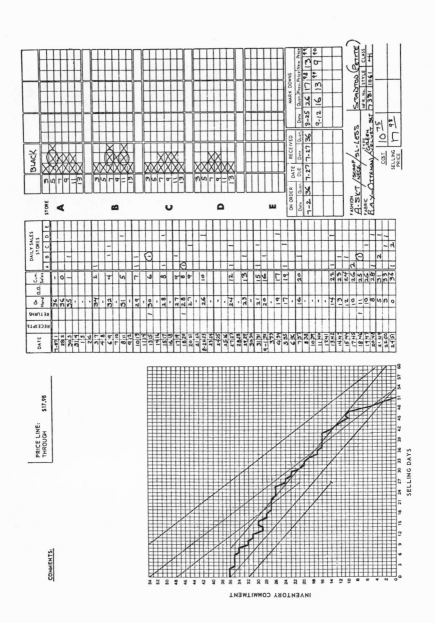

Exhibit 126. Style life inventory management.

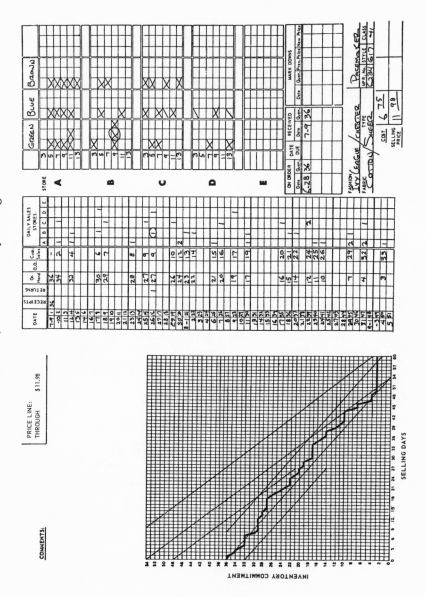

Exhibit 127. Buyer's reorder exception report.

MFGR. NAME	NO.	STYLE	COST	RETAIL	UNITS					DESCRIPTION	DATE R.O.	DUE	NOW SHIPPED	R.O. UNITS	AMT.
					DATE REC.	AMT. REC.	SOLD	ON	PLAN R.O.						
A Company	289	1104	$10.75	$17.98	8-8	24	5	19	36	Basic Wool	8-22	9-1	AF	36	$648.
B Company	7381	1046	10.95	17.98	8-8	24	8	16	36	Long-Sleeve-Crepe Wool	8-22	9-1	AF	36	648.
C Company	7424	708	12.75	22.98	8-15	18	4	14	18	Wool Flannel - Puritan Collar	8-22	9-1	AF	18	414.
D Company	1320	848	16.75	29.98	8-10	12	5	7	17	Short Sleeve - Basic Wool	8-22	9-1	AF	17	510.
E Company	7381	798	10.75	17.98	8-15	36	11	25	21	Wool Salt & Pepper	8-22	9-1	AF	21	378.
F Company	1684	222	19.75	35.00	8-16	6	3	3	14	Knit-Wool	8-22	9-1	AF	14	490.
G Company	3078	1432	35.75	59.98	8-1	8	6	2	8	Suede Jumper	8-22	9-1	AF	8	480.
H Company	7474	1841	14.75	25.00	8-15	16	8	8	18	Wool-Mohair	8-22	9-1	AF	18	450.
									TOTAL 168						$4018.

STYLE LIFE INVENTORY MANAGEMENT
REORDER EXCEPTIONS   DATE 8-22

Exhibit 128. Quarterly performance summary.

SPECIALTY STORE

JUNIOR DRESS DEPT.

ACTION INDICATED	ACTION TAKEN	NO. OF STYLES	UNITS	SALES $	GROSS PROFIT	
					% OF SALES	$/ STYLE
STAND PAT	———	140	2,048	$ 46,491	33%	$111
REORDER	———	47	882	18,846	37	147
REORDER	REORDER	60	2,025	46,574	37	287
MARKDOWN (18 DAYS)	MARKDOWN (38 DAYS)	60*	789*	17,199	26	75
		307	5,744	$129,110	34%	$144

* RETURNED TO VENDOR   23   197

Exhibit 129. Quarterly performance summary.

8 STORE GROUP

JUNIOR DRESS DEPT.

ACTION INDICATED	ACTION TAKEN	NO. OF STYLES	UNITS	SALES $	GROSS PROFIT	
					% OF SALES	$/ STYLE
STAND PAT	———	228	1,815	$13,670	32.5%	$19.92
REORDER	———	253	1,916	16,783	35	23.16
REORDER	REORDER	119	1,914	17,815	35	52.79
MARKDOWN (16 DAYS)	MARKDOWN (25 DAYS)	320*	2,230*	16,436	22	11.07
		920	7,875	$64,704	31.1%	$26.73

* RETURNED TO VENDOR   47   192

than offset by the time savings realized from the elimination of daily sales reports. Costs may be further reduced through mechanization, as described in the next section. Potential benefits in terms of significant reduction in the percentage of merchandise sold at markdown are indicated by the performance reports.

DATA PROCESSING ASPECTS

Style life inventory management (SLIM) can be implemented manually or it can be mechanized through punched-card tabulating, punched-card computer, a magnetic tape system, or a computer involving mass storage devices such as disks, drums, magnetic cards, or strips.

A prerequisite to the automation of SLIM controls is an operational unit control system. Incorporating the control procedure during design of the unit inventory system, and programming and converting them together, is probably the most efficient approach. Failing that, a SLIM program can be overlaid on almost any unit control system which maintains unit sales and stock information.

The input medium will, of course, depend on the medium in use within the store. Consider, for example, a department store using a magnetic tape computer of the 360 Model 30 class, with punched-card input, at a monthly rental of about $7,500. Where cards are used as input to a daily unit control system, the control calculations can be triggered to analyze every active master record; that is, every style for which a sale or customer return has been recorded for the day. This would mean that inactive styles that are likely to be markdown candidates would not be tested daily. On a weekly cycle, a short program is called in to analyze every style. If the buyer wishes specific styles analyzed, he makes up finder cards, which are then punched and read in to trigger the control calculations. This is, in a sense, random inquiry with a delayed response and without the trappings of data transmission and remote terminals. There is complete flexibility with respect to input.

An additional input is the buyer acknowledgment, wherein the buyer responds to the action signal, by either taking the indicated action or making a positive indication that he will not. These, too, are punched into cards and entered as a system input.

The SLIM Record

The basic requirements for data are not significantly different from the requirements for a conventional unit control system. In addition to such information as department, vendor, class, style number, price (original and markdown), on order, and on hand, the record contains special dates such as start date (day style goes on the floor) and reorder date, counts of the number of times the various systems signals have been produced, the initial order quantity, buyer acknowledgments, and perhaps several other items depending on the options selected. A maximum of 20 numeric characters is a conservative estimate of the additional data required to be maintained in the file.

Processing Logic

The highlights of the processing logic are outlined in Exhibit 130. The control program begins with the conventional housekeeping steps, which correspond to clearing one's desk before tackling a new job. Then a test is made to determine if the style has been on the floor longer than its estimated style life. If it has, and if the buyer has not yet been informed of this fact, the buyer is signaled and all further action signals for the style are turned off. The next step is a test for special instruction, including instructions from the buyer. For example, "no reorder" would tell the computer that no matter what the signal, this style is not to be listed for reorder.

Exhibit 130. Schematic of SLIM processing logic.

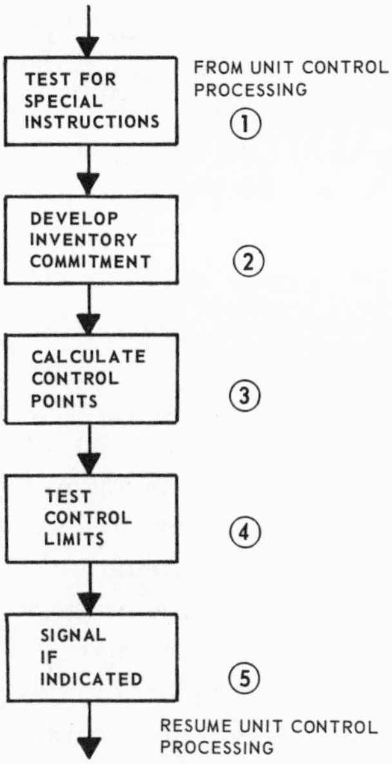

If there are no special instructions, the actual inventory on hand plus inventory on order is computed. Next the control point(s) are calculated and compared with the on-hand plus on-order position. On the basis of this comparison, the system identifies reorder, markdown or stand pat (no signal) conditions. Finally, the record is updated to reflect the action recommended and is written on the file.

There are basically two reports—the buyer's report, produced daily, and the manager's report, produced weekly, biweekly, or with whatever frequency is deemed appropriate by the merchandise manager.

The buyer's report, which is the primary exception or action report, follows the format of Exhibit 126, and lists, for those styles which require evaluation of action signals:

Department.
Style.
Vendor and vendor No.
On hand.
On order.
Cumulative sales.
Action signal (reorder or markdown).
Recommended reorder quantity.
Control history (times reorder or markdown signaled).
Special instructions.

The manager's report would include the above, but can be programmed to highlight systems signals and buyer response. This would identify those styles for which the buyer overruled the system and provide a basis for review and follow up.

Additional analyses of systems operation can also be produced as a byproduct of the control system, such as performance in terms of the gross profit contribution of controlled styles.

FOOD STORE MANAGEMENT

Similar systems, in some respects even more sophisticated, are in various stages of development and implementation in major supermarket chain operations. Typically, these aim to evaluate assignment of shelf space (facings) or freezer space by item, and periodically report action signals in terms of indicated increase or decrease in space allocation. Items failing to qualify for minimum space become candidates for deletion through substitution by new product offerings.

More advanced systems provide action indicators also for upgrading or downgrading of item location within a limited shelf area, and for price adjustment action. The large number of items and store locations in a major food chain makes use of computer power mandatory.

Input for the system includes, for each item, its cost, price, sales volume, and space utilization. From these data, profitability is calculated, per unit and per week, and converted to corresponding profit per facing inch.

Through a series of analyses, the system develops and periodically updates historical ranges of performance for each commodity group. When an item falls outside the normal range for its group with respect to sales volume or profit contribution, appropriate action is signaled. Action is taken by the store manager or central buying office in accordance with these signals after consideration of special factors which may not be fully reflected by operating statistics, such as the competitive environment and long-range plans for development or promotion. In addition to individual items, commodity groups as a whole are also periodically summarized and evaluated.

In each of the preceding illustrations, the intent is not to diminish the judgmental factor in merchandising—quite the contrary. By careful analysis of the buyer's and merchandise manager's own approach of marketing logic, those facets of his or her job which lend themselves to routine analysis have been isolated and mechanized in a way which focuses attention where it is most needed—on the exceptional items which require action.

14

MARKETING INFORMATION SYSTEMS
IN ADVERTISING AGENCIES

In many respects, the processes by which an advertising agency goes about planning and executing advertising strategy on behalf of its clients closely parallel the activities that take place within the marketing function of the advertiser. Where media advertising is an element in the overall marketing mix, the agency must develop a media plan that is consistent with the market plan for the product in question. The market planning process, in turn, draws upon both agency and client data sources to quantify the position of the product within the marketplace and the prospects for the product over the next year or more.

HOW AGENCIES USE SYSTEMS

It is helpful to view the overall advertising planning and execution process as comprising four distinct steps.

1. Preparing marketing plans, identifying the audience, and broadly defining the level and character of advertising to be provided.
2. Developing media plans which define in detail what advertising vehicles are to be used.
3. Scheduling and purchasing the space, time, and other elements required to execute the media plan and paying for all such outside services.

4. Preparing postbuy analyses to evaluate the quality of the plan as actually executed and to verify the performance of suppliers.

This chapter will deal primarily with steps 1, 2, and 4. The mechanics of scheduling, billing, and paying are more appropriate to discussions of complex transaction systems.

The marketing plan (step 1) is usually viewed as the responsibility of company marketing management, while the media plan (step 2) is usually recommended by a selected advertising agency and approved by the client's management. Advertising agencies, however, often undertake the development of marketing plans for smaller clients that lack experienced marketing personnel; they usually participate to varying degrees in the marketing planning activities of larger clients as well. All the agency's suggestions, of course, are subject to review, modification, or even rejection by the client.

The questions to be answered during the marketing and media planning process are simply stated as follows.

1. What group(s) of potential purchasers are we most anxious to serve?
2. What volume of our product or brand or service can we reasonably expect to market to these groups?
3. What strategies should we follow with respect to
   Allocating our sales force effort;
   Pricing the product;
   Packaging and displaying our product;
   Distributing the product to maximize its availability for purchase;
   Promoting our product by means of special inducements to wholesalers, retailers, consumers, or some combination of these;
   Advertising the product?

Although advertising appears last on this list, it is obvious that detailed advertising plans cannot be developed without first (or concurrently) planning all the other marketing strategies. All these programs, taken together, constitute a market plan.

HOW PLANS ARE DEVELOPED IN A REPRESENTATIVE AGENCY

It should be understood that the procedures described represent a composite view. Each step described receives consideration in some form by every agency, but the mode and degree of formality applied varies greatly. Our principal objective here is to identify those specific areas of analysis for which organized systems exist in at least some agencies, even though no single agency has operating systems in every one of the areas identified.

Geographic Strategy

Exhibit 131 deals with the development of a market plan for a particular brand. The primary information inputs are shown on the left. The geographic strategy for the brand is developed by first constructing a file of data on demographic characteristics. Derived from census data and trade publications, this file is usually on a county-by-county basis and contains estimates of current population, the income, ages, household sizes, and estimated spending patterns of the population, and some indicators of the relative importance of one county versus another. We should keep in mind that this file is often a book or set of tables and need not be on a computer tape.

The advertising industry's requirements for detailed information about the marketplace have created a sizable peripheral group of syndicated data suppliers, some of which are referred to in Exhibits 131, 132, and 133. In Exhibit 131, NDI and NFI refer, respectively, to the Nielsen Drug Index and the Nielsen Food Index, which are reports of retail movement prepared by the A. C. Nielsen Co. SAMI refers to Sales Areas Marketing, Inc., which reports on the wholesale movement of products from supermarket warehouses to retail outlets. BRI and SIMMONS refer to the Brand Rating Index and W. R. Simmons, Inc., which monitor the buying habits of a population sample. Also in Exhibit 131, BAR (Broadcast Advertiser's Reports), LNA (Leading National Advertisers), ROME (Rome Reports), and MEDIA REC (Media Records) indicate sources of data on the advertising spending of companies and brands in specific media such as print, television, and radio. At the bottom of Exhibit 131, ARB (American Research Bureau) and the other companies listed in that box and in Exhibit 132 (Hooper, Audit Bureau of Circulation, Pulse) provide data on the estimated audiences of individual advertising vehicles—how many people watch specific television programs or read specific magazines.

A number of these syndicated services have adopted the county as their basic geographic reporting unit, although their reports often contain information on Standard Metropolitan Statistical Areas, or on geographic areas defined in terms of television, newspaper, or radio markets. When advertisers or agencies purchase this information, they may relate retail product movement (for example) to internal reports of sales volume.

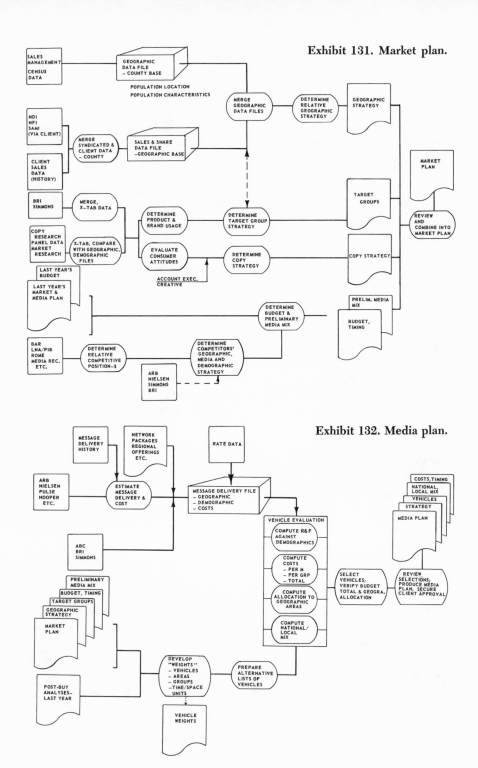

Exhibit 131. Market plan.

Exhibit 132. Media plan.

The resulting file of information, also on a geographic basis, contains actual sales for one brand and estimates of that brand's share of total market sales.

Merging the population file and the sales/share file facilitates determination of geographic strategy. For example, a segment of the merged files might show the following data.

County No.	Size	Households (000)	Sales ($000)	$ per Household	Estimated Retail
265	A	210	142	.68	5.1%
307	A	421	197	.47	3.2
1106	A	306	106	.35	4.3
1277	A	280	170	.61	6.0
188	B	120	85	.71	6.8
192	B	97	70	.72	6.4

Inspection of this segment shows, for example, that per-household sales (assuming households to be representative of purchasers in this case) are significantly less in counties 307 and 1106 than they are in counties 265 and 1277, although the counties are all approximately the same size. The same two counties, 307 and 1106, also show lower market shares. In addition, it appears that the brand is performing somewhat better in smaller (B) counties than in larger (A) counties. These factors, for all counties served by the company, affect the development of geographic strategy, although there is no single best strategy which can be derived from these data alone.

Target Groups and Copy Strategy

Both market and media plans require definition of what segment of the population is to be the focus—the "target group"—for the marketing effort. Syndicated information again contributes to this process. In Exhibit 131, BRI and SIMMONS refer to research organizations that report statistically which people are exposed to which media and what those people buy. For example, a cross-tabulation of the data may indicate that households with incomes over $15,000 are responsible for most purchases of color television sets and that the heads of these households are more likely to read magazine A than magazine B over a four-week period. Obviously, the greatest benefit from this type of data is obtained from consideration of alternative target groups and assessment of their importance in buying specific products. A number of agencies have converted the voluminous printed reports to magnetic tape and are thus able to retrieve and cross-tabulate with ease.

Additional inputs in the determination of target group and copy strategy are the specialized research studies and copy tests conducted by the agency. These help both client and agency monitor the attitudes of consumers toward brands and their response to varying kinds of sales messages.

Media Mix and Timing

Normally, the primary starting points for development of next year's advertising budget are this year's advertising budget and competitors' current expenditure levels.

Analysis of competitive advertising spending is becoming a more important input to the planning process. As indicated in Exhibit 131, several syndicated services collect and sell summaries of spending in various media. Thus an advertiser can buy a reasonably accurate set of estimates on his competitors' spending on a nationwide and local market basis. A further step involving the manipulation of larger volumes of data will yield the strategy of the competition. For example, a competitive spending report might show:

Brand	National Television ($000)	Local Television ($000)	Magazines ($000)	Radio ($000)
A	2,500	1,000	500	—
B	2,000	500	—	200
C	2,100	1,200	700	—
D	1,000	2,000	100	700

Supporting detail can pinpoint spending by station, time, and program type for broadcast media, and by publication, issue, and audience type for print media. Strategy can be evaluated by combining dollar estimates with audience estimates:

PRECENT OF SPENDING

Brand	Women 18–35	Women 35+	Urban	Rural
A	30	70	65	35
B	60	40	50	50
C	55	45	75	25
D	45	55	70	30

Similar techniques are used in some agencies to determine the geographic strategies of groups of brands. All the required information is available from published or syndicated sources.

Let us summarize the planning process and the systems supporting it to this point. The market plan for a brand normally specifies how much money will be spent for all marketing activities, including advertising. Where advertising is a major marketing expense, particular attention is directed toward devising efficient and competitive strategies for allocating funds geographically, for directing advertising's efforts toward specific groups of consumers, and for identifying the media through which the messages should be transmitted. Systems in this phase of the planning process rely both on internal data (sales statistics, previous budgets, market research) and on syndicated data of population, media audiences, market shares, buying habits, and competitive advertising spending.

The process of setting advertising budgets and policy resembles more the legal process in which divergent briefs are prepared, submitted, and adjudicated, than the scientific process of deriving conclusions from known and accepted fact.

There is no uniformity or consensus as to economic criteria to be applied, such as the maintenance of a prescribed dollar level of expenditures per case, per consumer, per household, or per brand, or of a prescribed ratio to competitive expenditures. Neither are there generally accepted cause-effect relationships, theories of effectiveness, or universal principles to guide apportionment of advertising dollars among media. Rather, the examination and reevaluation of advertising mechanisms and rationales is an inherent part of the annual marketing planning effort. The systems in existence are designed essentially to provide the factual grounds on the basis of which different groups in the client and agency organizations can advance their diverse and sometimes conflicting approaches, to be ultimately resolved at a high management level.

Within this framework, market planning systems have been developed by many agencies, both large and small. In fact, most of the systems have similar structures, and the industry has engaged in considerable duplication, or "reinventing the wheel." For this and other reasons, there have been recent efforts to provide syndicated systems by organizations offering both the programs and time-sharing facilities to agencies seeking to avoid development and equipment costs.

THE MEDIA PLAN

Media planning—that is, the detailed specification of how advertising dollars are to be applied to specific media vehicles, such as TV and radio stations or magazines, and to specific seasons or weeks—occurs to some extent coincidentally with and as a part of marketing planning.

The major effort in this area, however, gets under way after the marketing plan, comprising overall budgets and broad allocations to media categories and time periods, has been completed and released for implementation.

A flow diagram of information required for a media plan is shown in Exhibit 132. The developed market plan, with specific objectives and policy guidelines, is a major component leading to the media plan. Another key input is an analysis of how the last media plan turned out. These analyses usually indicate the actual costs of delivering messages to given geographic and demographic segments and the performance of various advertising vehicles in fulfilling the logistical requirements of the agency. For example, a series of television spot announcements might be purchased by an agency for broadcast in a particular time segment at a specified weekly or daily frequency. The network or local stations selling the time may not deliver the time as purchased because of preemption by special programming or through oversight. Similarly, any purchase of time or space is based upon an assumed audience estimated either by a syndicated service or by the vehicles themselves. After the purchase, new estimates are available and must be compared to original plans to determine the effect of changes on the overall costs of delivering messages. When errors or poor estimates are substantially different from the anticipated purchase, stations and publishers attempt to supply equivalent time and space.

With an analysis of last year's media buy and this year's market plan in hand, agency media planners exercise their judgment concerning the relative value of specific vehicles. In many cases, systems have been established to formalize the subjective evaluation of magazines, geographic areas, groups of consumers, and segments of broadcast time. Because of editorial image, geographic concentration, readership overlap with other media employed, or other reasons, an advertising agency may recommend one magazine over another for use in a particular campaign despite the fact that the estimated target audience reached by the rejected magazine is larger or less costly per individual reader than that for the accepted one.

In either a formal or informal fashion, the addition of the agency's subjective evaluation results in a series of lists containing possible vehicles for use in an advertising campaign. The next critical step is to evaluate these lists exhaustively to determine the most efficient media plan for the campaign. As in the market planning process, syndicated estimates of readers, viewers, listeners, and costs are used in a variety of ways to develop quantitative measures of campaign efficiency. Elaborate techniques involving sequential selection of vehicles and their simulation of message delivery have been developed by some larger agencies. The key computational steps leading to the final media plan are shown in Exhibit 132. All these steps, such as computing the costs, geographic dispersion, and audience delivery, require large volumes of input data. It is this input problem that has complicated systems development. For example, in order to accumulate a file of the geographic, demographic, and cost characteristics of the major magazines, television and radio networks, and local broadcast stations it is necessary to devise a common set of geographic and demographic pigeonholes into which each vehicle's characteristics can be put. Since the syndicated services which monitor these vehicles collect their data in different ways, the process of developing comparable data across all vehicles is extremely complicated.

As noted earlier, in several of the larger agencies, complex media planning systems have been constructed, incorporating logical concepts of the mechanics of advertising influence. These are generally viewed as having proprietary value by virtue of unique logical concepts and also because they represent sizable investments because of their inherent complexity. These large-scale models do not always perform in the ways their developers intended. Practical limitations of file size, computer time, and input preparation, and particularly the need for continual updating, have frustrated, and in some cases halted, their continuing application.

Referring again to Exhibit 132, the vehicle evaluation steps are carried out both sequentially and, in some cases, simultaneously to determine specific vehicles to be used, the number of insertions or messages to be delivered, geographic dispersion of messages, specific costs and budget goals, and the impact on specific demographic groups in terms of reach and frequency.

Media Buying

Following the client's review and approval, the media plan is ready for implementation. The final phase of actually carrying out the plan represents the greatest challenge for current systems development effort. There are hundreds of vehicles, dozens of ways to purchase space or time within each vehicle, and literally thousands of schedules, invoices, bills, and reports that must be processed in order to complete the implementation of the plan for a major brand. Only a very few of the largest agencies have successfully dealt with the problem of systemizing this process using the computer. Exhibit 133 shows the major steps required from the time the plan is approved through the buying process and concluding with payments to the media, the talent, and the agency.

Exhibit 133 also shows the preparation of a postbuy analysis, using

Exhibit 133. Buying plan.

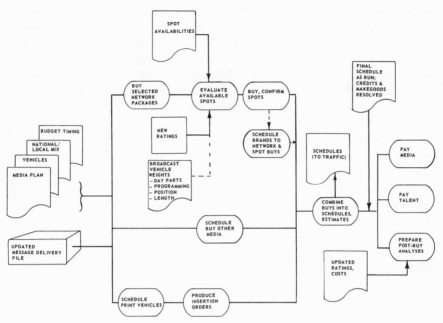

the most recent audience estimates and actual media costs. Like other follow-up activities, this process is more often conspicuous by its absence. Figuring out how the media plan was *really* executed and how those thousands (or millions) were spent is sometimes a painful procedure for agency and advertiser alike. The recent upsurge in independent media-buying operations, however, has put additional pressure on agencies to complete the cycle of planning, control, and evaluation. As noted earlier, the spot television buying process has been particularly difficult to simplify with the computer, and for that reason any postbuy analysis usually involves massive clerical effort to sort through estimates, ratings, invoices, cancellations, make-goods, and other documents that identify actual performance. An interim solution to this problem, assuming that the agency intends to provide postbuy information, is to establish the format for the analysis at the time the buy is made, enter the estimated data in much the same way as a budget would be detailed, and update the same document with actual activity data as it arrives.

Media Plan Evaluation

Another approach to both the media planning and postbuy processes is outlined in Exhibits 134, 135, and 136. In many cases, the advertiser cannot feel comfortable with the kinds of statistical information common to the agency, no matter how often the numbers are explained to him. This uneasiness is often reinforced by the agency's reluctance to clearly state assumptions behind its media planning concepts, or the agency's tendency to plunge into the other extreme of esoteric models of advertising response. The models may be valid, but their details take the advertiser further and further away from his basic business knowledge—the costs and profitability of manufacturing and selling his product on a unit basis.

Exhibit 134 shows the basic parts of a media plan that has been developed for (say) E-B brand of cake mix. The plan is designed to support the brand for a year, with special emphasis on a planned product improvement announcement and on scheduled trade and consumer promotions. At this summarized level, it is deceptively easy to pass judgment on the plan as being "consistent with objectives" or "within budgeted goals." In order to evaluate the plan more closely, and to get the agency and advertiser talking the same basic language, we have outlined an approach to examining the plan considering reasonable expectations of benefits under clearly stated assumptions.

The first part of this approach requires that the plan be broken down into major segments within each media type, as shown in Exhibit 135. Here the spot television budget in New York is illustrated by comparing an evening movie spot with a morning show spot. The movie, with its much larger total and target audiences, is substantially more expensive than the morning show. The advertiser can (and should) pose the question: Does that expensive spot justify its cost? Asked another way, the question becomes: What is the reasonable expectation of benefit from the more expensive spot?

The next step in the analysis involves an assumption about the relative values of repeated exposures. For purposes of the example, we have assumed a bell-shaped distribution curve for both spots, so that the 727,000 target audience viewers of the movie really consist of 91,000 women who are seeing the spot for the first time, 136,000 who are seeing it for the second time, and so forth. The value of these repeated exposures must be assumed, based on research findings or the instinctive judgment of both agency and advertiser. In this case, the assumption is that the first and second exposures are of critical value—these are the exposures that are most likely to directly influence the viewer to purchase the cake mix on her next trip to the supermarket.

Following this assumption, the cost of providing these key exposures can be calculated as shown. The movie exposure costs 2.2 cents; the morning show exposure costs 0.5 cents. Other inputs are now required,

Exhibit 134. Media plan.

	COST	%
I. REGULAR BRAND SUPPORT		
Nighttime network:	$ 900,000	26
Daytime network:	900,000	26
Spot television:	1,000,000	29
II. PRODUCT IMPROVEMENT		
ANNOUNCEMENT	250,000	7
Direct mail-coupon		
Life, Look, TV Guide		
Sunday supplements		
Outdoor		
III. PROMOTION SUPPORT		
Print:	400,000	12
	$3,450,000	100%

Exhibit 135. Example of a 30-second spot TV announcement, New York metropolitan area.

	EVENING MOVIE	MORNING SHOW
COST of SPOT	$5000	$400
RATING POINTS	22	6
AUDIENCE (000)		
Households	1263	385
Women 18-49	727	243
FREQUENCY (000)		
1st Exposure	91	30
2nd	136	46
3rd	273	91
4th	136	46
5th plus	91	30
1st + 2nd	227	76
COST/1st + 2nd Exposure	$.022	$.005

Exhibit 136. Example of a 30-second spot TV announcement, New York metropolitan area.

	EVENING MOVIE	MORNING SHOW
COST PER KEY EXPOSURE	$.044	$.010
If users=50%		
COST PER SALE	$.44	$.10
If switchers = 30% and		
one of three buys E-B		
Brand cake mix		

	DOLLARS	%
NET PRICE PER UNIT	$.50	100%
Variable mfg. cost ⟶	.23	
GROSS PROFIT	.27	54
Direct brand expenses		
Freight, commissions ⟶	.07	
CONTRIBUTION MARGIN	.20	40
Allocated selling expenses ⟶	.05	
MARKETING MARGIN	.15	30

as shown in Exhibit 136. Half the target audience, according to research studies, is now using *some* brand of cake mix while the other half does not use mixes or does not bake cakes at all. Other research findings indicate that 30 out of every 100 cake mix users will switch brands with each purchase and that the brand in question can be expected to attract one-third of these switchers. This logic is consistent with relatively stable market shares for major brands. In a stable share situation, each brand will gain and lose about the same number of regular purchasers over several purchase cycles.

Translating these research inputs (or assumptions) back to the media plan and the movie and morning show spots, it is possible to estimate the cost of influencing a member of the target audience to buy E-B brand when she switches. This influencing process is one of the primary reasons for advertising in the first place. (The advertising effort could also be directed toward the objectives of increasing the number of switchers or of increasing the number of mix users.)

Referring again to Exhibit 136, the cost per probable purchase through the movie is 44 cents, while the morning show is less than one-fourth that, 10 cents. The movie spot, under these assumptions, will result in an unprofitable sale, all other things being equal.

Of course, not all other things are equal. The prestige of the movie, the relative buying power of the movie audience, and the presence of other family members are factors that merit consideration before the movie spot is dropped from the media plan. More important than these, however, are the repeat purchases that an "influenced switcher" might make once the first E-B purchase has been made and presumably found satisfactory. If the movie spot produces three or four purchases rather than just one, its value goes up. These differences in the influencing power of media are the hardest to quantify.

By bringing the media costs down to the unit purchase level, two desirable purposes have been accomplished. First, the advertiser has been exposed to the fundamentals of advertising response (whether the assumptions are right or wrong), and, second, he is now able to compare the costs of encouraging a retail sale to the profitability of that sale.

This chapter has not answered the problem of "how to advertise." As far as we know, the problem of planning and executing an optimum advertising strategy has not been solved. In order to devise such a strategy, it would first be necessary to prove conclusively one of the many theoretical explanations of advertising response. Equally important, it would also be necessary to translate that proven theory into terms which could then be used to evaluate advertising alternatives in ways that would be continually valid as social, economic, and competitive conditions change. The lack of a comprehensive, proven logic for advertising strategy should not stifle systems development. As we have mentioned elsewhere in this book, very few marketing management activities enjoy the reliable structure of manufacturing operations. Even under these circumstances of uncertainty, a great deal of highly successful and innovative systems development has taken place.

15

MARKETING INFORMATION SYSTEMS IN FINANCE AND BANKING

Marketing information systems concepts have extensive applicability in the finance and banking areas. Benefits from marketing and sales activities, for which a sound marketing information system is required, are potentially greater for this industry than for many others. Because of the nature of the industry, marketing information systems may be installed more rapidly.

To date, however, the development of such systems has received a low priority relative to operational systems. Reducing the costs of handling transaction records and improving their accuracy has instead received the major share of attention. Cost savings were attractive, and computer processing was more accurate and timely than manual processing. However, with the increase in competition for patronage in recent years and the increasing cost of doing business, the stage for more rapid development of marketing information systems has been set. This development effort has been aimed at supplying sales and marketing with information required to plan and execute the strategies leading to increased profits.

In addition to competitive pressures, the massive data processing expenditures themselves have forced financial institutions toward analyzing ways of better utilizing their equipment. There is a limit to the amount of cost reduction which can be achieved in the operations area. Better sales information, however, provides an opportunity to increase profits by increasing sales or by redirecting sales efforts.

FACTORS POINTING TOWARD GREATER USE
OF MARKETING INFORMATION SYSTEMS
BY FINANCIAL INSTITUTIONS

Need	*Opportunity*
Overabundance of detail information on many aspects of operation.	Effective organization of data readily available in new form to fit management needs.
Complete overview of individual accounts using multiple services.	Classify account responsibility and critical activity and structure reporting accordingly.
Summarization of total activity related to a special area of service.	Effective use of computer capacity to reclassify, sort, and extract information for product or service line management.
Flexibility to respond to market changes.	Incorporate optional and special reporting methods in anticipation of expected needs.
Growing cost of data processing and information handling.	Efficient design and control of utilization of equipment and personnel.

Other reasons also exist for both the increasing emphasis and the increasing potential benefits of using marketing information systems. These factors will be reviewed in the discussion throughout this chapter.

MARKETING INFORMATION SYSTEMS IN A BROKERAGE HOUSE—SALES PERFORMANCE REPORTING

Levitz & Co. (not the real name), an old-line Wall Street house, decided a better system of sales performance reporting was needed. For years its management had relied on personal observation and its ability to review each representative's output personally. As the firm grew, trading volume increased and additional service lines were added. With these changes, management's personal involvement in all areas of the firm's operations became more and more difficult. A performance reporting system was clearly needed.

Such a reporting system had to satisfy two needs: periodic management reports and summaries for planning purposes. The information would have to be reported by service line and by branch so that responsibility could be clearly established. Levitz had hired specialists to develop and manage its service lines, but again had no way of regularly determining profitability by line.

As a result of the company's recognition of these limitations, a branch reporting system was designed in order to provide Levitz management with the specific information required to plan and measure performance. The basic building block of this system, shown in Exhibit 137, is the registered representative performance report. Three major categories of information were provided.

1. Information dealing with the status of a representative's accounts. Here, such data as the number of accounts, conditions of these accounts, and the like are shown.

2. A category dealing with profitability, which provides information on income and selected expenses. Because errors and extensions are costly to Levitz, this information is also shown here.

Exhibit 137. Levitz & Co. registered representative (RR) performance report activity sheet.

Date: MARCH, 197X
Branch —— 01

RR —— John Jones
Date Registered —— 6/10/7X
Levitz Trained —— Yes

ACCOUNT STATUS SUMMARY

| | | NUMBER OF ACCOUNTS | | | | | | OPEN ORDERS | | EQUITY* | |
| | | GROSS COMMISSION CATEGORIES | | | | | | | | | |
	TOTAL	A	B	C	DORMANT	NEW	LOST	NO.	$ GROSS	$ TOTAL	TURNOVER †
CURRENT YTD	121	21	29	42	27	42	23	1	230	962,000	2.2
PREVIOUS YTD	110	17	33	30	30	35	19	2	380	903,040	2.4

PROFITABILITY

| | | $ GROSS COMMISSIONS | | $ INTEREST INCOME | | ERRORS | | | | |
| | | | | | | TOTAL LEVITZ | | CHARGE TO RR | | |
	NUMBER TRADES	AVG./ TRADE	TOTAL (000)	ACTUAL	PLAN	NO.	COST	NO.	COST	NUMBER OF EXTENSIONS
CURRENT QTR	209	123	25.7	1,050	1,000	2	100	1	50	0
CURRENT YTD	596	125	74.5	3,130	3,000	4	200	3	150	0
PREVIOUS QTR	184	119	21.9	800	900	1	50	0	0	1
PREVIOUS YTD	540	120	64.8	2,500	2,600	5	450	3	350	2

EVALUATION

| | | GROSS COMMISSIONS | | RANK—FIRM | | RANK-BRANCH GROSS |
	CONTRIBUTION TO PROFIT	TOTAL	AVG./TRADE	GROSS	DATE REGISTERED	
STANDARD YTD	43,800	73,000	130			
VARIANCE YTD	900	1,500	−5			
RANK YTD				32	3	1

* TOTAL VALUE OF SECURITIES HELD BY REPRESENTATIVE'S ACCOUNTS.

† TOTAL SECURITY VALUE TRADED BY REPRESENTATIVE'S ACCOUNTS DIVIDED BY EQUITY.

3. An evaluation of the representative in relation to his peers and others in the firm.

The information concerning the representatives was then summarized for the branch manager, as shown in Exhibit 138. This report shows a summary of each representative's activity by service line. This data was then totaled to provide the branch manager with a summary of his branch's performance. Of greatest interest to the branch manager were the gross commission level and the average commission per trade. With the expansion in the number of branches, the firm's profits per dollar of gross commission had been declining. The present system did not permit a calculation of a commission per trade figure. Because of lack of management control, representatives, though meeting the gross commission objectives, were doing so with numerous small trades. The result was that the average commission earned was below Levitz's cost of executing the transaction.

Because the branch managers needed relative performance measurement, the gross commission rank for each branch and for the firm as a whole was also shown. Levitz encouraged competition among the representatives and the ranking provided a means of reporting their relative performance. It also provided similar incentive for the branch manager.

Sales mix information was also shown on this report. During the design of the new performance reporting system, it became evident that some branches' sales were heavily weighted toward a limited number of service lines. This could not be explained on the basis of market potential. The sales mix objective had been established by management during the annual planning meeting. While the overall mix was in balance, the performance at individual branches varied widely. It was the desire of the marketing manager to know where these deviations occurred so that he could react to individual situations on a timely basis.

It was the intent of management to regard each representative and branch as a profit center. The reports were designed to focus on those items which influence profitability, such as average commission per trade, interest income, and selected expenses.

Exhibit 139 is a representation of how the branch reports were summarized to the sales manager level. This responsibility reporting structure provided management with the means to measure and control the performance of its branches. Branches requiring corrective action were quickly spotted and, by the nature of information reported, the type of action required was indicated.

Organizationally, Levitz turned to its service line managers to provide the impetus needed on a service line basis. These managers were

Exhibit 138. Levitz & Co. branch performance report.

BRANCH –01   REGISTERED REPRESENTATIVES IN:
FIRM –– 824
BRANCH –– 10

| RR | | GROSS COMMISSIONS | | | RANK | | TOTAL NUMBER TRADES | GROSS COMMISSION % | | | OVER THE COUNTER | | ERROR COSTS CHARGED TO | | INTEREST INCOME | |
NAME	NO.	$	% TO PLAN	AVG./ TRADE	FIRM	BRANCH		NYSE	ASE	BROKER	HOUSE	RR	BRANCH	ACTUAL	PLAN
M. JONES 123															
CURRENT YEAR — MO		8,500	110	73	34	2	116	51.0	39.0	7.5	2.5	0	50	200	300
YTD		90,034	105	76	31	1	1,184	50.2	39.8	7.0	3.0	100	100	2,500	2,600
PREVIOUS YEAR — MO		8,100	101	74	30	3	109	43.6	41.2	8.7	6.5	50	0	200	250
YTD		83,200	104	75	25	5	1,109	46.1	42.0	7.7	4.2	75	200	2,450	2,500
W. SMITH 456															
CURRENT YEAR — MO		7,225	93	68	94	6	106	62.1	35.0	2.0	.9	50	0	162	200
YTD		76,529	89	66	102	5	1,160	60.8	35.1	3.5	.6	200	50	1,038	1,800
PREVIOUS YEAR — MO		6,885	86	67	85	5	103	73.6	22.2	4.1	.1	100	50	184	200
YTD		70,720	88	67	83	4	1,056	71.4	23.8	4.6	.2	300	100	1,764	1,800
BRANCH TOTAL															
CURRENT YEAR — MO		80,000	105	70	6	—	2,270	55.3	34.7	5.4	4.6	600	450	3,058	3,100
YTD		917,031	101	80	10	—	11,451	51.1	38.9	5.2	4.8	1,500	980	27,621	28,000
PREVIOUS YEAR — MO		78,009	96	75	8	—	2,100	56.8	33.2	5.3	4.7	400	300	2,864	2,700
YTD		865,000	98	79	9	—	10,328	53.2	36.8	5.3	4.7	1,200	850	25,138	24,000

Exhibit 139. Levitz & Co. branch reporting system summaries.

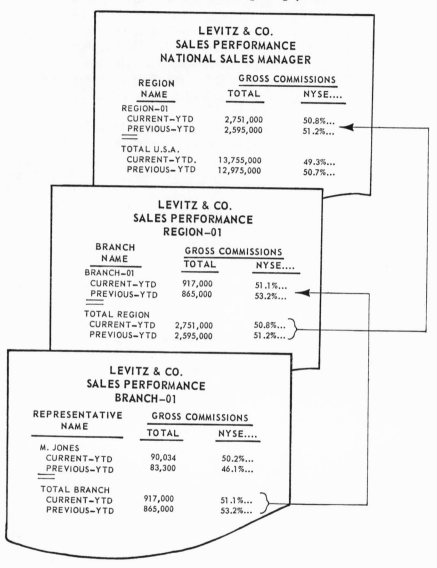

responsible for a particular service line and could be expected to develop programs leading to improved sales if sufficient market potential existed. This would be achieved through training programs, promotional programs, and sales contests. To coordinate the service line managers' activities with those of the branch manager, the basic transaction data was reported by service line. This was presented on an exception basis, as shown in Exhibit 140. Further information, if needed, could be requested in the form shown by Exhibit 141. Exception reporting was used to reduce volume of paper and to draw attention to problems

Exhibit 140. Levitz & Co. service line performance exception report of branches varying from gross commission plan.

Date: __OCTOBER 197X__
Service Line — Over the Counter

REGION BRANCH	MONTH ORIGINAL PLAN $	ACTUAL $	ADJUSTED PLAN $	% VAR. FROM ADJUSTED PLAN	YEAR TO DATE ORIGINAL PLAN $	ACTUAL $	ADJUSTED PLAN $	% VAR. FROM ADJUSTED PLAN
BRANCHES BELOW PLAN								
REGION 01								
BRANCH 03	74,000	70,241	73,000	−3.8	805,000	789,638	801,000	−1.4
BRANCH 06	110,000	103,862	108,500	−4.3	1,200,000	1,193,860	1,194,000	0
BRANCHES ABOVE PLAN								
REGION 01								
BRANCH 01	80,000	80,000	78,900	1.4	890,000	917,473	885,600	3.6

Exhibit 141. Levitz & Co. service line performance report, over the counter department.

On request
Date: __OCTOBER 197X__

REGION BRANCH	% TO LEVITZ	TOTAL	% HOUSE	OVER THE COUNTER SERVICES STOCKS	OPTIONS	BONDS CORPORATE CONVERTIBLE	NONCONVERTIBLE	U.S. GOVT.
REGION — 01								
BRANCH — 01								
COMMISSIONS (000)								
ACTUAL — MO	6.0	8.0	25	2.2	1.9	1.8	1.1	1.0
YTD	5.4	91.7	30	25.1	23.4	28.3	10.9	4.0
PREV. YR.	5.4	86.5	31	24.3	18.0	22.1	12.0	10.1
PLAN — MO	5.5	8.0	25	2.0	2.0	2.0	1.1	.9
YTD	5.3	89.0	29	24.5	22.0	22.0	10.0	10.5
VARIANCE	.1	2.7	1	.6	1.4	6.3	.9	−.4
AVG. COMM. PER TRADE								
ACTUAL — MO	70.7	7.0	—	86	84	82	60	40
YTD	76.9	8.0	—	91	86	88	59	44
BRANCH — 02								

quickly. Data was shown on the report when either monthly or year-to-date performance exceeded preselected criteria. Response time of these periodic performance reports is aimed to coincide with the time period within which action should be taken. The illustrated reports have a monthly time cycle.

The data for these performance reports originates from the original transaction entry data. In the area of information capture, financial institutions generally have a head start on many other industries but often fail to take full advantage of this. In the Levitz system, along with current data, historical information is maintained for comparative purposes. This historical information is also used for preparing the annual plan, which is usually updated quarterly.

Performance data of past activity provides the basis for planning future activity. To help in the planning process, Levitz developed a series of planning summary reports, an example of which is shown in Exhibit 142. Here, a year's activity appears on one report. The gross commission mix is shown for each branch by service line. The actual and plan are both historical information (past year), whereas the forecast data for the coming year represents a mechanized approach to provide a basis for the service line manager's planning. The forecast is based on past performance and includes seasonal and other trend factors.

Many other kinds of financial information continued to be available for the service line and branch managers. This sales reporting segment, however, represented a new way of looking at performance, and it enabled the manager at each level to take actions on a more timely basis. By emphasizing profitability, the entire management team could direct its efforts more effectively toward activity of greatest benefit to Levitz.

MARKETING INFORMATION SYSTEMS APPLICATION IN A BANK

National Bank (again not the real name) required information on its customers, on market penetration, and on several other aspects measuring the performance of its marketing activities. Though some limited information was available, the marketing staff and senior management required more specific and specialized data in these areas.

Customer and market information reports were primarily aimed at providing more data on such areas as market share, account turnover, and prospects. As promotions or advertising programs were instituted, information on their effectiveness was required. The same was true of new service introductions. While the sales performance reports indicated

Exhibit 142. Levitz & Co. planning summary report, over the counter department.

Annual or on Request							OVER THE COUNTER SERVICE		
								BONDS	
							CORPORATE		
MONTH	TOTAL	BROKER	HOUSE	% HOUSE	STOCKS	OPTIONS	COVERTIBLE	NONCONVERTIBLE	U.S. GOVT.
JANUARY									
GROSS COMMISSIONS (000)									
ACTUAL	99.3	50.5	48.8	49.1	27.2	25.3	30.7	11.8	4.3
PLAN	96.4	46.7	49.7	51.6	26.6	23.8	23.8	10.8	11.4
FORECAST	97.0	45.3	50.7	52.3	27.4	24.1	25.6	11.1	10.7
AVG. COMMISSION PER TRADE									
ACTUAL	99	96	102	—	113	107	109	72	52
FEBRUARY									
TOTAL YEAR									
GROSS COMMISSIONS (000)									
ACTUAL	1,192	617.5	574.5	48.2	326	304	368	142	52
PLAN	1,157	551.9	605.1	52.3	319	286	286	130	137
FORECAST	1,100	509.3	590.7	53.7	322	300	320	140	120
AVG. COMMISSION PER TRADE									
ACTUAL	104	101	107	—	118	112	114	77	57

areas where strategic actions were required, these additional reports measured the results of the actions taken.

The customer profile analysis, shown in Exhibit 143, provides information about account size and turnover by category using Standard Industrial Classification (S.I.C.) codes. It shows performance in convert-

Exhibit 143. National Bank, customer profile analysis by type of customer.

Date: JULY 197X
Service Line: DEMAND DEPOSIT ACCOUNTS
Market: NORTH SIDE

S.I.C.	INDUSTRY	MONTH TO DATE			YEAR TO DATE		
		LAST YEAR	THIS YEAR	PERCENT CHANGE	LAST YEAR	THIS YEAR	PERCENT CHANGE
20	FOOD MANUFACTURING						
	NO. NEW ACCTS.	10	11	10.0	73	67	−8.2
	NO. LOST ACCTS.	4	4		28	30	7.1
	TOTAL AVG. DEP. ($000)	826	873	5.7	844	859	1.8
	TOTAL SER. CHRGS. ($000)	19	22	17.4	138	149	7.9
22	TEXTILE MANUFACTURING						
	NO. NEW ACCTS.	15	16	6.7	108	112	3.7
	NO. LOST ACCTS.	7	9	28.6	64	66	3.1
	TOTAL AVG. DEP. ($000)	1,183	1,211	2.4	1,195	1,225	2.5
	TOTAL SER. CHRGS. ($000)	27	30	13.5	204	210	2.8
	TOTAL ALL CUSTOMERS						
	NO. NEW ACCTS.	1,180	1,250	5.9	8,390	8,840	5.4
	NO. LOST ACCTS.	1,260	1,140	9.5	8,260	8,910	7.9
	TOTAL AVG. DEP. ($000)	17,995	18,674	3.6	17,770	18,430	3.7
	TOTAL SER. CHRGS. ($000)	122	125	2.9	848	863	1.8

Exhibit 144. National Bank, customer performance report, trust service line.

Date: MARCH 197X
Responsibility: W. ADAMS

CUSTOMER TYPE	YEAR TO DATE				% GOAL LAST PERIOD	GOAL TOTAL YEAR
	GOAL	ACTUAL	OVER/ UNDER	% GOAL		
TRUST						
COMMERCIAL GROUP						
NUMBER SOLD	14	10	−4	72	77	70
DOLLAR VALUE (000)	10,000	8,000	2,000	80	79	50,000
PROFIT CONTRIBUTION	50,000	40,000	10,000	80	69	250,000
CORPORATE GROUP						
NUMBER SOLD	18	11	−7	61	58	90
DOLLAR VALUE (000)	15,000	9,700	5,300	65	56	94,000
PROFIT CONTRIBUTION	67,000	63,000	4,000	94	85	325,000
RETAIL GROUP						

Exhibit 145. National Bank, market penetration by service line.

Date:_____03-20-7X_____
Selling Unit:____EUCLID_____
Responsibility:___G. WHITE_____

DEPOSITS	197X-4	197X-3	197X-2	197X-1	197X
101 DEMAND DEPOSITS					
INDIVIDUALS					
TOTAL MARKET POTENTIAL	27,700	28,000	28,200	28,400	28,500
ACCOUNTS AT BRANCH	8,600	8,720	8,900	8,850	8,820
BRANCH MARKET PENETRATION	31%	31%	32%	31%	31%
BUSINESSES					
TOTAL MARKET POTENTIAL	460	470	485	505	515
ACCOUNTS AT BRANCH	260	265	275	280	285
BRANCH MARKET PENETRATION	57%	57%	57%	56%	55%
OTHER DEMAND DEPOSITS					
TOTAL MARKET POTENTIAL	—	—	—	—	—
ACCOUNTS AT BRANCH	—	—	—	—	—
BRANCH MARKET PENETRATION	—	—	—	—	—
TOTAL DEMAND DEPOSITS					
TOTAL MARKET POTENTIAL	28,160	28,470	28,685	28,905	29,015
ACCOUNTS AT BRANCH	8,860	8,985	9,175	9,130	9,105
BRANCH MARKET PENETRATION	32%	32%	32%	32%	31%

ing new demand deposit accounts. The total number of accounts in the market and their average size are also shown. This information was obtained from external sources.

A somewhat different type of customer performance report was prepared for the service line manager of the trust department. This is shown in Exhibit 144. The number of accounts and their average size and profit contribution are shown. These figures are reported against goal figures which the product manager helped establish.

A comparison of actual performance to total potential was prepared whenever external data could be collected. An example is shown in Exhibit 145, showing market penetration by service line. This external data was placed on the computer files and mechanically compared to internal data for planning and control purposes. This is an example of information which is especially necessary in the development of annual plans.

Exhibit 146 provides information on new and lost business. This report shows account turnover by branch for various categories of accounts. The reasons for the turnover were also reported. These provided

Exhibit 146. National Bank, new and lost business analysis, regular savings.

Date: MARCH 197X
Group: RETAIL
Responsibility: M. BLACK

SELLING UNIT	THIS MONTH				YEAR TO DATE			
	NUMBER OF ACCOUNTS			TOTAL AVG. BALANCE CHANGE	NUMBER OF ACCOUNTS			TOTAL AVG. BALANCE CHANGE
	NEW	LOST	CHANGE		NEW	LOST	CHANGE	
EUCLID	16	4	12	$ 39,355	34	13	21	$ 106,590
BEDFORD	10	6	4	16,345	26	14	12	41,511
LAKEWOOD	9	12	−3	6,345	21	19	2	−645
TOTAL	211	110	101	$411,595	655	241	414	$1,411,619

SUMMARY LOSS ANALYSIS

REASON	THIS MONTH		YEAR TO DATE	
	NO.	%	NO.	%
MOVED	28	25	49	20
SWITCHED BANK	16	15	35	16
TRANSFERRED TO ANOTHER BRANCH	15	14	41	17
UNKNOWN	51	46	116	47
TOTAL	110	100%	241	100%

Exhibit 147. National Bank, prospect report.

Date: 03–21–XX
Requested by: G. WHITE
Area: EUCLID SERVICE AREA
Criteria: HAVE DEMAND DEPOSIT ACCOUNT BALANCE OVER $300
NO TIME PAYMENT LOAN
3-YEAR-OLD AUTOMOBILES
File: CENTRAL

NAME	ADDRESS	CITY	STATE	ZIP	TELEPHONE
JOHN A. CHESTER	567 CIRCLE DR.	CLEVELAND	OHIO	44124	123–4567
PETER R. DAVIS	12 N. ELM	CLEVELAND	OHIO	44109	321–7654

Total customer prospects: 1,573

important background information for one of the bank's crucial areas
of performance—customer service.

National's extensive data files also proved to be a source for identifying new prospects for the bank's service lines. In the report illustrated
in Exhibit 147, selection criteria are defined and printed along with
the computer-produced list of accounts meeting these criteria. These
lists are used either for personal contact or for promotional mailings.

Exhibit 148 is another type of prospect report National Bank developed as a business generator. This sales call report was designed to
help maintain bank relationships and to help in identifying opportunities
for selling the bank's services. Information was kept on major customers,
using tickler data to remind an officer when and for what reason an
account contact should be made. Should a scheduled call be missed
or overlooked, it could be highlighted in subsequent reports.

The next group of marketing information reports deals with the
measurement of special activities, such as promotions, sales activities,
and performance of new services. Strategic actions, such as a promotion
of savings accounts, affect only a limited number of accounts. These
can be separated, identified, and reported upon during a relatively short
time span, and, after the event, the report may be discontinued. An
illustration of a promotion progress report is shown in Exhibit 149. Here,
the actual number of new accounts for a special promotion are compared
to plan and to forecast. Specific activity of this nature is controlled
more closely because of the short time span involved. Information can
be summarized for future reference as shown in Exhibit 150. Additional
information on retention and cost is also presented, calculated in terms
of cost per retention as opposed to cost per initial capture.

As new service needs are identified and a development effort under-

Exhibit 148. National Bank, sales call report.

Date: __FEBRUARY 197X__
Requested By: __W. JONES__

CUSTOMER	PRESENT ACCOUNTS	AVERAGE SIZE	PROSPECT FOR	LAST CONTACT			TECHNICAL SUPPORT	KEY DATA
				PERSON	TYPE	DATE		
JOHN A. ADAMS	DDA	$ 400	CHARGE CARD	L. BROWN	PHONE	01-05-XX	M. STEWART	BIRTHDAY
165 NORTH MAIN	REG. SAV.	$10,000	TRUST					03-10-XX
CLEVELAND 44137	SAFE DEP.							
216/123/4567								
BILL'S TOBACCO	DDA	$ 5,000	CHARGE SERVICE	G. JOHNSON	PERSON	10-01-XX		NONCONTACT
3242 MAPLE								IN 30 DAYS
CLEVELAND 44125								
216/765/4321								

Exhibit 149. National Bank, promotion progress report, demand deposit account promotion.

Date: 007-06-7X
Service Line: DEMAND DEPOSIT ACCOUNTS
Responsibility: R. SMITH
Promotion No.: 00105

	WEEK								
	1	2	3	4	5	6	7	8	TOTAL
NUMBER OF NEW ACCOUNTS									
FORECAST W/O PROMOTION	75	75	75	75	75	75	75	75	600
PLAN WITH PROMOTION	100	150	200	300	400	400	300	150	2,000
ACTUAL	85	140	195	305	420	—	—	—	—
OVER/UNDER FORECAST	10	65	120	230	345	—	—	—	—
OVER/UNDER PLAN	15–	10–	5–	5	20	—	—	—	—
% OF PLAN THIS PERIOD	85	94	98	101	105	—	—	—	—
EXPECTED % OF TOTAL PLAN TO DATE	5	13	23	38	58	78	93	100	100
ACTUAL % OF TOTAL PLAN TO DATE	4	11	21	36	57	—	—	—	—

Exhibit 150. National Bank, promotion effectiveness report.

Date: NOVEMBER 197X
Service Line: DEMAND DEPOSIT ACCOUNTS
Responsibility: R. SMITH
Promotion No.: 00105

CAPTURE
FORECAST OF TOTAL NEW ACCOUNTS (06–01–XX TO 07–31–XX)   600
ACTUAL NUMBER OF NEW ACCOUNTS (06–01–XX TO 07–31–XX)   2,113
NEW ACCOUNTS FROM PROMOTION   1,513

RETENTION
ACTUAL NUMBER OF NEW ACCOUNTS (06–01–XX TO 07–31–XX)   2,113
NUMBER ON FILE AS OF 10–31   1,322
% RETENTION FOR THIS PROMOTION   63
HISTORICAL % RETENTION OF DDA   72

COSTS
TOTAL DIRECT COSTS OF PROMOTION $ 9,272.78
AVERAGE COST PER CAPTURE $ 6.13
AVERAGE COST PER RETENTION $ 7.01

taken to market them, performance and control information must be available. Approval of the development of a profitable service is based on its development within selected cost levels. The new service development manager receives a report on the status of active projects in terms of actual time and cost compared to plan, with an estimate to completion, as shown in Exhibit 151. When the new services become a standard part of the line, their performance measures are incorporated into the reports discussed previously.

Finally, a general report of activity requiring prompt action is prepared for each manager with responsibility for an individual selling unit, as shown in Exhibit 152. As an exception occurs, it is referred to the account manager or officer directly concerned. If it is a key or major account (KAM), personal calls may be in order; for smaller accounts, a mailed notice may be used. In addition to reporting problems, the system also reports unusual activity of a KAM account. This could include items such as a very large deposit or the purchase of another bank service, which is used as a basis for contacting the customer.

Because National Bank was assuming a more aggressive posture with

Exhibit 151. National Bank, new service development status report.

Date: ___MARCH 197X___

SERVICE	SERVICE NUMBER	TIME TO PLAN			COST TO PLAN			ESTIMATE TO COMPLETE				
		PLAN	ACTUAL	O/U PLAN	PLAN	ACTUAL	O/U PLAN	DAYS	COST	DATE	TIME VAR.	COST VAR.
INCOME TAX PREPARATION	12	40	31	9	3,600	2,950	650	15	1,000	04-21	−6	−350
CASH-DISPENSING MACHINE	11	17	18	−1	2,000	1,650	350	10	500	OPEN	−11	−150

Exhibit 152. National Bank, exception report.

Date: _02–28–7X_
Group: _CORPORATE_
Selling Unit: _WEST_
Responsibility: _T. WOOD_

NAME	KAM	ACCT/ID#	DAYS SINCE OCCURRENCE	NATURE OF EXCEPTION
1. ABC BREWING CO., INC.	*	123456	4	LN. PAYMENT PAST DUE 4 DAYS: $475.00 DUE
2. MOTOR OIL CO.	*	00–12345	1	CD MATURES 05-19-XX ($100,000)
3. BAKER PROCESSING, INC.		00–1234567	1	NO DDA DEPOSIT IN 15 DAYS
4. SMALL MFG., INC.		00–1234567	3	DDA OVRDRWN BY $253.76
5. INDUSTRIAL CHEMICALS, INC.	*		1	COMP BAL ($ 1,000) CUR BAL ($782.97)
6. PAPER DISTRIBUTORS, INC.	*		1	NO CONTACT IN 30 DAYS
12. T. WOOD		47492	1	EXP VOUCHERS FOR JAN. NOT RECEIVED

respect to soliciting sources of funds and users of funds, an increased emphasis on the marketing approach was required. National Bank was able to build its marketing information system on much of the data gathering, storage, and retrieval mechanisms which were part of the transaction processing and financial reporting systems. Of particular importance was the analysis of activity for selected segments of its customers or service lines, such as prospects or promotion effectiveness.

Each of the two systems described for Levitz apply also, in principle, to National Bank, and conversely the two systems described for National Bank could apply to Levitz as well. Periodic performance reporting, both detailed and in summary, was illustrated in the Levitz case study. Performance analysis reports and special performance and control reports were illustrated in the National Bank case study. The two cases show that the principles of marketing information systems apply to financial institutions in a manner very similar to other types of businesses discussed elsewhere in the book.

16

ORGANIZING THE MARKETING INFORMATION SYSTEMS EFFORT

Previous chapters have described and illustrated the elements of a productive marketing information system. Such a system can be of great benefit to the marketing manager once it is installed and producing the information he needs to plan and operate on both a short- and long-range basis. The marketing manager's involvement is required, however, to insure that this happens.

This chapter will describe the basic approach to implementing an information system and its parts, and the marketing manager's role in the process. A systematic and planned approach is required. Certain guidelines, developed through experience, significantly reduce both the time and effort needed to install a system. The discussion will be grouped by subject:

Organizing for the systems effort.
Planning the effort.
Effective project administration.
The approach to systems design.
Requirements for implementation.

ORGANIZING FOR THE SYSTEMS EFFORT

The ultimate goal of the marketing information system is to promote and protect market position and increase corporate profitability. As the systems effort progresses, it should be subject to continuous review to assure that evolving design concepts properly relate to this objective. To achieve this, a top-level steering committee should be established to provide overall policy guidance in line with corporate objectives. The committee also represents the place where any problems or conflicts arising out of the systems effort can be resolved. The committee should consist of those directly responsible for corporate policy and should include the major functional areas of the company. The committee normally reports to the top executive, who may act as chairman but more frequently delegates this task to the most qualified member.

The basic task of the committee is to provide overall management guidance in the proposal, planning, and execution of individual systems projects. The committee serves to identify business factors, to define the scope and nature of problems, to consider the requirements for further investigation, and to communicate with the proper level of management.

The following are the specific functions of the committee.

1. Set corporate objectives for systems applications.
2. Create and charter task forces to perform studies, prepare systems designs, and implement the installation of systems in specified areas of operation.
3. Review project definition, expected overall approach, and time and budget allotments submitted by the task forces.
4. Establish priorities among scheduled projects.
5. Select among alternative proposed projects.
6. Approve a proposed systems development schedule.
7. Review follow-up reports on systems presently undertaken.
8. Initiate audits of completed applications to insure continuing effectiveness.

The steering committee may be divided into permanent and temporary members. Permanent members could include the executive vice president, marketing vice president, manufacturing vice president, controller, and data processing manager (or manager of management information systems). Temporary members should be included to provide specialized information and background as needed. The committee should meet as often as necessary to review the objectives, but not less than once a month.

The working elements within this committee structure are the task forces, which are created by the steering committee and assigned to formulate and execute in detail a particular plan. The membership of a given task force would include user groups and data processing personnel. Note that both functional and technical skills are represented. Chairmanship of the group would reside with the principal user. A task force, as we have discussed here, typically operates as a unit until a specific project has been completed. Note that marketing is involved during this entire process.

The steering committee and task force organization are shown graphically in Exhibit 153.

The committee structure shown in Exhibit 153 may also accommodate participation by outside consultants at all levels of the organization. These can provide technical competence and a level of experience that the company may not need to acquire permanently. Having helped to

Exhibit 153. Organization of the steering committee.

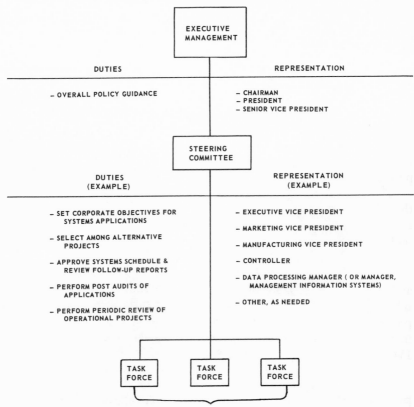

PERFORM ASSIGNMENTS AT REQUEST OF STEERING COMMITTEE

NOTE: CONSULTANT PARTICIPATION CAN OCCUR AT ANY LEVEL OF THE ORGANIZATION STRUCTURE.

Exhibit 154. Marketing information system task force.

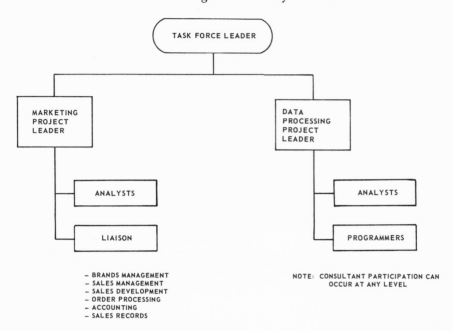

install similar systems in other organizations, consultants may be aware of pitfalls or useful shortcuts, and they often bring to the task an important degree of objectivity.

The concept of management involvement is of key importance. Often, the success of an entire systems project hinges upon it. If management feels itself bypassed, or its experience not properly consulted or utilized, both a lack of confidence in the system and an overall resentment toward the system can result.

It is important that specific organization charts of the task force and systems project be developed. Such charts define reporting responsibility and identify specific individuals and their connection with the project. These organization charts also help to promote management involvement. An example of a task force organization is shown in Exhibit 154.

PLANNING THE EFFORT

With management involvement, a comprehensive long-range master systems plan can now be developed, as described in Chapter 8. Under the direction of the steering committee, task forces work to determine both present and future corporate information requirements. These findings serve as the basis for determining the scope and objectives of the company's systems activities. Most systems effort involves significant initial one-time costs, and sufficient utilization of the output is required to amortize the expense of the effort. The economic benefits must therefore be clearly identified at the outset.

While formulating the long-term systems plan, the opportunity for short-term systems improvements becomes apparent. Priorities for their implementation should be established by the steering committee. These priorities depend upon the compatibility of the long- and short-range plans, the immediate information benefits to be gained, and the cost benefits of the activity.

The next step in the systems effort is to establish controls over completion of both the long- and short-range projects through the use of project schedules. A formal system of scheduling serves several purposes. Initially, it helps in the development of bench marks—realistic target dates, projected manpower requirements, and dollar expenditures for a particular project. These bench marks serve as the basis for periodic reports to management; the current status of a project is compared to estimated cost and progress. Periodic reports will provide the steering committee with a warning if a project begins to exceed its budget or if it encounters serious delays. Such reporting is thus useful in keeping a project on track or in providing early information for a change of direction if an error in judgment has been made.

Effective scheduling of a project requires detailed work programs, time budgets, regular progress reporting, and uniform documentation standards. A completed project schedule should include the following.

1. A list of tasks which must be completed.
2. The estimated number of man-days needed to complete each task.
3. The time period required to do the job with the personnel available.
4. The specific personnel assigned to the task areas.
5. The specific monthly progress expected in each task area.

EFFECTIVE PROJECT ADMINISTRATION

The success of any project as extensive as an information system rests upon close coordination and control of the effort. Detailed planning and close control serve to insure fulfillment of the systems objectives, eliminate duplication of effort, reduce completion time, and allow necessary revisions as the project progresses. It is important that each project be reviewed regularly and uniformly. All master plans require adjustments reflecting changes in internal organization or operations, external business conditions, developments in data processing technology, and the marketing managers' requirements.

Project administration is judged by measuring the expenditure of time and money against that budgeted to achieve the project goals. Budgets and time estimates must be realistic in terms of capability and financial support. The project's milestones should be designated to measure meaningful completion stages in the development of the system.

A detailed work program is an essential element in project control. This serves to break down each major work segment into its components and explains the actual work to be performed in greater detail. It also provides a guide for assignments and work during the project and identifies the documented results of each step.

A detail work program includes a man-day estimate for each step, along with projected staffing levels. In addition, approximate starting and completion dates should be estimated, taking into consideration the interrelationships of all activities, priorities, and deadlines. The program schedule and work assignments should be adjusted to minimize the number of different personnel assigned and to level the workload where possible.

A summary manpower schedule is shown in Exhibit 155. This schedule lists the major project phases along with their estimated man-

Exhibit 155. Summary, manpower schedule, proposed system.

PHASE	MAN-DAYS BY MONTH							TOTAL MAN-DAYS
	1	2	3	4	5	6	7	
1. PROJECT DEFINITION	5	7						12
2. PRELIMINARY SYSTEM DESIGN	28	28	20					76
3. DETAIL SYSTEM DESIGN		30	40	5				75
4. PHYSICAL PREPARATION					1			1
5. PROGRAMMING AND TESTING			10	70	50	20		150
6. CONVERSION PREPARATION					24	15		39
7. SYSTEM TEST						21		21
8. CONVERSION						25	20	45
TOTAL	33	65	70	75	75	81	20	419

Note: Organization and administration functions will add about 10% to total project time (40–45 days in this example).

Exhibit 156. Sample page for proposed system, detail work program.

Segment Task Numbers	Project Step Number and Description	Responsibility	Current Estimate			
			Man-Days	Time Schedule		Prerequisites
				Start	Complete	
03.06.	Marketing Department:					
	01. Interview the employees in the Marketing Department-	Joe Campbell	10	3- 2-X1	3-19-X1	Interview schedule to be cleared with Marketing Manager first. Also, arrange to issue Task Analyses work sheets
	a. Determine number of employees					
	b. Review the procedures noting all exceptions to the normal processing					
	c. Obtain filled-in copies of all source documents-					
	(1) Determine what controls are established over the documents					
	(2) For each document prepare a Source Document Data Sheet					
	d. Obtain filled-in copies of all reports-					
	(1) For each report prepare a Report Data Sheet					
	e. Determine what files are maintained in the department-					
	(1) For each file obtain a filled-in copy of the document					
	(2) Prepare a Master File Data Sheet for each file					
	02. Prepare summary lead schedules-	Joe Campbell	1	3-23-X1	3-23-X1	
	a. Source documents					
	b. Reports					
	c. Master Files					
	03. Flow chart the procedures	Joe Campbell	3	3- 3-X1	3-19-X1	Pick up Task Analyses

days of effort by month. Periodic reports are prepared comparing actual effort with over and under estimate figures shown to the present date. Such a report provides management with a compact summary comparison of actual and estimated effort.

The detail work program may take several forms. First, the work program is listed by project steps with appropriate assigned personnel and estimated time requirements (Exhibit 156). The program is then summarized by assigned personnel, each person designated for involvement receiving his own listing of the work to which he is assigned and its related data (Exhibit 157). Such information informs all concerned of their planned participation, involvement, and accountability.

Control of a project is exercised through feedback and review of the actual time spent compared with estimated. A time report provides regular and uniform documentation of time spent on the project. These should be periodically required of every individual involved on the work program. The time reports should be summarized on a form such as the project analysis chart in Exhibit 158. Such project analysis also provides an estimated completion date for the project as compared with the original completion date. These reports list project steps, the personnel assigned, hours originally planned, and actual performance for the entire project. Time reports may also be summarized by individual, thus providing information on the progress of each individual assigned to the project and an analysis of the workload of the individual. This individual form is essentially identical to the project analysis form and is illustrated in Exhibit 159.

Effective administrative control of a systems project cannot be emphasized enough. The extra time taken in the initial phases of the project to establish reporting and documentation standards can only prove beneficial.

THE APPROACH TO SYSTEMS DESIGN

Once the effort has been planned and provision made for properly administering the project, preliminary systems design can be undertaken. This phase of the activity consists of outlining the reporting requirements, designing the processing system, developing the installation schedule, preparing an economic analysis, and reporting to the steering committee.

In evolving the planned new system, thorough analyses of present systems must be made. Without adequate knowledge of the existing system, there is always a probability that the new system may not have

Exhibit 157. Individual task assignments.

Steps Assigned to: Joe Campbell   924523
              (name)   (Empl. Number)

Number	Project Step Description	Start	Complete	Man-Days
			Current Estimate	
			Time Schedule	
02.00.00	Project orientation and training	2-26-XX	2-27-XX	2
03.06.00	Review of present requirements--Marketing Management			
	01. Conduct interviews	3- 2-X0	3-19-X0	10
	02. Prepare summary lead schedules	3-23-X0	3-23-X0	1
	03. Flow chart the procedures	3- 3-X0	3-19-X0	3
	04. Review flow charts, etc. with interviewees	3- 5-X0	3-20-X0	2
	05. Summarize costs of present system	3-24-X0	3-25-X0	2
	06. Determine information requirements	3-26-X0	3-30-X0	$\underline{2}$
				20
04.00.00	Preliminary system design			
	01. Design new reports	3-31-X0	4-17-X0	10
	02. Develop top-level concept	4- 6-X0	4-10-X0	5
	04. Verify the system concepts	4-20-X0	4-24-X0	$\underline{5}$
				20
05.00.00	Analysis of computer equipment requirements			
	03. Prepare and issue Spec Book	4-27-X0	5- 8-X0	10
	04. Evaluate vendor proposals	5-18-X0	5-22-X0	5
	05. Prepare comparative summary and recommendations	5-25-X0	5-29-X0	$\underline{5}$
				20
06.00.00	Analysis of economics			
	01. Estimate proposed system operating costs	5-11-X0	6- 3-X0	8
	02. Develop estimated operating savings	6- 4-X0	6- 8-X0	3
	03. Estimate one-time conversion costs	5- 9-X0	6-15-X0	$\underline{5}$
				16

considered all the existing requirements and the manner in which they are currently met.

Detailed interviews with all users should be conducted. At this time, samples of current reports and information requirements should be reviewed in detail. Each piece of information is examined for use, source, presentation form, and flow. Users are thus forced to forgo generalities and to define specific needs. It is not uncommon in such investigations to uncover redundancies and so-called required information which cannot specifically meet need-to-have requirements. Current reports may often be reduced in size, if not totally eliminated. Additional and more pertinent information requirements as to content, form, and distribution may also be discovered.

Reporting requirements of the system may now be summarized. A list of the necessary outputs is compiled, noting combinations, eliminations, and additions of reports. In determining the reports of a system, key concepts to be considered should include:

1. The use of exception reporting. Action reports should only be generated when adverse conditions require a manager's action.
2. A single report serving multiple uses.
3. Reports tailored to an individual's needs, where practical.
4. Information presented in an easy-to-read and relevant form.

Each of the reports is then designed and samples made for the manager's approval. This process may extend over a considerable time, particularly if the same reports are to serve several users.

With report content made final, the necessary input data, its sources, and the means by which it is to be collected is determined. The reports and necessary source documents may be summarized in matrix form, noting for which report(s) the particular input data is required. In addition, the systems from which the source documents come, such as the order entry system, should be fully documented in a flow chart. Frequency and estimated volumes should be noted. The marketing manager should be familiar with all phases of this work to insure that no reports or information needs are overlooked.

In coordinated marketing information systems, consideration should be given to the concept of a centralized data base. This represents a central store of information kept by the company. Such a base would contain data on a wide range of functional activities, including marketing, manufacturing, accounting, and the like. Since these files serve the needs of the entire organization, the marketing information section must be integrated with other company information. The data file structures are determined with this in mind. File structures should also include

Exhibit 158. Project analysis chart.

SEGMENT	TASK	STEP	DESCRIPTION OF SEGMENT TASK, OR STEP	ASSIGN TO:	REQUIRED START DATE	MAN HOURS	TARGET DATE	MAN HOURS THIS WEEK	MAN HOURS TO DATE	ESTIMATE REMAINING HOURS	EXPECTED COMP. DATE	REMARKS
03	02	02	Prepare summary lead schedule	Jim Kennedy	3/23	8	3/23	7	7	-0-	3/23	Done
	02	05	Summarize costs of present system	Jim Kennedy	3/24	16	3/25	20	20	-0-	3/26	Done
	02	06	Determine info reqmts.	Jim Kennedy	3/26	16	3/30	6	6	16	4/1	
03	05	Review	marketing dept. procedures									
	05	01	Interview	Norm Cheek	3/23	8	3/23	5	5	-0-	3/26	Done) Bill Swan
	05	02	Prepare summary lead schedule	Norm Cheek	3/26	8	3/26	-0-	-0-	4	3/31	will assist Norm
	05	03	Prepare flow charts	Norm Cheek	3/24	8	3/24	9	9	-0-	3/26	Done) this week
	05	04	Review flow charts, etc., w/users	Norm Cheek	3/25	4	3/25	-0-	-0-	4	3/30	
	05	06	Determine info reqmts.	Norm Cheek	3/25	12	3/26	3	3	12	4/2	
03	06	Review	marketing mgmt. requirements									
	06	02	Prepare summary lead schedule	Joe Campbell	3/23	8	3/23	-0-	-0-	8	3/31	
	06	04	Review flow charts, etc., w/users	Joe Campbell	3/5	16	3/20	3	18	2	3/30	
	06	05	Summarize costs of pres. system	Joe Campbell	3/24	16	3/25	14	14	-0-	3/26	Done
	06	06	Determine info reqmts.	Joe Campbell	3/26	16	3/20	16	16	-0-	3/26	Done

Note: ORIGINAL PLAN spans REQUIRED START DATE, and ESTIMATE OF EFFORT (MAN HOURS, TARGET DATE). ACTUAL PERFORMANCE spans MAN HOURS THIS WEEK, MAN HOURS TO DATE, ESTIMATE REMAINING HOURS, EXPECTED COMP. DATE.

Exhibit 159. Personnel analysis form.

EMPLOYEE NAME __Jim Kennedy__

| APPLICATION OR SYSTEM | | | DESCRIPTION OF SEGMENT, TASK, OR STEP | START DATE | ORIGINAL ESTIMATE OF EFFORT | | ACTUAL PREFORMANCE | | | | REMARKS |
Segment	Task	Step			MAN-HOURS	TARGET DATE	MAN-HOURS THIS WEEK	MAN-HOURS TO DATE	ESTIMATE OF REMAINING HOURS	EXPECTED COMPLETION DATE	
APPLICATION OR SYSTEM NAME: Marketing Dept. Study											
03	02	02	Prepare summary lead schedule	3/23	8	3/23	7	7	-0-	3/23	Done
03	02	05	Summarize costs of pres. system	3/24	16	3/25	20	20	-0-	3/26	Done
03	02	06	Determine info reqmts.	3/26	16	3/30	6	6	16	4/1	
			GENERAL SUPERVISION AND ADMINISTRATION								
			GENERAL EDUCATION AND RESEARCH								
			CURRENT SYSTEMS								
			HARDWARE AND SOFTWARE SUPPORTS								
			STANDARDS AND PROCEDURES								
			GENERAL MEETINGS				1	19			
			NONDEPARTMENTAL ACTIVITIES								
			EXCUSED OR UNASSIGNED TIME								
			ILLNESS				8	8			
			VACATIONS AND HOLIDAYS								
			TOTALS		48		42	60	16		

an allowance for future expansion; the additional cost of providing some idle storage space at the outset is often minor compared to that of subsequent expansion. Without a reserve for expansion, the entire data bank may have to be redesigned, and this can involve extensive reprogramming and additional conversion time.

Simultaneously with file structure design, the processing approach must be selected. Alternative approaches to be considered include batch processing and on-line processing. Batch processing consists of grouping transactions or data input into batches, either by fixed time period or by fixed amounts of data to be processed. Examples include orders received or remittances applied, which may be presorted into a sequence identical with that of the master files for processing as a group. Generally, this is done where master files are large and there are long intervals between processing runs. In on-line processing, transactions are processed as they are received, rather than in batches. This provides for immediate update of the master data files and demonstrates the most rapid response time. Of the methods described, on-line processing is usually the more expensive.

Processing modes determine the equipment necessary for the system and the turn-around time associated with it. On-line processing demonstrates short response times but requires direct access storage devices (magnetic disks or drums). Batch processing, however, utilizes magnetic tape devices (or other sequential storage mediums) which are generally cheaper than the direct access devices. Magnetic tape has high storage capacity, low unit cost, low storage costs, but long turn-around times.

The selection of the processing mode involves, then, a balancing of the value applied to the timeliness of information against machine and processing costs. It is obviously important that the marketing manager participate in these decisions, since only he can evaluate the information needs of his business.

The discussion of the approach to systems design is not complete without briefly describing the subject of evaluating the economics of an installation.

Complete evaluation includes assessment of both real and intangible benefits, and covers the useful life of the system as nearly as possible. It also serves as a basis for evaluating the results of the installation once completed. Generally, three types of costs are estimated: those related to operating the proposed system, those related to operating the present system, and those related to the one-time costs of installing the new system. With these three elements, a summary of expected economics is developed. Usually, the intangible benefits or factors are presented as supplementary information. The marketing manager's greatest contribution is made in the areas of operating the proposed system and evaluating intangible benefits. Exhibit 160 provides an economic analysis representative of a marketing project.

REQUIREMENTS FOR IMPLEMENTATION

Upon approval of the project, the detailed work program, as shown by the sample page in Exhibit 156, and an installation schedule for the new system should be made final. Again, the objective is to prepare a well-considered document. Once developed, the installation schedule provides a yardstick for measuring progress during the installation, helps management determine action required to offset delays, and serves as a basis for estimating future installations.

After formalization, the installation schedule should be published. This is an important link in communication between management and those associated with the project. Such a procedure helps to achieve a better understanding of the project between the implementers and the appropriate users and management. As work proceeds, findings should be presented to all levels of management so that their continued involvement is assured.

The detailed system design segment of the installation includes all the work required to complete the design of the system and to document it for those responsible for its implementation and use. The task at this point in the installation is to define precisely how to implement these elements.

The overall system is successively broken down into more and more detailed specifications until adequate documentation of individual program requirements is available for the programmers. These detailed specifications also make system documentation available to all those involved in the project.

The installation schedule itself depends on the work done during the design phase of the installation. The segments of installation are identified and analyzed, and again comprehensive estimates of manpower effort are made. Once completed, the organizational capabilities and needs are assessed, and a general timetable is established.

There are two primary steps in the preparation of detailed program specifications. The first is to identify program segments. In this step, the functions that each program performs are identified and documented. The second step is to write up the program segments. In this step, the programs are designed to carry out the functions effectively and efficiently.

Exhibit 160. Economic analysis summary.

Description	Period of Preparation 1st Year	Period of Preparation 2nd Year	Period of Conversion and Thereafter 1st Year	2nd Year	3rd Year	4th Year	5th Year
OPERATING COST CONSIDERATIONS							
Cost of current system if no change made							
Personnel	$150,206	$165,081	$181,525	$199,706	$219,816	$242,064	$266,685
Equipment	76,809	76,809	76,809	76,809	76,809	76,809	76,809
Other	1,794	1,911	2,036	2,169	2,311	2,463	2,626
Total	228,809	243,801	260,370	278,684	298,936	321,336	346,120
Cost of proposed system plan							
Cost of current system during phaseout							
Personnel	150,206	165,081	23,070	3,552	–	–	–
Equipment	76,809	76,809	6,215	–	–	–	–
Other	1,794	1,911	93	–	–	–	–
Total cost during phaseout	228,809	243,801	29,378	3,552	–	–	–
Cost of proposed system							
Personnel			137,507	160,824	165,286	181,372	197,083
Equipment			120,476	120,476	25,916	25,916	25,916
Other			3,921	4,175	4,446	4,734	5,042
Total cost of new system			261,904	285,475	195,648	212,022	228,041
Total cost of proposed plan	228,809	243,801	291,282	289,027	195,648	212,022	228,041
Net operating cost reduction/(increase)	–	–	(30,912)	(10,343)	103,288	109,314	118,079
ONETIME INSTALLATION COST CONSIDERATIONS							
Project personnel		97,136	9,875				
Other -- (identify major items)		10,433	150				
Total onetime installation costs		107,569	10,025				
Net savings (cost) by period	$ –	($107,569)	($ 40,927)	($ 10,343)	$103,288	$109,314	$118,079
Cumulative savings/(cost)	$ –	($107,569)	($148,506)	($158,849)	($ 55,561)	$ 53,753	$171,832

The steps described to this point are heavily data processing oriented. The marketing manager may question his contribution in such an environment. As a member of the task force or steering committee, he must be familiar with the progress of the work. As a user, he must insure that the output meets his needs and specifications. The output of systems such as we have been describing can only be as good as the user's involvement.

From the detailed program specifications, the programming and debugging required for each program may proceed. This phase of the work represents detail block diagramming, coding, test data preparation, and debugging of the individual programs. It is during this phase that the most detailed documentation is developed to assure both a consistent and accurate approach to program documentation and testing. To get maximum programmer productivity, further standards should be developed which are specific to the computer being used. Only through a complete set of specifications and a consistent set of standards with respect to specifications, changes, test data creation, and testing procedures will this goal be attained. The objective is to provide cohesive and logical work documentation to aid the programmer and simplify later revisions. To maintain progress and insure complete communication, active supervision is essential.

Each program and subsystem must be tested separately. A test procedure should be developed and executed to guarantee that the newly designed system meets the original requirements and that it can operate satisfactorily. Testing should generally be performed in two stages. The first stage should be a simulation of actual operation involving the use of test data. The marketing manager can provide some of this data and help to insure that the system is properly tested. The simulation should involve all those persons who are expected to use the new system when it is in operation. Included in the test data should be a number of erroneous transactions to test the various validation routines. The second stage of testing uses live data. Sample transactions are selected from the existing system for processing. Initially, a few transactions are used, but these are gradually increased to approximate the size of an average run, which may be monthly, weekly, or daily batch sizes depending upon the processing cycle. Test data should be included to test the extremes of individual or batch quantities. All data errors that have been signaled should be rerouted through the entire processing procedure to check for possible omission of required duties or functional oversights. Here also, close coordination by the marketing manager is required to help evaluate the significance of the errors or omissions that may occur.

As the conversion date nears, a program for training users should be initiated. As an example, order entry clerks can be familiarized with new formats and data requirements. Such training helps insure that personnel involved have the knowledge and skill required for using the new system. The training program should be completed immediately prior to the conversion effort. During the period of the preconversion training, operating schedules should be formulated to insure that all outputs are produced properly so as to best utilize personnel resources.

Throughout all this, the marketing manager should be thoroughly familiar with the status, capabilities, and operations of the new system. This permits the marketing manager to make an unhurried and thorough evaluation of the new system under close control. As processing is fully evaluated and approved, actual turnover to the new system is performed.

CONVERSION APPROACHES

There are three distinct types of conversion approaches which affect the personnel and the effort required for conversion activities. The direct conversion approach without parallel operations is the preferable method. However, if there are some parallel operations or if a pilot test of the new system is used, the additional personnel and increased effort that are required by the use of these alternatives should be considered in planning for the conversion activities.

Parallel Conversion

Parallel conversion involves the operation of both the old and the new system in parallel (before a complete cutover is made) until the new system is proved satisfactory.

Past experience indicates that a properly planned and executed system test obviates the need for parallel operations. In many cases, it is not possible to run the two systems in parallel since the new reporting requirements incorporated in the new system cannot be compared with the results of the old system. Furthermore, parallel systems involve duplication and are, therefore, expensive to operate. The volume of data which has to be processed and verified could impose severe time restrictions on the personnel and require an inordinate amount of overtime. In addition, parallel systems often confuse the situation by having two different procedures in operation at the same time. If systems are run in parallel for any length of time, confidence in the new system may begin to wane.

Pilot Conversion

With the pilot conversion approach, a new system may be put into test operation as soon as it has been system tested, but without effecting a full cutover, in order to get problems resolved and provide hands-on training. For example, one area of marketing may be selected for the pilot test of an application, perhaps for simplicity and ease of reconstruction, if required. This approach is similar to system testing, but generally involves current data rather than data from an old period.

Direct Conversion

Under direct conversion, the new system is converted without operating it in parallel with the old system. An important prerequisite for starting the conversion under this and the other approaches is that the system test is complete and the results of the test have been adequately reviewed and approved by the marketing manager.

This chapter has dealt with the "how to" of organizing and undertaking a systems effort. It has presented highlights so as to provide some insight for the marketing manager into the data processing function. The systems applications described elsewhere in this book typically follow the installation procedures outlined in this chapter. However, there are numerous variations in these procedures based upon current circumstances, which are best handled by the data processing expert. After all, the marketing manager's chief concern is that the information he needs be provided on a timely basis for decision and control.